INDIA-CHINA RELATIONS
CHANGING PROFILE IN THE 21ST CENTURY

INDIA-CHINA RELATIONS

Changing Profile in the 21st Century

Y. Yagama Reddy

GYAN

India-China Relations Changing Profile in the 21st Century

ISBN : 978-81-212-1141-3

Published in 2013 in India by
Gyan Publishing House
23, Main Ansari Road, Daryaganj,
New Delhi - 110002
Phones : 23282060, 23261060

Fax : (011) 23285914
E-mail: books@gyanbooks.com
website: gyanbooks.com

Laser Type Setting : Rajender Vashist, Delhi
Printed at : Chawla Offset Printers. Delhi

Contents

Preface

China and India, surmised as the only two 'civilisational states' by Samuel Huntington in his 'Clash of Civilisations', could not stand for world hegemony of a single culture. Their common historical experience has made these sovereign nations share views on many important international issues on the lines of promoting a multi-polar world; thereby they are expected to evolve as 'natural allies' in the contemporary international system and sustain their relations for harnessing their potentials. The first Indian Prime Minister Jawaharlal Nehru mused on China's cooperation to build up an Asian balance that would offset the influence of the superpowers. Rabindranath Tagore's vision for mutually beneficial interactive relationship between the two civilisations and his desire for 'India-China fraternity' greatly inspired Nehru as to observe in his *Discovery of India* that "the name of China will be written in golden words in future whenever the question of most-trusted friends would arise". Tan Yun-Shan, who led the China Bhavan for many years at Shantiniketan and immensely contributed to India's understanding of Chinese civilisation and modern development, hailed Sino-Indian relations as "the most important of the most important". The millennium-long cultural contacts and fraternal friendship between India and China impressed Jawaharlal Nehru so much as to envision "a worthy model for sustenance of the Asian way of harmony and co-existence", as enshrined in the *Panchsheel*, the Five Principles of Peaceful Coexistence, signed by Prime Minister Jawaharlal Nehru and Premier Zhou En-Lai.

The geography-imposed obstacles and the non-expansionist nature of the Indian culture made these two geographically proximate nations oblivious of each other's existence until the advent of European influence in the 19th century. China and India, termed as 'non-identical conjoined twins joined at the Himalayas', have attuned their security apparatus to the precepts of geographical causation. As a consequence, the potential prospects for sustainable partnership between these geographically proximate nations have been eclipsed by a spiral of misgivings and mistrust manifesting in overt and covert hostilities in the latter half of the 20th century, what is to be termed as "protracted geopolitical conflict" in Sino-Indian relations. It is simply the geographical ambience getting subdued by the geopolitical ambivalence. The Sino-Indian border dispute is an issue complicated by misunderstanding and misperceptions that perpetuated trust-deficit and the consequent estrangement for over three decades since the 1962 border war. The perceptional gap between the two sides is so wide that neither side could make unilateral concessions; and the relationship between the two Asian giants during the second half of the 20th century underwent a Cold War of its own; about the same time, neither China nor India does wish to be locked in a status of confrontation with each other.

As the two largest developing countries, China and India have many common interests in global issues, like shared views on national sovereignty and dignity and challenges posed by globalisation. In the context of the centre of gravity of the world economy gradually shifting to Asia in the 21st century, China and India, reckoned as the 'pillars' of the Asian economic landscape, are looked upon as the 'twin engines' for Asia's growth and the 'key drivers' of Asian economy. The distinction of China and India as Asian giants owes much to their historical legacy and geographical landscape; and their eminence as potential centres of political power and economic strength subscribes to the concepts of Asian Century and New Asia.

Notwithstanding their fundamental clash of interests rooted in history, strategic culture and geopolitics, the rapprochement process between the two countries had begun in the late 1980s. Emphasis on "peaceful and friendly ties based on the Panchsheel" was the bottom-line of the talks between the Indian Prime Minister Rajiv Gandhi and Deng Xiaoping, during the former's visit to China in December 1988. Agreement on the Maintenance of Border Peace and Tranquillity (signed during the Prime Minister P. V. Narasimha Rao's visit to China in September 1993) and the Agreement on Confidence Building Measures along the

Line of Actual Control (concluded during the President Jiang Zemin's visit to India in 1996) did testify to the realisation of mutual accommodation and cooperation as being the only rational and realist option for them. Bringing stability and security to the Asia-Pacific region was the responsibility vested with India and China, as declared by the visiting Premier Zhu Rongji to India in 2002. Commitment to multipolarity and to "channel globalisation in the right direction" was the hallmark of the agreement reached between the visiting Indian Prime Minister Atal Behari Vajpayee and his counterpart Wen Jiabao in 2003. The Declaration, "A Shared Vision for the 21st century", signed on 14 January 2008, during the visit of the Indian Prime Minister Manmohan Singh to China, underscored the need for both sides "to look to the future in building a relationship of friendship and trust, based on equality", and for developing the strategic and cooperative partnership for peace and prosperity between the two countries. The spirit of good neighbourliness in the Sino-Indian relations is manifested in high level political interactions, increasing bilateral trade, joint military exercises and boundary-demarcation talks.

Yet, these two Asian powers continue to "suffer from a trust-deficit", as evident from the oft-recurring border violations, military developments across the Himalayas, Chinese extensive transport network in the Tibetan plateau and strategic encirclement of India by China, popularly termed as 'string of pearls'. The maritime rivalry is not all together ruled out, because of ostensible safeguarding the sea lanes of commerce and communications. Unlike China, India is constrained by geographical setting that becomes inimical to the Indian war-logistics; and therefore, India can ill-afford to have a hostile and indignant China on its borders, nor could it gain any substance by entering into an anti-Chinese alliance. Whatever the reality of the limitations of the concept of "India balancing China", China seeks to play its own balancing game and to push its own agenda till opposed. Though China has neither intention nor capability to contain India or to prevent it from emerging as a major power, New Delhi should make China to recognise India's importance. India has to be a little more specific about its own 'core interests' vis-à-vis China's 'national core interests'. Before entertaining the idea of 'competing or cooperating with China', India must respond firmly and strongly to Chinese actions that encroach on India's sovereignty and territorial integrity. If India's goal is to "gain its rightful place in the comity of nations" in a globalised world, it is absolutely imperative that India replaces its reactive policy towards China with a proactive one.

The other Asian states, which too had for long been obsessed with inward looking, have also given credence to the policy of inclusiveness. The Asian community of nations has thus evolved on to the stage of demonstrating its wherewithal for achieving regional integration and forging new partnerships, besides getting its relations with the traditional partners fortified. The overarching multilateral framework, composed of several trans-regional, regional/sub-regional bodies, keeps open a multitude of possibilities for partnerships on win-win situation. Thus, the evolving open regionalism subscribes to a pan-Asian group or simply the Asian Solidarity. It is about the same time that India's proactive Look East Policy enabled India's economy to get integrated itself with the Asia-Pacific region and catapulted India to the centre stage of Asia-Pacific security architecture by winning the trust of the regional players.

In the wake of New Asian solidarity and new global order gaining momentum, a fit case for an academic discourse is the Sino-Indian relationship marked by several instances of irritants, intercepted by positive gestures. An International Seminar in October 2009, organised by the Centre for Southeast Asian and Pacific Studies (CSEA & PS), provided an opportunity for interface among the scholars and statesmen to deliberate on various issues of concern and interest for these two Asian powers oscillating between the imminent prospects of cooperation and provocative challenges. The presentations and the discussions thereof at the Seminar facilitated the authors to evolve quality papers, which upon being edited meticulously are included in this anthology.

Apale De, while highlighting the post-cold war non-traditional security challenges as countenanced by India and China, seeks to examine the level of bilateral convergence or divergence between the two Asian neighbours in tackling these intimidations.

Binod Mishra weighs up the cooperation over the other 'C's–Conflict, Competition and Containment– in the Sino-Indian bilateral engagement for creating a stable South and Southeast Asian region on which these two great powers heavily depend in order to ensure their resource security and to fulfill their ambition of great power status.

A. Chandrasekaran and P. Govinda Reddy underline the need for India and China to sink their differences, pool all their resources and come together with an understanding that "together we will prosper" in pursuit of accomplishing the task of blossoming of "One Asia".

While being skeptical of using the India's Northeast region as a spring board for the defence of the nation's geo-strategic space in the context of China's military activities in the Tibetan region, Deepa Karthikeyan looks for India to acknowledge the importance of its Northeastern frontier, both in the larger Sino-Indian context and within the national framework.

While assessing the factors that favoured the promotion of spirit of unity and understanding among the BRIC nations to advance global prosperity and growth stability so much as to evolve as the "guardian of the interests of developing countries", Lakshmana Chetty amply portrays the emergence of BRIC nations as the world's new political and economic centres of gravity in the context of expectations over BRIC as an effective engine of the world economy.

Mohan Kumar Reddy terms the strategic and security cooperation between India and Vietnam *sine qua non* in the context of India's regional strategic imperatives, India's integration with ASEAN and India's enhanced relations in the Asia-Pacific region.

While dealing with the implications of the transformed world scenario in the context of the New Global Order that brought New Delhi and Beijing closer to each other, Mohor Chakraborty in her comparative analysis observes that the NDA government adopted more pragmatism in China policy, while lack of China-focus was primarily attributable to the domestic strains of coalition politics that the UPA government countenanced.

Munirathnam Reddy considers cultural diplomacy as an important component of the Sino-Indian relations not merely for resolving the contentious border dispute, but also for revitalising the bilateral partnership in terms of maintaining peace and enhancing economic cooperation.

Nalini Kant Jha and Subhash Shukla emphasize peace with neighbours, stability in Asia and substantial cooperation between India and China as being necessary for regional peace and stability and to turn the 21st century into the

Asian Century as well as for India to establish itself as a global player in world politics.

Nirmala Devi critically examines the economic diplomacy of China and its implications for India in consequence of the spread of China's influence through massive economic aid to the members of the SAARC region and growing China's trade and investments in India.

M. Prayaga evaluates the rejuvenated and diversified China-Vietnam relations and their impact on the India-Vietnam relations which are time-tested and burgeoning in a multitude of areas in the context of post-Cold War scenario.

L. Premashekhara who feels the need for developing a comprehensive understanding of the historical facts among the Indian public that India has been the gainer in its border row with China calls for a pragmatic approach for the resolution of the border problem between the two Asian giants by legitimising the Line of Actual Control as international border and formally establishing "Dull Frontiers" which, apart from serving India's interest, will remove the threat of any armed conflict.

A. Subramanyam Raju, while assessing the energy demands in India and China and their dependence on external sources, analyses the competition as well as cooperation between them in addressing their energy requirements as well as the possibilities for their cooperation with the neighbouring countries in the energy sector.

Tridib Chakraborti analyses the relations of India and China relations in the post-Cold War years in Southeast Asia through the prism of a mosaic of parameters, including a plethora of challenges and openings, their foreign, economic and strategic objectives, as well as their emergence as economic power-houses due to their pragmatic and modernisation programmes.

B.C. Upreti looks at the strategically important trans-Himalayan region as having the vast potential as regards economic cooperation for India and China, the two important trans-Himalayan countries. In view of the commercial interests and strategic concerns for India and China in Central Asia as well as geo-economic prospects of the trans-Himalayan region, Upreti advocates that India-China cooperation would promote the trading prospects and offer vast opportunities for the utilisation of natural resources as well as help in the resolution of the border disputes that can bring peace and stability in the region.

In the context of India and China juggling for a position of strength and influence in the Indian Ocean and the issues that could lead to conflict/confrontation in the Indian Ocean region (IOR) as well as the areas for cooperation which open to both the countries, R.S. Vasan examines the character and dimensions of engagement and estrangement between the two countries and their geo-political and -strategic ramifications in the IOR.

Vijay Kumar Reddy underscores the need for India and China to foster their strategic and cooperative partnership for peace and stability so that the growing economic and trade relations between the two emerging Asian powers would not become hostage to the differences on certain other contentious issues.

Y. Yagama Reddy looks at the "protracted geopolitical conflict" in Sino-Indian relations for the last 50 years as being influenced by the formidable Himalayan mountain system that thwarts human efforts at exercising an effective control over the borders. Giving credence to the precepts of geographical causation of history that makes it hard for China and India to confront one another on the long contentious border crisis, Reddy weighs up the principle of rapprochement that would portray their competence in the Asian balance of power vis-à-vis new global order.

I feel very much obliged to the contributors for their earnest academic support in the form of participation in the seminar and submission of the revised papers for this compendium. The freedom of expression of the contributors has never been subdued in the process of editing the papers; and thus the views expressed in these papers are essentially those of the contributors, but not of the editor.

The splendid support I received from my colleagues in the Centre (CSEA & PS) was at the base of all the accomplishments words have, therefore, become scarce to acknowledge the saga and spirit of cooperation of my colleagues. What deserves plentiful appreciation is the scholarly contribution of Prof Lakshmana Chetty— former Director of CSEA & PS and former Dean, Faculty of Arts, Sri Venkateswara University— to get all these papers edited meticulously and promptly. The technical assistance of my colleague in the Centre, Dr Prayaga, who has spared all that time and energy, is highly commendable and duly complimented. The financial support of the University Grants Commission to the Centre under 'Area Studies Programme' has made it possible to carry on an array of academic activities including the October 2009 Seminar. I feel rather privileged to have this book published by Gyan Publishing House, New Delhi, known for its proven expertise and unflinching quality-consciousness in the arena of publication of scholarly works.

Y. Yagama Reddy

List of Contributors

1. **Ms. Apala De,** Junior Research Fellow, Department of International Relations, Jadavpur University, Kolkata.
2. **Dr. Binoda Kumar Mishra**, Fellow, Maulana Abul Kalam Azad Institute of Asian Studies Kolkata.
3. **Prof. A. Chandrasekaran,** Professor Emeritus, Department of Indian History, University of Madras, Chennai – 600 005.
4. **Deepa Karthikeyan**, Research Fellow, Centre for Asia Studies, Chennai.
5. **Prof. A. Lakshmana Chetty**, Former Director, Centre for Southeast Asian and Pacific Studies, Sri Venkateswara University, Tirupati – 517502.
6. **Prof. P. Govinda Reddy,** Professor, Department of Anthropology, University of Madras, Chennai – 600 005.
7. **Dr. L.R. Mohan Kumar Reddy**, Reader in History, S.V. Arts College, Tirupati.
8. **Mohor Chakraborty**, Senior Research Fellow, Department of International Relations, Jadavpur University, Kolkata.
9. **Prof. P. Munirathnam Reddy**, Centre for Southeast Asian and Pacific Studies, Sri Venkateswara University, Tirupati – 517502.
10. **Prof. Nalini Kant Jha**, Director, Madanjeet Singh Institute for SAARC, Pondicherry University, Puducherry.
11. **Dr. Subhash Shukla**, Guest Faculty at the Department of Political Science at Allahabad University.
12. **Prof. T. Nirmala Devi**, Director, Centre for SAARC Studies, Andhra University, Visakhapatnam.
13. **Dr. M. Prayaga**, Assistant Professor, Centre for Southeast Asian and Pacific Studies, Sri Venkateswara University, Tirupati – 517502.
14. **L. Premashekhara,** Associate Professor, Department of Politics and International Studies, Pondicherry University, Pondicherry – 605 014.
15. **Dr. A. Subramanyam Raju**, Associate Professor, Centre for South Asian Studies, Pondicherry University, Pondicherry – 605 014.
16. **Prof. Tridib Chakraborti,** Department of International Relations, Jadavpur University, Kolkata 700032.

17. **Prof. B.C. Upreti,** Centre for South Asia Studies, University of Rajasthan, Jaipur.

18. **RS Vasan,** Head, Strategy and Security Studies, Center for Asia Studies, Chennai.

19. **Dr. G. Vijay Kumar Reddy**, Assistant Professor, Centre for Southeast Asian and Pacific Studies, Sri Venkateswara University, Tirupati – 517502.

20. **Prof. Y. Yagama Reddy**, Former Director, Centre for Southeast Asian and Pacific Studies, Sri Venkateswara University, Tirupati – 517502.

1

Non-Traditional Security Threats of India and China in Post-Cold War Era: Issues of Terrorism and Energy Security and the Way-Out

Apala De

Introduction

In the history of world politics, the nation-states in their existence had faced a number of challenges from within and outside and these threats varied from time to time. Since the end of the Second World War, most of the Third World developing countries in course of their own survival occasionally faced threats, not only at the domestic level, but also from outside their territory, which were predominantly trans-national in character. The threats which these countries had confronted are presently termed as non-traditional security threats that had come into limelight since the fall of the former Soviet Union. The term non-traditional threats generally includes climate change, water scarcity, ethnic strife, low-intensity conflict, terrorist onslaught, poverty, forced and illegal migration, underdevelopment, transnational crime, maritime piracy, drug trafficking, serious communicable diseases, environmental degradation, natural disasters etc. This host of non-traditional security threats that afflict the people of the world, rich and poor alike, may be classified into four types and they are as follows:

1. **Territorial non-conventional threats** include incursion by population groups, resource extractions, fishing, and diversion of water etc.
2. **Economic non-conventional threats** refer to the marginalisation of geographically disadvantaged countries, intellectual property rights etc.
3. **Political non-conventional threats** mean corruption, piracy, illegal narcotics and small arms trade etc.
4. **Environmental non-conventional threats** refer to global warming, climate change, trans-boundary pollution, depletion of natural resources including mineral, marine and water resources.

However, on many occasions, two or more threats operate together making the situation even worse. This situation is further aggravated by the emergence of the processes of globalisation and liberalisation as well as the evolution of a new global order. There is no doubt in the fact that these non-military factors account for most of the domestic and regional instabilities, violence, death and deprivation[1]. In addition, endemic political hostility, decay in democratic institutions and practices, terrorist activities, ethnic and communal violence, cross-border migration and their repercussion on domestic and inter-state politics; have combined together to create complex matrix of conflicts, instability and insecurity, both at micro and macro levels under the unmarked global circumstances.

The emergence of India and China in the new global order as strong powerhouses has been a sensational story. Huge population, underdevelopment, poverty, and war with neighbours have branded these two countries as trivial global players in international politics during the cold war era. Their status as emerging powers has been acknowledged by the major global players in the post-cold war years only. The combined size and population of India and China make them the largest geographical and human resource mass on the planet. India and China have centuries old cultural, religious and trade links. They also became nation-states almost simultaneously and share a past of colonial and imperialist subjugation from which they were liberated after a prolonged struggle. Paradoxically enough, these two countries fought a war with each other over the disputed frontiers. This particular conflict episode, the continuing border dispute between the two countries and China's rapid growth in military power, created intermittent anxieties about her future relationship with India. This uncertainty on several instances failed to prove the benign image, which China tries to display towards many other countries of the world. There are many strategic thinkers who always felt that China is the major future threat for India. However, with the emergence of the new millennium order and its changing dynamics through information technology and economic interdependence, both India and China have pragmatically realised the need to adopt these tectonic changes, in order to develop as economically stable and politically lasting entities. The leadership of both these countries is aware of the need to ensure social and economic well-being of their peoples, because they believed that security and stability are the two essential pillars for development. They sensed that independent behaviour in internal and external relations is no longer feasible in the international arena. The need to assure the neighbours of their interests through confidence building measures, placing ancient disputes in correct perspective, reaching for consensus instead of conflict resolution by force, are the need of the day. Both India and China appreciate the need for military strength commensurate with their security and the anxieties of their neighbours.

The reality after the Cold War is of a world order based on equity amongst the states and constructive engagement through trade and economic development. Even as some hegemonic mindsets are still there, the future of inter-state relations is well set on the course of cooperation. China and India recognise the need for cooperation and for moving away from the old animosities through mutual agreements. They have resolved to find solutions to their disputes through negotiations. Indian initiatives in South Asia and Chinese efforts in finding solutions to its issues of contention with Russia, Japan and USA and in the Asia Pacific are evidence of their new awareness. In some ways, China is adding a healthy dose of "Idealist" balance to its policies. India, on the other hand, is introducing an element of "Realist" pragmatism to its policies. They are in the process going beyond the culture constraints of the past. Kautilya and Sunzi would have both approved of such a reorientation[2]. The purpose of this paper is to highlight the post-Cold paper will also discuss how the two Asian neighbours are tackling these problems and whether there is any bilateral convergence or divergence between them for overcoming these intimidations.

Energy Security as a Field of Competition between China and India

The issue of energy remains a major bone of contention to all countries in the new global order. Energy consumption, through conventional and non-conventional means has been a major subject-matter of study for all the countries in international relations. Most of the developed and developing countries are presently concentrating on how to preserve energy for their economic development and prosperity. India and China are no exceptions to this common ground. In the energy business, more than in any other aspect of international economic activity, the bravest are the most fortunate. While the Indian establishment spent five years worrying over the construction of a natural gas pipeline from Iran to India via Pakistan, China took just ten months to propose, construct and operationalise a thousand kilometers oil pipeline from Kazakhstan to Xinjiang. As soon as this pipeline was completed, China's National Petroleum Corporation (CNPC) expressed its eagerness to lay another gas pipeline along the same route. "We completed the 4,500 km-long pipeline from Xinjiang to Shanghai in just two and a half years." Chin Geng, President of the CNPC told India's Petroleum Minister, Mani Shankar Aiyar, and a group of top Indian executives in Beijing in January 2006. The Indian side was very impressed. Recently India is trying to compensate for its earlier lack of interest with an ambitious proposal for a pan-Asian gas grid that would extend the two connections—Iran-India and Kazakhstan-China—linking Asia's major energy producing regions with the consuming ones. At the meeting, in New Delhi in November, 2005, of the principal North and Central Asian energy producing and consuming countries, India unveiled an ambitious $22.4 billion pan-Asian gas grid and oil security pipeline system. The grid has four principal elements:

- The first would extend the existing Baku-Tbilisi-Ceyhan pipeline system — originally conceived by the U.S. as a means of shipping Central Asian hydrocarbons westward — down to the Red Sea via Syria, Jordan, and Saudi Arabia, allowing Caspian crudes to be exported easily to the Indian Ocean littoral.

- Second is the famous Iran-Pakistan-India pipeline, with the possibility of two additional sourcing spurs, one from the Caspian-Turkmenistan region to Iran, the other from Turkmenistan via Afghanistan.

- The third element would be a pipeline system connecting eastern India to Myanmar and south-western China with one connection running from Sittwe on the Burmese Bay of Bengal coast to Mizoram, Manipur, and Assam into China, eventually connecting up to the West-East China gas pipeline near Shaanxi, the other from Yangon to Kunming.

- The fourth element would involve the laying of pipelines that would connect the Sakhalin deposits in Russia to Japan, China, and South Korea.

Pipelines aim to deliver gas, crude or products but this is not necessarily a zero sum game. The underlying economic logic of a grid is that the capital costs can be more easily absorbed and amortised and energy supplies calibrated to match demand variations in the consuming countries without too much effort. But there is a political logic as well. As Asian grid will create mutual dependencies, giving countries a stake in the political and economic stability of one another, and hasten the process of regional integration. If at all Asia is to make progress towards creating an Asian counterpart to the International Energy Agency (IEA) and develop a regional market for the energy with its own price markers, the construction of physical infrastructure such as pipelines is essential[3]. The energy officials and policy makers of China felt that the route to greater Asian cohesiveness lies through cooperation in the energy sphere with India and other developing countries. The Chinese strategic community felt that the USA was pressurising India to detach itself from Iran. China was also apprehensive about the US design to coordinate with all the countries around Iran and isolate her. Hence the Chinese were of the opinion that if India sacrificed Iranian pipeline in the hope of securing nuclear energy from the US, it might end up with nothing, for the reason that the Iranian and Central Asian pipelines will be the strategic lifeline for Indian energy security in the near future. This is because the Chinese interpret the emerging of the US policy towards Asia as partly motivated by the emergence of the Shanghai Cooperation Organisation (SCO) as a framework for all-round cooperation—from anti-terrorism to economic exchange, including the issue of energy security. India, Pakistan and Iran have already joined the SCO as observers. The emergence of SCO as a substantial consortium will pose a strategic challenge to US interests in the region. Thus SCO is an indirect initiative taken up by China to keep out the USA, on the one hand, and securitise its energy needs, on the other.

To meet China's quickly growing energy demands, Chinese leaders have struggled between a market-oriented approach and a state-centered approach. The market-oriented approach seeks energy security through enhanced integration of national and international markets ...state intervention would be limited to the diffusion of information in a multilateral context, the support of innovation, and, for some, the management of a strategic oil reserve which would be used in case of momentary supply disruption[4]. In contrast, the state-centered approach is based upon neo-mercantilist thinking that relies on bilateral diplomatic contacts with oil producing countries to beef up energy security by the use of national resource and state-owned enterprise investments in overseas energy assets and tight control of exports and imports of energy products. Although market-oriented economic reform has been the direction of post-Mao reforms, the market-oriented approach has not gained momentum in the energy sector because the Chinese leadership has considered China's energy security strategically 'too important to be left to market forces alone'[5]. Taking over offices in 2002, 'President Hu Jintao and Premier Wen Jiabao decided that ensuring reliable supplies of petroleum and other scarce resources was not only crucial to sustained economic development, but also integral to China's national security. In 2003, Premier Wen Jiabao formalised seven small search groups to prepare for the first time a long term energy security strategy at the national level. Since then energy security has been prioritised by the Beijing leadership as a national security agenda in their national and foreign policy domain[6]. This resulted in a series of zone of conflicts that have emerged between China and some Asia-Pacific countries.

In fact, China has not hesitated to flex its muscles against competitors for energy resources. In this case, 'Beijing's obsession with energy—and its assertion of a Chinese-style Lebensraum doctrine—could render the country at loggerheads with many of its neighbours'. China's thirst for foreign energy has sparked concerns from some of China's neighbours. Though Beijing's claims over Taiwan remain the focus of world attention, China is embroiled in unresolved territorial maritime and land issues with many of its neighbors. Given that China's military capability is growing apace with its economy, the potential for military conflict over the disputed regions is similarly on the rise. While China up till now has attempted to address these issues diplomatically, the fact that many of the unresolved border disputes involve potential energy reserves might prompt China to use military force to resolve issues of strategic and economic interest. To avoid the seas and the perilous straits, China has examined a range of options from the plausible to outlandish, including pipelines to Burma and Pakistan or even a Panama-style canal across Thailand. In addition, China is transforming its armed forces, particularly China's naval capacity, well beyond what is required to protect its coasts and the Straits of Taiwan. Some Western observers point out that China has built up a sizable submarine fleet as well as made efforts to conclude agreements on the use of port facilities along the tanker routes in the South China Sea and in Burma, Bangladesh, and Pakistan. Thus the energy imperative has gradually changed Beijing's attitude towards the disputed islands.

Like China, energy preservation of India also remains a major foreign policy agenda in the 21st century. However, India's preservation of energy resource outside its territory has not at all been a success story like what China achieved so far. It is a fact that India is more vulnerable than China, given that it imports more than 70% of its crude oil needs as opposed to

China's 40%. Although Indian oil companies have been attempting to aggressively maneuver and expand internationally, with the aim of tripling the annual flow of oil from overseas assets to 20m barrels by 2010, more often than not they find themselves unable to compete with Chinese business and strategic mindset. It has been complained by Indian companies that Chinese energy companies are not only comparatively cash-rich but also receive solid financial backing from the central government. The Indian experience with respect to Petro Kazakhstan was a sad experience because the Chinese bid ($4.18 billion) was no match to that of India ($3.98 billion). China's flexing of its well-oiled muscles demonstrates the depth of the competition between the two Asian titans at a time when world energy supplies are already tight and the economies of India and China are galloping upwards[7]. Thus, this advantage of China to preserve its energy by various means has occasionally created serious tension between the two Asian giants.

Counter-terrorism as a Major Area of Cooperation between India andChina

With the end of the Cold War, ethnic conflict resurged along with religious extremism. Most of the third world nation-states experienced low-intensity conflict, terrorist activities perpetrated by neighbours or incited by some extra-regional powers. New terrorism was not only different in character but the targets of the terrorists also shifted along with the motives. The concept of new terrorism actually came into limelight and was coined a new name after the 11 September incident of 2001. This idea of new terrorism aimed at creating fear psychosis in the minds of the several thousands of innocent civilians designated as soft targets by attacking a handful of them. This new brand of terrorism does not have any specific political demands such as independence from foreign subjugation; they are either religious fanatics or sycophants, who benefit from instabilities and troubled regions. There is nexus between the narcotics dealers, the human-traffickers, the illegal arms sellers and the terrorists. The Golden Triangle and the Golden Crescent are perhaps the best examples. Both India and China are located in areas, where these problems have assumed alarming proportions. The mafias often commit crimes in one territory and escape to another state. If these two states do not have mutual understanding, intelligence sharing or Treaty of Extradition, they fail to check criminal activities across and along the border areas that are generally porous and not properly monitored. Being two of the major global players, India and China have decided to carry out joint military exercises to check terrorism on the one hand and build stronger ties between themselves. Recent history shows that these two countries have been repeatedly attacked by terrorists who were either supported or sent from outside. As a matter of fact, India has been facing such situations in Kashmir and the North-east for several decades. But terrorism as an issue of global concern was not established before the attack on the twin towers of WTC on September 11, 2001.

Beijing has strong reasons to express its condemnation of terrorism. China seeks to present itself as a responsible rising power on the world stage. Chinese leaders believe the selection of Beijing as the site for the 2008 Olympic Games reflects the international community's confidence in China's continuing reform and stability. China's admission to the World Trade Organisation in 2001 demonstrates China's commitment to embracing and upholding the rules of international trade and investment. A strong and forceful stand on international terrorism will put China in good stead in the community of nations. President Jiang Zemin's consultations with his Russian, British, and French counterparts, along with his conversations with President Bush, are part of China's efforts to build a positive international image. These efforts also help refute charges that China has 'one foot in the terrorists' camp' due to arms transfers to states that harbour or sponsor terrorist groups and organisations.

The latest attack on Mumbai, the economic capital of India, once again proved that much has been left to achieve in terms of counter-terrorism tactics. The death of several police men and armed officials clearly points to the fact as to how poorly they were equipped. Similarly, in China in a terror attack four days ahead of Olympics, two Islamic militants rammed a truck into a group of Chinese border guards and lobbed grenades, killing at least 16 of them in restive northwest Xinjiang province, heightening security fears before the mega event. Sixteen personnel were also injured in the attack by Uighur separatists, which took place when two assailants ploughed a truck into the policemen. The two militants, who were later arrested, alighted from the vehicle, tossed explosives and hacked to death the guards with knives in front of a hotel, 200 meters away from border armed division, as reported by the Xinhua news agency. Fourteen policemen were killed on the spot and two others died on way to hospital. The authorities suspected the involvement of the banned "East Turkistan Islamic Movement" (ETIM) which was planning terrorist attacks during August 1 to 8, ahead of the opening ceremony of Olympics, Xinhua said. The separatist Uighur group had nearly also claimed responsibility for a spate of bombings, including the May 5, 2008 strike in the eastern city of Shanghai which killed three persons and an attack on police in Wenzhou, also in the east, and had threatened more attacks. China has been bracing for terrorist attacks from Islamic militants, especially

ETIM, in the run-up to Olympics, deploying over one lakh security guards, besides over one million volunteers and installing 300,000 cameras to ward off any security threat. The attack put security forces nationwide on alert. The attack was one of the deadliest in recent years in Xinjiang province, where local Muslims waged a sporadically violent rebellion against Chinese rule. It was felt by the Chinese government that radical Muslims who are fighting for what they call an independent East Turkistan in Xinjiang posed the single greatest threat in the present juncture. The community, known as Uighurs, which was fighting against the Chinese government felt that the suppression has aggravated tensions in Xinjiang, making them feel even more threatened by an influx of Chinese and driving some to flee to Pakistan and other areas where they have readier access to extremist ideologies. One militant group, the Turkistan Islamic Party, pledged to target the most critical points related to the Olympics. The group is believed to be based across the border in Pakistan, with some of its core members having received training from Al Qaida and the Pakistani Taliban, as felt by the Chinese government. It was also felt by them that with more than 100,000 soldiers and police guarding Beijing and other Olympic co-host cities, terrorists were more likely to attack less-protected areas.[8]

Thus, the issue of terrorism remains a major concern for both India and China and how to overcome this menace has become a principal agenda for both New Delhi and Beijing. To get relief as well as to tackle this problem, India and China, in different international platforms, have expressed their deep concern for this issue and principally agreed to overcome this peril through different initiatives. One of the important outcomes of this initiative was the First Annual Defence Dialogue held in Beijing in November 2007. In this meeting, both the governments agreed in principle to discuss this issue thoroughly. The fruitful understanding between India and China bore its fruit when the Second Annual Defence Dialogue (ADD) was held on December 15, 2008 at New Delhi. This meeting laid the foundation for better understanding and international cooperation to defeat terrorism and non-traditional threats sponsored by religious fundamentalism. In this meeting, the Chinese officials expressed the opinion that India-China relations are no longer a zero-sum relationship and that growing defence cooperation enhanced mutual trust and confidence. The Chinese government vehemently condemned the terrorist attack in Mumbai in November 2008 and conveyed condolences for the victims. It was agreed in this meeting that both the countries will carry out joint exercises on counter-terrorism in each other's soil and thereby to strengthen their existing bilateral ties on this issue more and more. They agreed that the relationship between the two countries has moved beyond bilateralism and has significance for the stability and growth of the world at large. The two sides also shared views on global and regional security including piracy off the coast of Somalia. The Chinese side shared its experience in areas like disaster relief and the successful conduct of the Beijing Olympics mega sports event. Both the countries also agreed to pursue annual visits, deputing observers to witness exercises and evaluate defence cooperation. Thus, the Annual Defence Dialogue is an important mechanism for holding bilateral talks on defence cooperation between India and China and is also a forum for exchange of views on regional and security issues between the two countries.

Chinese Foreign Minister Tang Jiaxuan reiterated China's principles on counter-terrorism and pledged its efforts to work jointly with the international community in the fight against terrorism. Addressing the United Nations Security Council Ministerial Meeting on Counter-Terrorism, he said that the purpose of the war on terror is to free mankind from the threats to peace and security. Counter-terrorism aims at maintaining peace and security of mankind. All measures, ways and means employed by the international community must be helpful in easing and resolving tensions both at the international and regional levels. The universal development and common prosperity constitutes the basis of counter-terrorism. Uneven distribution of resources and income has made the peoples of the Third World countries, easy prey to the manipulation of terrorists. Only if common development can be achieved by facilitating each other's economy, the root causes of terrorism can be eradicated. He stressed the need for closer communication and integration among civilizations, adding that this is the guarantee of counter-terrorism. Counter-terrorism should, he noted, provide different civilizations with a new opportunity to learn from each other through mutual exchanges, a new starting point for their dialogue and integration, and a new engine for their common progress and prosperity, rather than a cause for greater ethnic hatred, racial conflict, and clashes of civilisations or rupture between peoples. Tang said the key to counter-terrorism is stronger and deeper international cooperation. The success of international campaign against terrorism requires clearly-defined and joint actions, guided by the principles of the UN Charter and universally recognised norms of international law, he added. He noted that China, as a responsible country that loves, treasures and endeavors to defend peace, has implemented in real earnest the relevant Security Council resolutions and joined the majority of the international anti-terrorism conventions. He said China is also a victim of terrorism, citing the example of the 'East Turkistan' terror groups that had long collaborated with al-Qaeda and committed numerous terror attacks in China's

Xinjiang and neighbouring regions of Central Asia. The Minister called for an integrated approach with due regard to properly handling such issues as development and regional conflicts, emphasizing there should be no 'double standards' in counter-terrorism[9].

Conclusion

Chinese Premier Wen Jiabao and Indian Prime Minister Manmohan Singh signed a joint document at Beijing, vowing to promote the building of a harmonious world. India and China are the two largest developing nations on earth representing more than one-third of humanity. Both China and India bear a significant historical responsibility to ensure comprehensive, balanced and sustainable economic and social development and to promote peace in Asia and the world as a whole. They are convinced that it is time to look to the future in building a relationship of friendship and trust, based on equality, in which each is sensitive to the concerns and aspirations of the other, under the banner of Panchsheel. China-India friendship and common development will have a positive influence on the future of the international system. These relations are neither targeted at any country, nor will affect their friendship with other countries. The two sides believe that the continuous democratisation of international relations and multilateralism are important objectives in the new century. They support and encourage the processes of regional integration that provides mutually beneficial opportunities for growth, as an important feature of the emerging international economic system as well as to overcome the threats which emanate from intra and inter levels. To strengthen their ties, as well as to overcome the threats faced by both of them, they view each others' participation in regional processes and agree to strengthen their coordination and consultation within the regional cooperation mechanisms, including the East Asia Summit[10]. It is a fact that both India and China on many local, regional and international issues, have displayed good understanding, especially with reference to non-traditional threats faced by them. But, this good understanding between New Delhi and Beijing is not at all sugar-coated. On many occasions, serious differences have developed between them with reference to energy consumption, boundary issue, space for strategic and naval movements in the Indian Ocean region, issue of Tibet and sharing of waters, etc. Thus, the soft power posture which China followed in the post-cold war years towards India and vice-versa should be given justice in the true meaning of the word if both countries look pragmatically at problems which are common in nature.

References

1. Abdur Rob Khan. *Globalisation and Non-traditional Security in South Asia.* Academic Press and Publisher Limited, Dhaka, 2001, p.1.
2. *The Hindu*, 25 January 2006.
3. nic.in/ks_41061.htm (Accessed on 7.9.2009).
4. Christian Constantin, 'Understanding China's energy security', *World Political Science Review*, No. 3, 2007, p.11.
5. Heinrich Kreft, 'China's quest for energy', *Policy Review*, October-November 2006, p. 65.
6. Jaewoo Choo, 'Energy Cooperation problems in Northeast Asia: Unfolding the Reality', *East Asia*, Vol. 23, No. 3, Autumn 2006, p. 96.
7. Kreft, N. 5, p. 67.
8. *The Indian Express*, 24 August 2005.
9. http://islamicterrorism.wordpress.com/category/china/ accessed on 27.9.2009.
10. *Beijing Time*, 21 January 2003.

2

Cooperation and Discord in India-China Relationship: Key to the Future of South and Southeast Asia

Binoda Kumar Mishra

It is no coincidence that the two most populous countries of the world, having ancient cultural contacts and sharing close proximity do not share a patterned relationship between them. History certainly has a hand in shaping their bilateral relations. The single historical event of clash in 1962 looms large in determining their mutual perceptions. The historical cultural connections between the two countries are also a cause of some major frictions between the two countries. The spread of Buddhism to China from India did not establish strong connections rather, the exceptional rise of Buddhism in Tibet has brought strains between them. Despite not having a very friendly attitude towards each other, India and China have moved from a position of conflict to major collaborators in some aspects of their bilateral engagements. Now the question is how to explain the changing relationship between the two countries and what lies ahead? These are important ponderings because the shape of the 21st century international system largely depends on the future juxtaposition of these two countries.

India and China in the Emerging International Order

Something important is happening in Asia which the whole world is watching with eager and anxiety. The two most populated countries of the world have started their march towards the core of international economic system and seem to be marching at a fair speed. Their combined march can be compared to the "rise of Europe during the 19th century or the burst of the US in the 20th century".[1] It may be early into the present century but there are unmistakable allusions that the current century is going to be shaped largely by the actions of these two Asian giants. Some see the rise of India and China as a single phenomenon 'the rise of *Chindia*' and some are interested in the implications of the rise to these two powers.[2] The fact that both India and China are growing at a sustained rate, despite fluctuations in global economy, is the primary cause of anxiety for many who find it difficult to comprehend that two drastically different systems are performing similarly and spectacularly in the global economic sphere. The anxiety is due to it being unprecedented and lacking any reference to any other global phenomenon. Those, who believe in the 'End of History' theory, find the rise of China beyond any plausible explanation and those who see India, through J.K. Galbraith's eyes, as a 'functional anarchy' find it difficult to account factors for such a sustained growth. The second reason for the increasing anxiety among those who are watching this rise is the uncomfortable bilateral history and the geopolitical issues involving both these countries. The rise of India and China is giving jitters to the Westerners who fear job loss and many other deprivations. But India and China, on the other hand, have a tough task at hand as they house one third of world's population and aspire to provide them the standard of life comparable to the West. It is under this background that this paper intends to look at the points of convergence of interests and the potentials of rift between the two Asian giants and their future implications for the region. Before embarking upon the complex India-China relationship, it is imperative to have a sound understanding of the two systems and their style of operations, particularly foreign policy formulation. While China has experienced republican and communist political systems, India has the experience of colonial system followed by democratic political system. About the Chinese style of operation a small anecdote will make it clear. Once, Henry Kissinger asked Deng Xiaoping, "What do you think about the French Revolution?" Deng's answer was, "It is too early to say."[3] Thus, it is clear that the Chinese take a very long-term view of their interests and plan. Therefore, any analysis of Chinese approach has to be highly circumstantial. On the other hand, India is perceived not to have any long-term vision behind her foreign policy and rather is believed to have an *ad hoc* or a contingent approach. Given the history and its influence over present mutual perceptions, the paper at first discusses the historical flash points and their contemporary relevance for Sino-Indian bilateral relationship. Then the contemporary engagements between the two nations are discussed to assess the exact nature of the evolving Sino-Indian relationship and its possible implications for their immediate neighbourhood called South and Southeast Asia.

History and Potentials of Conflict

Tibet

Tibet remains an anxious point between India and China. The traditional buffer between India and China during the British Indian period turned into an issue having the potential to offset the Sino-Indian relations at any point of time. A look at the history of Tibet and its relation with India and China is warranted for objectively appraising the importance of the Tibet issue for both India and China. In India, the first Prime minister, Pandit Jawaharlal Nehru is still criticised for his policies towards China over Tibet. His policy towards Tibet has been made out to be the most controversial and the weakest of his foreign policy choices. Nehru's acceptance of Chinese suzerainty over Tibet in 1950, after the Chinese occupation of Tibet and further acceptance of Chinese sovereignty over Tibet, while granting asylum to Tibetan spiritual leader Dalai Lama, are seen as confused and against his pledge to oppose imperialism any where. I do not intend to argue that Nehru was right in every aspect so far as the Tibetan autonomy is concerned but a historical analysis of the Tibet question would make it clear that there was nothing better any one could have done.

Historically, the nature of China and Tibet interactions have been complicated but it is true that China has periodically established her suzerainty over Tibet, starting from the Mongolian Yuan domination of China and Tibet together during the thirteenth century. Further formal Chinese control to Tibet was extended during the reign of Qian Long Emperor (c. 1735 – 1795) of Qing or Manchu Dynasty who "stationed two Qing imperial envoys (*amban*), with the protection of Qing garrisons in Lhasa."[4] This control of China proper over Tibet declined with the Western incursions into China during the nineteenth century and "Tibet increasingly became independent, reducing Chinese hegemony over Tibet to nothing more than a symbol."[5] But there were no serious efforts from the Tibetan side to completely sever ties with China proper. Even during 1911-1949, though the Chinese Republican governments hardly paid any attention to Tibet except claiming Chinese sovereignty over Tibet, the government in Lhasa did not try to obtain *le jure* legitimacy for their independence. Only after the communist revolution in China, the Chinese Communist Party forcefully asserted

Chinese sovereignty over Tibet. The nature of assertion of the Chinese Communist Party took every one by surprise. For the first time, China denied the autonomous status of Tibet which was contrary to Mao's earlier position. In 1936, in an interview, Mao reportedly said that Tibet together with Outer Mongolia and Xinjiang "will form autonomous republics attached to China federation" after "the People's Revolution has been victorious."[6]

With this background, China occupied Tibet under the pretext of liberating the later. Nehru was among the firsts to recognise Chinese 'suzerainty' over Tibet against the wishes of many, both inside and outside the country. There were wide ranges of suggestions given to Nehru that included attacking Tibet pre-emptively and occupy it and/or extend international recognition to Tibet. Thus, Nehru's stand seemed to be appeasing the Chinese and sacrificing the Tibetans' cause for his communist preferences. If one looks at the Tibet issue independently, one may conclude, like many of his critics that he acted in a un-statesman like manner. But a critical understanding of Tibet question and Indian interest in the matter needs references to other interests of India vis-à-vis China, most importantly the border dispute with China. The India-China border dispute would form a separate section of this paper but suffice it to mention here that the Indian argument on the India-China border issue rested on the principle of inheritance from the British. The only legal document India had made the basis of her geographical claims vis-à-vis China and Tibet was the tripartite Simla Agreement of 1914. The controversial McMahon Line was agreed and recognised by all the three parties to the treaty namely: India, China and Tibetan representatives as the geographical boundary between India and Tibet autonomous region of China. According to this same agreement, the Chinese Suzerainty over Tibet was established and recognised by India, China and most importantly by the Tibetan representatives.

Nehru, throughout his interactions with China, was mindful of possible problems China might pose for India. "He had experience of Communist Regimes and knew that they could be sweet reasonableness itself or pig-headed with conceit in turn."[7] He rightly anticipated the victory of the Chinese Communist Revolution and wrote to the provincial Prime Ministers of India in a letter dated 16 September 1949:

> In China the Communist armies are marching rapidly towards Canton and there can be little doubt that they will reach there before long. Probably by 10 October, which is a special date in Chinese history and is called the double tenth, a new central Government might be proclaimed in China. The question of

> recognition of the new regime will then have to be considered. We are in no way opposed to such recognition....[8]

Just after the victory of Chinese Communist Party, in another letter dated 31 December 1949 to the provincial heads of India, Nehru warned about the Chinese Government. He wrote: "the problem of China has troubled us greatly ... China has a strong centralised government and no country can ignore it for long."[9] The use of the words "troubled us greatly" suggests that he was apprehensive of trouble with China. While he was rightly apprehensive of the mind of the Chinese Government, he was quite clear about the China Tibet relationship. Even before extending recognition to the Communist Government in China, he wrote to the provincial heads of on 1 December 1949 that:

> Our policy has been rather vague about Tibet. It has been an inheritance from British days. We have recognised the autonomy of Tibet under some kind of vague suzerainty of China. Strictly speaking, in law, we cannot deny that suzerainty. We would like Tibet to be autonomous and have direct dealing with us and we shall press for this. But it is clear that we cannot bring any effective pressure to change the course of events in Tibet. Therefore, we must be cautious about the steps that we might take so as not to get entangled in enterprises, which are beyond our strength. We have accepted certain facts as they are....[10]

There is no evidence to suggest that any one in the country opposed to his observations during that time except Vallabhbhai Patel. Patel clearly opposed Nehru in his policies towards China in general and on Tibet in particular. He was of the view that the Chinese incursion into Tibet constitutes a direct threat to India's security and he was right in his assessment. He suggested to Nehru in a letter "to instigate a serious military and intelligence appreciation of the Chinese threat to India and to begin long-term steps to increase India's military readiness, to improve communications with frontier areas, to strengthen administration in the frontier regions and to consider policy in relation to the McMahon line, which had settled India's north-eastern frontier in 1914".[11]

Nehru in his note on his formulation of China Policy, which he forwarded to Patel, maintained that Pakistan is the major enemy. Though he discounted in his note the Chinese threat, it does not mean that he was not aware of the possibility of the kind of threat Patel was hinting at. But he was fully convinced that India was in no position to prepare for a military confrontation with a country like China, at least for some time then as the cost of such military preparedness would further weaken India's general defence position. He was precise in his formulation that "there are limits beyond which we cannot go ... and spreading out of our army in distant frontiers would be bad from every military or strategic point of view".[12] About the second suggestion that Nehru should 'consider policy in relation to McMahon line,' no one knows what Patel meant by that as he passed away soon after this exchange. But if he, as many others, felt that Nehru should have negotiated the McMahon line with China, then there would have been a contradiction in the suggestion itself. As mentioned earlier, the legality of India's geographical claims in the north-eastern region rested on the Simla Agreement of 1914 and any deviation from that would have undermined the principle of inheritance from the British and thus would have opened up more problematic fronts.

Despite the relative peace between India and China over the Tibet issue, China remains worried about Tibet and thus India, because if there is any country in a position to extend its influence over Tibet, it is India. The Chinese have extracted substantial concession from India over Tibet and India is no longer ready to give any more. China thus remains anxious over Indian intensions since 1.2 lakh Tibetans along with their spiritual and political leader Dalai Lama continue to live in India. A clear picture over Tibet and India-China relationship can emerge only when the Chinese wait comes to an end. The Chinese are waiting for the death of the present Dalai Lama with the hope that with his death the movement will come to an end. China's anxiety is due to the fact that if Tibet manages to get independence, then China will be on a slippery slope of independence declarations that could start from Tibet, through Xinjiang, Hong Kong and end in Taiwan.[13] Secondly, it is only India that can have any influence over Tibet which, for the Chinese means huge loss vis-à-vis India within the region and outside.

Sino-Indian Border Dispute

The other major problem India and China have in between them is the dispute over border. They fought over the border issue and the dispute still remains unresolved. In this case also Nehru is faulted for not picking the allusions of Chinese operations in Tibet and not understanding the Chinese sinister design of occupying Indian land. From the nationalist point of view, Nehru's China policy can be called disastrous as it led to a humiliating defeat for India. But for a judicious analysis, one needs to look at the then prevailing larger international picture and the options available to Nehru which could be pursued without compromising India's new found political sovereignty.

Given her population, her rich culture and long history of civilization, India regarded China as a sister civilization.[14] Nehru's reading of China was historically conditioned and he firmly believed that there could never be a situation when India and China would have a clash of interests on any matter. He further believed that the peace-loving Chinese would never force war on a country like India. His faith on the peace-loving nature of Chinese people rested on a peculiar notion. In a letter to his daughter, Nehru related the construction of the Great Wall of China to Chinese distaste for war. Describing the utility of the Great Wall of China, Nehru argued that the Chinese people preferred to spend a huge amount on a project that would not protect China from any major attack but would be a guard against petty attacks. This, according to him, shows that the Chinese were against maintaining standing armies.[15] Secondly, in Nehru's vision, China and India deserved to get meaningful positions in the international system owing to their population and it is China and India that would lead the Asian resurgence. Much before India's independence, in his conception of a South Asian federation he included China as a major player. In his autobiography Nehru projected a federation of nations including the present 8 South Asian countries, China and Burma (Myanmar).[16]

Nehru's initial China policy was based on these simple understanding that he had about China. During his visit to China in August 1939 and his interactions with Marshall Chiang Kai-shek and Madam Chiang, he was convinced that the Chinese do not attach much importance to geography and thus was sanguine that under no circumstances both nations would have problem regarding the border. His understanding of China and her people was valid till the communist revolution took place in China. Once the revolution was successful and the communists established firm control over the country, they maintained secrecy in every matter and none in the world outside of China had any knowledge of the happenings in China. For understanding the Chinese policies one had to rely on the official policies announced by the Chinese government and the statements made by the leadership of the Chinese Communist Party (CCP). The border dispute between India and China evolved from the point of discovery and was made ugly by systematic Chinese actions. A brief description of the evolution of the borer dispute would help in understanding the nature of the conflict and the high stakes of both India and China.

India did not share a border with China proper till the Chinese occupation of Tibet in 1950. Once China made Tibet a part of China, it shared a long border with India, which according to the Chinese authorities had never been delimited. The Sino-Indian border dispute had two specific issues: the Aksai Chin desert and the North Eastern Frontier Agency (NEFA). Though Aksai Chin had remained a bone of contention between the two countries, China never acknowledged that there was a dispute with India on the border questions till 1958. In all their references to the border question with India, the Chinese leadership maintained the view that there is no border dispute with India but "small" border issues. The Chinese leadership was careful in not to antagonise Indian leadership as he was leading the campaign for PRC's entry into the UN. "The Chinese leadership played on Nehru's Asian, anti-imperialist attitude, his proclivity to temporise, and his sincere desire for an amicable Sino-Indian relationship. Chou's strategy was to avoid making explicit in conversations and communications with Nehru, any Chinese border claims, while avoiding any retraction of those claims which would require changing Chinese maps".[17]

The history of Aksai Chin goes back to 1865 when W.H. Johnson drew a line to link Demchok in the south with Karakorum pass in the north. This line included the Aksai Chin desert in the domain of the Maharaja of Kashmir. There have been alterations to this boundary on strategic grounds but never established formally. The most important of these alterations is the MacCartney-Macdonald line of 1899 that excludes most of Aksai Chin from the British domain. The Chinese seemed not to have responded to any of these developments. Further, the British reasserted the validity of the Johnson line in response to a survey conducted by Russian experts for the pro-Soviet Sinkiang government of the warlord Sheng Shih-tsai.[18] This was the latest claim on the line that India inherited from the British on her border claims so far as the Aksai Chin is concerned. As all others, India asserted her boundary as demarcated by the Johnson line last decided by the British under the principle of inheritance.

The second section of the border that turned out to be disputed is the India-China border from Bhutan to the border between China and Burma known as McMahon Line. The history of McMahon Line is not as old as the Aksai Chin desert. The British Indian authorities called for a Conference to demarcate the boundary between British India, Tibet and China. According to the Chinese, they participated in the Conference reluctantly but the Tibetans participated eagerly. The result of the Conference was the famous McMahon Line. This line, for all practical purposes remained the boundary line as no party involved in the Conference disputed even when this line figured in the Survey of India map of 1937. There are several signs to suggest that China accepted this line as the boundary of India. There seemed to be no change in this stand of China even after the Communists came to power in China and occupied Tibet with force despite protests from India and other countries.

During the initial years, the Communist leadership never made their objection to McMahon line explicit. In many instances, the Chinese leadership had opined that there is no major border dispute of China but only some minor issues which can be solved amicably. In New Delhi in November-December 1956, Chou sought to create the impression with Nehru that China would accept the McMahon line. Nehru reminded the Chinese premier his observation of 1956 in a letter to Chou. Nehru reminded him that: "...the Chinese government is of the opinion that they should give recognition to McMahon Line. They had, however, not consulted the Tibetan authorities about it yet. They propose to do so".[19] The Chinese, however, changed their position to make matters rigid and complicated. They harped on the point that the Simla treaty was a clandestine one and China never ratified the treaty. Chairman Mao Zedong described the Indian leadership as only a transitory liberal bourgeoisie that was bent upon pushing unjust imperial treaties on China's middle kingdom pride.[20] The issue became an emotional one between the Chinese and the Indian authorities. It is argued that the Chinese were ready to negotiate if Nehru wanted to negotiate. The argument may be true and literature focusing on the Chinese stand gives the impression that the Chinese were willing to settle the border without reference to the Shimla agreement. One cannot conclude firmly whether the Chinese were actually interested to agree to Indian demands on the border issue, but assuming that they were ready for a compromise, there were two problems.

The negotiation offer involved trading the claims over territories. China wanted India to give up of her claim over Aksai Chin in return China would recognise the McMahon line. Nehru was convinced personally that some kind of compromise was essential for settling the border and tried to prepare the Indian public to accept this fact. He argued that Aksai Chin is a snow desert where a blade of grass does not grow. Nehru understood clearly that Aksai Chin was a difficult terrain and had limited economic and strategic utility for Indian Union. Many security experts in India and abroad vindicate his understanding of the region that China cannot make a comical attack on India from that point. But this was not acceptable to Indian public. In Indian political circles, negotiating with the Chinese was considered as compromising India's sovereignty. Secondly, negotiating with India's inherited border would have created further complications in the Northeastern part of the country and that were questioning their merger with the Indian Union. Thus, the only alternative India was and is left with is to stand firm on her claims knowing fully well that this might drag India into a conflict with China. The position on the border remains the same even today. Even today, the Chinese are asking for negotiation on the border issue without reference to the Shimla agreement and no political leadership in India is ready to agree to such terms of negotiation.

The claim over Arunachal is important to the Chinese for two reasons:

1. It would prove Chinese control over Tibet.
2. Control over Tawang on the ground of it being the birth place of 6th Dalai Lama would legitimise Chinese control over the Institution of Dalai Lama and thus Buddhist Tibet.[21]

In the present circumstances when India is also rising along with China and aspires to be a great power in her own right, a solution to the boundary question seems to be a far cry. We see hard positions being formulated in Indian policy circles anew. There are suggestions that India should assert herself vis-à-vis China over the border question. India should raise the issue of Shaksgam valley (5,180 sq. km. of PoK) transferred to China by Pakistan in 1963. India should also show concern over the Karakoram Highway linking PoK with Xinjiang province. India is also advised to stake a claim over Mt. Kailash and Mansarovar over similar religious ground as Chinese are doing related to Tawang.[22] However, on the positive side, both India and China have chosen to restrain from allowing escalation of tension over the border issue. On the negative side, in the words of B. Raman, "[o]ver the years, diplomats and statesmen all over the world have perfected the art of creating an illusion of dramatic forward movement in bilateral relations, while, in fact, remaining stuck in the same place",[23] and India and China seem to be perfecting this art in relation to the border dispute.

Allusions of Co-operation or Illusions?

The new century is said to have brought in significant changes in the bilateral relationship between India and China. The process of, so called, rapprochement began with the visit of the Chinese Premier to India in 2005. India declared 2006 as India-China friendship year. The Chinese response to this was 140 border incursions during October 2006 – September 2007.[24] The *Bhai – Bhai* rhetoric led both to a war. But it is said that now there is a new impetus to the bilateral interactions between India and China, that can be best described as India China Buy-Buy. Currently India-China bilateral trade is set to cross $60 billion. This is quite healthy despite India having huge trade deficit vis-à-vis China. China has replaced EU and US and become India's largest trading partner (India is China's 10th largest trading partner). Some optimists point out that there is still more potential in their bilateral trade. This is being projected as a sure indication of Sino-Indian rapprochement. But a closer look at this increasing trade between the two countries would suggest that it is hardly contributing to the change in mutual distrust even in the economic spheres. Border trades between the two countries are in operation at three points namely: Shipki La in Himachal Pradesh, Lipu Lekh in Uttaranchal (1992-93) and Nathu La in Sikkim (2006). The trading has not been up to the mark as both India and China have reservations in increasing the items to be traded. The scope of trade is also being kept limited to the population of the border districts only.

Secondly, the economic component that is closely associated with trade is investment. We do not see much improvement in investment in each other's country. Indian investment in China is 130 million USD in comparison to Chinese investment in India during April 2000 to March 2009 is just 10.85 million USD (0.01 percent of India's total FDI inflow).[25] Cautious by the other country is the allegation that restricts mutual investment. While India tries to protect its sensitive sectors such as telecommunication and port development, China protects her sensitive areas. China does not allow Indian IT companies to operate in areas such as Tibet, Xinjiang and Sichuan.[26] (The hardware and software rhetoric is yielding virtually no results). We can downplay the significance of low level of investment as a sign of persisting distrust between India and China. We can look at other levels where there seem to be a greater propensity towards mutual cooperation. It is the concept newly in fashion called 'regionalism'. One of the manifestations of Indian and Chinese foreign policies in the recent years (after the end of Cold War) is their attempt to engage other countries (neighbours in particular) in multilateral arrangements both at regional and sub-regional levels. There are a number of such regional and sub-regional arrangements, such as SCO, Mekong-Ganga, Greater Mekong sub-regional Cooperation, BIMSTEC, and BCIM.

We can pick up the behaviour of India and China in any of these arrangements in which both are involved to assess what they think of each other. I pick BCIM and the attempt is to evaluate how cooperative is India towards China in matters unrelated to their points of conflict. Initiated as Kunming initiative in 1999, it is a sub-regional arrangement that aims at creating an economic hub including Bangladesh, Myamnar, Southwest part of China and Northeast (NER) part of India. It is primarily an economic arrangement aimed at ameliorating the underdeveloped condition of NER and Southwest China along with Bangladesh and Myanmar. India is reluctant to commit itself to the initiative. Our theoretical understanding says that countries considering each other as rivals will not come together face to face at such smaller arrangements. If they consider each other as competitors, then they come together but remain worried about each other's (relative) gains rather than their own absolute gains. If they consider each other as friends then they wholeheartedly cooperate. If we look at India's approach towards BCIM, it becomes clear that India is more worried about the possible Chinese gains than absolute gains for India.

India has substantial economic incentives to interact with her eastern neighbours and a compulsion as well. India's NER is economically stagnated, and needs to be opened to the external world to improve the economic situation of the area. Economists from BCIM countries and outside have shown complementarities of the region in terms of resources.[27] They reinforce these resource complementarities with technological complementarities making the case for cooperation very strong.[28] China's interest in the arrangement is viewed as positive, and India is alleged to be acting as a spoilsport in the entire process. Such diagnosis is based on the Neo-liberal Institutional understanding of regional cooperative arrangements that there is a convergence of interest of BCIM countries in making the sub-region economically integrated. Such an analysis is based on the understanding that the states active in a particular issue-area must share common interests that can be attained only through cooperation.[29] But economy is not always benign in international politics. More importantly, inter-state economic calculations change in terms of their payoffs under different circumstances. If the parties to the economic arrangement are in friendly terms with one another, economic calculations remain benign as parties remain sensitive to their own gains in absolute terms, but if the parties to the arrangement are pitted in a situation of mutual competition, economic calculations change. The absolute gains may be termed as relative losses.

One cannot say that Indian policy-makers are unaware of the potential of the area turning into an economically prosperous region. But still India chooses to go slow and remain cautious. The address of the then India's Secretary (East), Mr. Rajiv Sikri, encapsulates India's approach.[30] He clearly spelt out that the Indian government is against structuralising BCIM. At the same time he called upon the Forum (BCIM) to come up with economically viable specific projects for the region.[31] In his own words, he proudly discussed the achievement of India engaging the other nations through various other Forums. Why then is India against any structural arrangement of BCIM? A reading between the lines of Mr. Sikri's address clearly reveals the apprehensions. The apprehensions are directly related to non-economic issues that bother India vis-à-vis the other members of the region. Some worries on the economic front are also visible in his address. His stress on economic viability of the specific projects is indicative of the fact that India does not wish to lose control of the economic situation in the region. The fear is of a loss in relative terms. Given the fragile peaceful relationship, India manages to have maintained with China, given the intermittent flare-ups on contentious border issues, and China's preposterous claims over Arunachal, it is natural that India apprehends economic trouble. What is shown as the economic threat is actually not the real threat perceived by the Indian policy-makers. It is said that in the event of economic integration, the cheap goods from China would flood the markets of India's northeast. This, at best, is a symptomatic manifestation of the real fear. There is no study available to calculate the relative payoffs for China and India from economic integration under BCIM, but the present advantages of China over India in terms of preparedness for availing of economic opportunities is jittery enough for India to apprehend that in the event of economic integration of the region, the total control of the regional economy would be in the Chinese hands. Such a possibility, under present circumstances, is disincentive enough for India to become unconditionally interested in such regional arrangements.

On an earlier occasion, Mr. Sikri had expressed the hope of travelling from Kolkata or Guwahati to Bangkok through Dhaka or Yangon.[32] Interesting to find out that China or her Southwest provinces did not figure in Mr. Sikri's scheme of things. Such exclusion is intentional, and points to the fact that India is not comfortable with the idea of directly engaging China within any multilateral arrangement. It is the notion of space that forces India to keep away China from regional arrangement, wherein India feels it may be proved to be a lesser player vis-à-vis China. Second important economic worry for India is the possibility of Northeast India becoming a periphery to Southwest China. At present, Southwest China may be as poor as India's Northeast and may not have any industries, but once the region opens up in terms of connectivity to the sea and to larger markets through Myanmar, India and

Bangladesh, the region may experience rapid industrialisation. But the same cannot be said about India's Northeast. Given the Chinese expertise in the manufacturing sector and the low (government controlled) wage structure, Southwest China may offer itself as the best destination for establishing industries. These industries are to be built on the resources of the region, i.e. Myanmar, Bangladesh and Northeast Region of India. In the ultimate perceptual analysis, India feels to be gaining less in comparison to China from the region's economic integration. This apprehension of relative loss becomes alarming in its possible political spin-offs. We see similar approach by China in East Asia Summit, in SCO, leave aside India's Mekong Ganga and China's Greater Mekong Sub-region Economic Cooperation Programme whereas each excludes the other.

Pursuing Energy

It is often cited that India and China are cooperating in energy sector which is their common interest to sustain their growth. But a closer look reveals that cooperation is the last thing in their pursuit of oil. Both have collaborated in four cases, viz., Sudan, Syria, Iran and Columbia. On the other hand, China successfully outbid India in four other oil fields such as, Angola, Kazakhstan, Ecuador and Nigeria. A critical analysis of the time line and the costs would reveal the underlined competition in energy sector. The seeming cooperation in energy sector are in places that are considered high risk zones by the western countries or are marginal players in oil sector. In Sudan (March 2003), India paid $750 million for 25% in the Greater Nile Oil Project while Chinese company CNPC paid $441 million for 40% of the share. In Syria (December 2005), both pay a total of $573 million for 37% share. In Columbia (August 2006), both spent $850 million for 50% share. In Iran (September 2006), India got only 29 % shares in comparison to China's 51%.[33] In contrast, in Kazakhstan (August 2005), China outbid India in a take over. Initial Chinese bid was $3.6 billion and the Indian bid was $3.9 billion, but the Chinese revised their bid overnight to $4.18 billion. In Ecuador (September 2005), China outbid India by 1.4 to 1.42 billion USD. In Nigeria (January 2006), China won by 2 to 2.3 billion USD.[34] In Angola (November 2004), China won the bid with 725 million USD to India's 310 million USD. It is clear that China is dictating the terms of cooperation to energy desperate India and the latter has no other alternative than to agree to the Chinese terms as in competition China can adopt all methods, such as unscrupulous bidding practices to providing economic and political incentives to the regimes to prevent India from obtaining any access to energy sources.

Open Competition and Containment

The Sino-Indian march towards the international core, with a burden of billion plus population, entails rationalisation of resource security. Added to this, both have the self-image of being great powers in the emerging international system. To ensure this resource security and to fulfil their ambition of great power status, both have to depend heavily on their immediate neighbourhoods called South and Southeast Asia. It is not an unfair wish on the part of any nation to maintain a favourable neighbourhood but a demand of exclusive possession of a region would certainly be resented by similarly ambitious nations. Since both India and China share the same neighbourhood, similar compulsions and similar self-perceptions, they are bound to compete directly and also over the neighbourhoods in all matters, whereas most important among them being security.

Power Projections

The contemporary security strategy of China related to its immediate region is to "prevent the rise of a peer competitor in Asia or cancel out any advantages that a competitor might have by making alliance with other states".[35] China remains worried that stronger powers at its neighbourhoods would pose a challenge to her control over restive peripheral provinces and there are realistic calculations that China may go out of the way to inflict substantial damage on any country that it feels is a competitor (potential opponent to its self-assumed hegemony) in the region. During the Kargil War, one Chinese official reportedly told a Western diplomat that "should India and Pakistan destroy each other in a nuclear war, there would be peace along China's southwestern frontiers for at least three decades and Beijing needs 20 to 30 years to consolidate its hold over restive Xinjiang and Tibet provinces.[36] There are similar observations over Chinese intensions by Western scholars as well. In her testimony before the US-China Economic and Security Review Commission on May 20, 2009, Lisa Curtis of the Heritage Foundation mentioned : "... Chinese officials also view a certain degree of India-Pakistan tension as advancing their own strategic interests as such friction bogs India down in South Asia and interferes with New Delhi's ability to assert its global ambitions and compete with China at the international level."[37]

An exact nature of Chinese threat to India is hard to measure in any absolute terms, therefore, states in an environment of uncertainty may, at times, over-react but such over-reaction is always considered prudent. In this context the Chinese actions from mid-1970s have been of considerable anxiety to India. From mid-1970s, China started bringing nuclear weapons and missiles into Tibet and parked them in the caves of Tibet on the pretext of those being a deterrent against the then Soviet or possible US attacks. But a careful analysis would suggest that these weapons are strategic assets only against India. This can be vindicated by the fact that the number of nuclear warheads in Tibet has not decreased after the end of the Cold War. More particularly, as China has a 'no strike' agreement with Russia[38] and an agreement with the US for not targeting US bases in the region, there can be no other rationale for China than targeting India.[39]

Nuclear Weapons have emerged as an independent variable in determining the India-China relationship over the years. From the very beginning, while India was pursuing her nuclear programme, it had projected China as the threat factor that can push India to cross the nuclear threshold. As early as January 27 February 1, 1962, Homi Bhaba, in the Pugwash conference in Udaipur, declared that "given the threat, China poses to her smaller neighbours, it is expedient for India to go nuclear weapons way".[40] On the other hand, China assisted India's arch rival Pakistan to lay her hands on nuclear weapons. From 1971 to '76, Zulfikar Ali Bhutto, first as foreign minister and then as prime minister, made three visits and finally China agreed in 1976 to support Pakistan in developing the weapon. It is, of course, directly related to India's Peaceful Nuclear Explosion (PNE) of 1974. China transferred the design of her own fist bomb which Pakistan tested in 1987. From then on, Pakistan is claiming to have possessed the technology to develop the nuclear bomb. The nexus still continues and China goes on assisting Pakistan in complete violation of her Nuclear Non-Proliferation Treaty (NPT) obligations. The Indo-US Nuclear treaty is being used as legitimising Chinese assistance to Pakistan.

Not only nuclear weapons, China has been assisting Pakistan in building missiles that can reach all parts of India. Every Chinese project that results in a Pakistani missile is claimed by Pakistan to be indigenous to Pakistan. We know for sure that nearly 70 percent of Pakistani battle tanks and 50 percent of combat aircraft are of Chinese origin. Currently, Pakistan is using the US aid to develop its conventional arms and the Chinese assistance to develop nuclear programme. As recently as 20 May 2009, Lisa Curtis exposed the Chinese help to Pakistan in developing missiles having the ability to carry nuclear warheads. As part of China's policy of arming Pakistan, it supplied conventional weapons to Pakistan which include JF-17 aircraft, JF-17 production facilities, F-22P frigates with helicopters, K-8 jet trainers, T-85 tanks, F-7 aircraft, small arms and ammunition.[41] It helped Pakistan "build a turnkey ballistic-missile manufacturing facility near the city of Rawalpindi and helped Pakistan develop the 750-km-range, solid-fuelled Shaheen-1 ballistic missile capable of carrying nuclear warheads.[42] In line with Indo-US nuclear deal, there are steady supplies of nuclear technology and materials to Pakistan by China. The Indo-US nuclear deal is civilian and well accounted for. But the same cannot be said about the clandestine Sino-Pakistan nuclear cooperation arrangement. There is desperation on the part of China to help Pakistan emerge as a nuclear capable state. At this juncture of time when Pakistan is reeling under the pressure of home-grown terrorism and severe political and financial crisis, China has agreed to construct two new nuclear reactors in Pakistan.[43] Thus, in the regional context the modernisation programme of China and its assistance to Pakistan can be seen to have two objectives: (1) gaining leverage over India, and (2) building Pakistan as a client state to box India into South Asia.[44]

Since the beginning of the current century, China has embarked upon a massive modernisation programme for its armed forces.[45] According to official figures, for the year 2008, China's defence budget of 418 billion Yuan (£35 billion) was an increase of 17.8 percent over 2007.[46] And "according to figures from Jane's, the military specialists, has risen by 178 percent in the past seven years".[47] China's budget for 2009 proposes a further increase of 14.9 percent over its defence expenditure of 2008.[48] There is a nuclear component to the Chinese nuclear modernisation. In an interview to Arms Control Today, Gareth Evans hinted at the nuclear component of China's modernisation programme and linked it to possible arms race in a triangular manner.[49] It is the Chinese modernisation programme that forces India to pursue an effective deterrence programme. Given the gap in the conventional military capabilities between China and India, it has become imperative for India to build credible deterrence with nuclear weapons. These sharp cumulative increases, in military expenditure by China, cannot be treated separately from the increasing competition between India and China to increase their sphere of influence in the combined region of South and Southeast Asia. In military terms, If India remains worried about these increased Chinese defence expenditures, China remains worried about India developing intermediate range supersonic cruise missiles

Brahmos (in collaboration with Russia) and intermediate range ballistic missile *Agni*. India alleges China of putting up signal intelligence post in Coco Island in Myanmar and China alleges India of upgrading her monitoring facilities in Mongolia. China has also expressed its anxiety over India's Blue Water Navy and its power to control the Malacca Straits through which 80 percent of Chinese imported oil flows. China also has expressed its worries over the possibility of India posing a threat to China in Southeast Asia and East Asia in collaboration with Vietnam and Japan.[50] Further, China is apprehensive that the 'arc of freedom and prosperity' — the US, Japan, Australia and India collaboration — is actually an "Asian NATO"[51] and a strategy to contain China. All these are sufficient grounds for India to believe that China's military modernisation is also targeted against India. China has also similar interpretation of India's foreign policies, particularly the Look East Policy.

Conclusion

The above discussion brings out the fact that there are four 'Cs' that characterise Sino-Indian relationship. Those are, Conflict, Cooperation, Competition and Containment. Feeding over a billion population certainly generates great scope for cooperation. It is increasingly being realised by both the countries that it is not going to be an easy task for them to fulfil the requirements of their population by themselves. They need to increase the scale of their resource base to support them in their effort to raise the standard of living of their populations. Both India and China are in the process of forming economic blocs involving other countries and each other to satiate their increasing requirements. China's compulsions lie in its lack of usable natural resources which, in comparison to India is 40 percent less. Given her population it has to look for resources beyond her territory. Similarly, India also has a vast population with limited resources. We see attempts to form sub-regional groupings involving countries geographically contiguous and otherwise. China on her part has been very pro-active and gone half of the world to connect with Latin American countries for commodities as basic as food substances (the Chinese Tofu comes from Brazil). Its compulsions are evident from the fact that it now out-consumes United States in four basic food and industrial commodities: grain, meat, steel and coal. So far as oil consumption is concerned, China is currently positioned second and may exceed the US at any time.

The objective assessment of their domestic situations would suggest that both would help themselves well, if they cooperate with each other. But at the same time, the aspiration to great power status and the historical issues seem to be weighing heavily in their minds. The high stakes, involved from both sides in the disputed issues, have the potential to engage both in perilous conflict. There is a cliché that great powers, either established or aspiring, even if good neighbours, do compete. And India and China seem to be behaving in no different way. Their immediate neighbourhood, i.e. South and Southeast Asia have to realise this fact to avoid unnecessary anxiety over Indian and Chinese actions vis-à-vis each other and towards the region. We will be better helped in any attempt to create a stable South and Southeast Asian region, if we give due importance to the competitive spirit of both India and China, which is both structurally dictated and domestically compelled. It is upto India and China to behave either like 18th century nations and use force to settle their disputes or as matured nations of 21st century or to explore civilised ways to mitigate their differences/disputes and compete with a positive spirit. The future of South and Southeast Asia is inextricably related to this decision of India and China.

References

1. David Smith, *The Dragon and the Elephant: China, India and the New World Order*, London: Profile Books, 2007, p. 171.

2. *Ibid.*

3. Sashanka S. Banerjee, *India's Security Dilemmas: Pakistan & Bangladesh*, London and New York: Anthem Press, 2006, pp. 224-25.

4. Chen Jian, "The Tibetan Rebellion of 1959 and China's Changing Relations with India and the Soviet Union," *Journal of Cold War Studies*, Vol. 8, No. 3, Summer 2006, p. 56.

5. *Ibid.*

6. Edgar Snow, *Red Star over China*, New York: Grove Weidenfeld, 1968, p.444, cited in, foot note No. 7.

7. Iqbal Singh, *Between two Fires: Towards an Understanding of Jawaharlal Nehru's Foreign Policy*, New Delhi: Nehru Memorial Museum and Library, 1998, p.187.

8. *Ibid.*

9. *Ibid.*

10. *Ibid.*

11. Cited in, Judith M. Brown, *Nehru: A Political Life*, New Delhi: Oxford University Press, 2003, p. 258.

12. *Ibid.*

13. Susan L. Craig, *Chinese Perceptions of Traditional and Nontraditional Security Threats*, March 2007, At http://www.StrategicStudies Institute.army.mil/, p. 95.

14. *Glimpses of World History*, *Centenary Edn*, New Delhi, OUP, 1989, p. 28.

15. *Ibid*, p.69.

16. *Jawaharlal Nehru: An Autobiography,* Centenary Edn, New Delhi: OUP, 1989, p. 608.

17. *The Sino-Indian Border Dispute, Section 1: 1950-59, CIA/RSS*, 2 March 1963, Released in May 2007, Available at, http://www.foia.cia.gov/CPE/POLO/polo-07.pdf

18. "*The Great India-China Game*", at http://www.rediff.com/cms

19. "Nehru's letter to Chou", 14 December 1958.

20. Swaran Singh, "India-China Relations: perception, Problems, Potential," *South Asian Survey*, Vol.15, No.1, 2008, p. 84.

21. Rajiv Sikri, *Challenge and Strategy: Rethinking India's Foreign Policy*, New Delhi: Sage Publications India Pvt. Ltd., 2009, p. 97.

22. *Ibid*, p.106.

23. B. Raman, "Our PM's visit to China: Core Issues Persist," *Chennai Centre for China Paper Studies, No. 99*, January 15, 2008.

24. "140 Incursions by China: ITBP Chief", *Tribune News Service*, New Delhi, October 23, 2007.

25. *Fact Sheet on Foreign Direct Investment (FDI): From August 1991 to May 2009*, Available at, http://www.dipp.nic.in/fdi_statistics/india_FDI_ May2009.pdf.

26. B. Raman, "India-China Ties: Positives and Negatives," *Chennai Centre for China Studies Paper No. 92*, January 7, 2008.

27. For a detailed analysis of the economic complementarities between Northeast India and Southwest China. See, Biswa N. Bhattacharyay and Prabir De,

"Promotion of Trade and Investment between People's Republic of China and India: Towards a Regional Perspective," *Asian Development Review*, Vol. 22, No. 1, pp. 45-70.

28. *Ibid.*

29. Robert Keohane, *After Hegemony: Cooperation and Discord in the World Political Economy*, Princeton: Princeton University Press, 1984, pp. 6, 247.

30. Address by Mr. Rajiv Sikri, Secretary (East) at the *6th Bangladesh-China-India-Myanmar Forum*, New Delhi, March 30, 2006.

31. *Ibid.*

32. Rajiv Sikri's address at a Forum organised by the Centre for Northeast India, South and Southeast Asia Studies, September 10-11, 2004, as cited by Sanjib Baruah, "The Problem," *Manipur Online*, November 23, 2005. Available at, www.manipuronline.com.

33. Chietigj Bajpaee, "The Panda and the Peacock," *China Security*, Vol. 3, No. 4, Autumn 2007, p. 109.

34. *Ibid.* Also see, Gillian GOH Hui Lynn, "China and India: Towards Greater Cooperation and Exchange." *China: An International Journal*, Vol. 4, No. 2, September 2006, pp. 273-74.

35. Christian Koch, "China and Regional Security in South Asia," in *The Balance of Power in South Asia*. Emirates Centre for Strategic Studies and Research, 2000, p.76.

36. Mohan Malik, "The China Factor in India Pakistan Conflict," *Parameters*, Vol. 33, No. 1, Spring 2003, p. 47.

37. Lisa Curtis, *China's Military and Security Relationship with Pakistan*, May 26, 2009.

38. *Sino-Russian Detargeting and No-First-Use Agreement*, September 1994.

39. US-China Non-targeting Agreement, June 1998.

40. George Perkovich, *India's Nuclear Bomb: The Impact on Global Proliferation*, New Delhi: Oxford University Press, 2000, pp. 60-61.

41. "Annual Report to Congress: Military Power of the People's Republic of China, 2009," Office of the Secretary to Defence, p. 57. Cited by Lisa Curtis, N.37.

42. "Pakistan Profile." *Nuclear Threat Initiative*, January 2009, May 14, 2009. Available at, http://www.nti.org/e_research/profiles/Pakistan/index.html. See Lisa Curtis, N.37.

43. Matthew Rosenberg, "Pakistan Secures China's Help to Build 2 Nuclear Reactors," *The Wall Street Journal*, October 20, 2008, Available at, http://online.wsj.com/article/ SB122445373748048283.html.

44. The two objectives are drawn from Brahma Chellaney's formulation of three objectives of China's proliferation activity. See, Brahma Chellaney: The India-Pakistan-China Strategic Triangle and the Role of Nuclear Weapons, *Proliferation Papers*, Security Studies Department, Institut francais des relations internationals, Winter 2002, www.ifri.org, p. 23.

45. The new national defence policy issued in December 2004 puts the increase of Chinese defence expenditure to 211.7 billion yuan (25.6 billion dollars) in 2004 from 170.8 billion yuan in 2002 and 190.8 billion yuan in 2003. See, Verna Yu, "New China Defense Policy Focuses Threat on Taiwan." *Space Daily*, December 27, 2004. Available at, http://www.spacedaily.com/news/china-05a.html.

46. Richard Spencer, "China's military ambition fuels Asian arms race," Available at, telegraph.co.uk, September 13, 2008.

47. *Ibid.*

48. China increases Defence Budget by 14.9% in 2009, *Xinhua*, cited in, *Asian Defence Industry Monitor*, March 4, 2009.

49. In his response to a question related to China's willingness in being part of the global nuclear elimination process, Evans replied, "[t]hat remains to be seen. China is engaged in fairly enthusiastic modernisation and expansion at the moment. He elaborated to explain China's concern over Taiwan and mutual concern between India and China would hold the key to nuclear game. See, Gareth Evans, "Getting to Zero: Interview with Gareth Evans, Co-Chair of the International Nuclear Non-Proliferation and Disarmament Commission." *International Crisis Group*, April 2009. Available at, www.crisisgroup.org/home/ index. cfm?id=6039&1=1.

50. For a detailed discussion on Chinese fears vis-à-vis India, see Jing-dong Yuan, "The Dragon and the Elephant: Chinese-Indian Relations in the 21st Century." *Washington Quarterly*, Vol. 30, No. 3, Summer 2007, pp. 131-44.

51. "Chinese Strategic Journals have been vehemently opposing the Japan-US-Australia-India 'alliance of democracies' concept, calling it as 'Asian NATO'." *China Daily*, January 16, 2007, as cited in D. S. Rajan, "India's Place in China's South Asia Strategy," *South Asia Analysis Group Paper, No. 3127*, April 1, 2009. Available at, http://www. southasiaanalysis.org/%5Cpapers32%5Cpaper3127.html

3

Twenty-first Century Responsibilities of India and China

A. Chandrasekaran and *P. Govinda Reddy*

Introduction

India and China are emerging powers which had made a significant mark, in the recent decades, in various fields of human activity. They have a glorious past and their civilisations are greatly note-worthy. But from the early modern period, India had been in the clutches of the English hegemony and China had also been in the grip of the European dominance, since the middle of the nineteenth century. It is the resurgent movement in Asia that had brought about freedom to Asian countries which soon began to develop themselves in various spheres. Noble ideas, such as Liberty, Equality and Fraternity, which became popular in France and other European countries in the 18th century, had found their place in the constitutional codes of the Asian countries. But the Cold War conditions and political developments in Asian countries jolted the concept of "One Asia". Particularly, activities such as suppression of democratic tendencies, violation of human rights, commission of genocide and aggression on neighbouring countries aggravated tense situation and aspects like regional integration through economic interdependence and strategic and security partnerships for peace and prosperity transcending all barriers had become illusions.

In such an atmosphere, India and China— whose population put together is more than quarter of the total world population and whose potentials are as great as that of the world powers— have to take up greater responsibilities to fulfill the dream of "One Asia". India and China have to bring about the Asian countries together for developmental activities and for Asian peace and prosperity. The Asian countries with the help and support of India and China can sink their differences, pool all their resources and come together with an understanding of the concept that "together we will prosper". India and China can take up these responsibilities to accomplish the blossoming of "One Asia".

Conditions in India and China

The rapid economic growth of East Asia is probably the most important development in the world economy in the recent decades. The growth of China has been particularly spectacular and has been intensively discussed and analysed in the press and by academics. The Indian growth has not been as spectacular as that of China. However, the last two decades have seen a tremendous transformation of the Indian economy. India and China are among the fastest growing economies today.

They are also the two most populous economies. India's current population of 1.17 billion is 'only' some 200 million behind China. The UN's 'medium variant' projections indicate that India will be equal to China in population by 2025, and each will contribute some 18 per cent of the world's total population. Further, it should be pointed out here that economists and policy-makers today are greatly interested to know the living standards in India and China. (Bhaskar and Gupta, 2007).

Both India and China were incessantly disturbed by the problems of food shortage, poverty and natural disasters. Yet, people laboured hard to get over all the problems. Workers in both the countries toiled greatly to improve the conditions. Particularly in India, per-capita income certainly remains low, and over a quarter of the population lives below the poverty line (Datt and Ravallion, 2002). More recently, data from the 2004/5 survey are available and the analysis by Dev and Ravi (2007) reveal that poverty reduction has continued at a very low rate in the recent times (since 1993). Rising educational levels of the labour force are instrumental in growth accelerations within the countries and differences across the countries, and the estimates for India and China are no exception. Education has greatly contributed to Indian growth. Education is the one influence on labour productivity growth that appears to have been a little stronger in India than in China.

The Chinese incursion in new areas of NEFA in Siang and Lohit divisions was reported in Shillong on August 31st, 1959. The reports said that a few Indian frontier outposts close to the McMohan Line manned by the Assam Rifles have been lost as Chinese infiltration continues. Prime Minister Nehru categorically declared in the Rajya Sabha that the incursion by the Chinese troops was, in his view, "a clear case of aggression" (*The Hindu*, 1.9.1959). Again Prime Minister Nehru revealed in the Rajya Sabha on September 4th 1959 that the Chinese government had accused India of committing aggression. The Chinese note received by the Government of India on September 3rd 1959 denied that China had committed any aggression and went on to accuse India of illegally occupying a number of areas. The Chinese Government had asked India to withdraw from the area which they claimed was Chinese territory. The Chinese had also accused India of sending armed patrols into Tibetan territory. The note mentioned a large number of places which the Chinese claimed were their territories. (*The Hindu*, 5th September 1959).

After the 1962 conflict with China, the Indian Government passed a resolution stating its determination to get back every inch of Indian territory occupied by China. One of the Chinese commentators cited this resolution in an article in Chinese media as a major obstacle in the way of reaching a solution. Nonetheless, resolution had expressed India's frustration and anger. But it cannot be described as a very useful move in terms of real politics or a statement of an achievable objective. This had clearly led to a deadlock in India-China relations. Both the countries are still looking for an amicable and mutually acceptable solution. But, at the same time, China has been so friendly with Pakistan offering support in all possible ways and China's involvement in Pakistan's nuclear programme, had caused considerable concern in India. (Acharya and Deshpande, 2003).

China's security interests through most of the 1950s and even the ones that pertained directly to India, were chiefly tied to the Peoples Republic of China's (PRC's) entry into the Cold War. China did have a strong interest in treating India as a friendly neighbouring state and that was indeed what India was. Chinese leaders were far from certain that India was truly friendly, because frontier and border questions left over by history still remain symbols of strained relations between these two countries (Hoffmann, 2006). Soon after independence, the Indian government began to consolidate India's frontier and border position. It did so not only under the leadership of Nehru but also under the influence of Deputy Prime Minister Vallabhai Patel, who, like Nehru, had been a giant of the Indian independence movement. But the consolidation initiative did not fructify. Perhaps much more could have been achieved, but Nehru himself became primarily concerned with repairing a relationship with China that had been strained by China's actions relating to Tibet.

Partly in this context, Nehru from 1951 followed a policy towards Tibet that some have described as appeasement of China, a label that is unfair. Although Nehru recognized China's sovereignty over Tibet, he also encouraged the Tibetans to uphold their autonomy, particularly the degree of autonomy allowed to them under the Tibetan government's 1951 agreement with China. Nehru also wanted to uphold and strengthen Tibetan morale, both within the exile community in India and within Tibet itself. In 1954 he told his intelligence chief, B.N. Mullik that if Tibetan refugees in India aided their compatriots inside Tibet, the Indian government would take no notice and would refuse to heed Chinese protests so long as the refugees did not act too openly. In 1958, however, Nehru, as part of an effort to maintain relations with China on a correct level, sought to curb the political activities of Tibetan refugees in India.

Nehru's policy of friendliness towards China in the 1950s was motivated by many aspects. Idealism was involved, as was a security calculus involving both Tibet and the Indian border. Nehru, "hoped fondly that friendship" between India and China would maintain "peace in Asia" and even "start a new phase in world affairs, with Asia giving the lead in a more humane as well as a more sophisticated diplomacy". Nehru's reasoning was that it might be possible to maintain a substantial amount of Tibetan autonomy via diplomatic means and by limiting tension between China and India. In connection with a 1954 agreement signed by India and China whereby India gave up its claim to certain special rights in Tibet inherited from the British, Nehru reportedly hoped that "with the last vestiges of [Chinese] suspicion against India removed, China might adopt a reasonable attitude and Tibetan autonomy could yet be saved in substance and India's own interests safeguarded".

Nehru was not naive about China but wanted to adopt his own brand of pragmatic idealism in dealing with China. On some occasions, he criticised China in strictly realist terms and indicated by negative comments he is known to have made privately to his intelligence chief, Mullik, in 1952 about the historical nature of China as a country. In the meeting with Mullik, Nehru argued that China historically had been aggressive and had desired to extend its boundaries by conquest or subjugation of territories on the Chinese periphery. In addition, China did not believe in dealing with other countries as equals. Nehru felt that once the Chinese had achieved a certain degree of internal economic and political stability, they would "try to extend their influence and leadership over the rest of Asia and even suzerainty over some of the peripheral territories". Nehru believed that the largest obstacle in China's path towards supremacy in Asia would be India.

Nehru expressed this view elsewhere too. But his quest for Indian-Chinese friendship was of paramount importance to him. He was once reconciled what he realised was an apparent contradiction in his outlook by telling Mullik in 1953 "that he really wanted to be friendly with China". But he feared and stated : "The Chinese might misuse that friendship and so we must always be on our guard". He brought his negative thinking about China to public attention after Indian-Chinese relations had deteriorated because of the 1959 Tibetan revolt and the growing dispute over the borders. But his early 1950s realist opinions of China, and China's assumption of authority in Tibet, had already contributed to his government's efforts to strengthen India's administrative and intelligence-gathering capacities along the Tibetan frontier. Among those efforts, quite possibly, was the 1951 Indian takeover of the British-claimed Tawang territory lying beyond Se La Pass.

Even before 1959, Chinese suspicions of Indian involvement in the unrest in Tibet probably contributed to a hardening of the China's position on border issues. The Chinese government regarded the Indian frontier town of Kalimpong as a focal point of the Tibetan revolt, because it was there that Tibetan émigrés and agents of the United States, Britain, Taiwan, and India were allegedly conspiring. In March 1959, the Chinese claimed that the rebellion in Lhasa "had been engineered from the 'command center' in Kalimpong". India's grant of asylum to the Dalai Lama in 1959 and other aspects of the Indian government's handling of both the Dalai Lama and the Tibetan issue at that time gave impetus to the deterioration of Indian-Chinese ties. Chinese leaders "believed that . . . India was meddling in China's Tibetan affairs in collusion with the United States, in an attempt to separate Tibet from China."

Another important contributor to the development of the border dispute was the way the India-China frontier came alive after the Tibetan rebellion of March 1959. This occurred partly because of the movement and stationing of Chinese and Indian security personnel. They acted in a competitive fashion, and incidents were bound to occur, particularly because jurisdictions and border markings had never been jointly defined. The Indians hardened their stance on the borders after a major incident occurred not in the Assam Himalaya but near the Aksai Chin. The conflict spiral possessed a momentum of its own and culminated in the Indian-Chinese border war of October–November 1962.

In March 1959, the Dalai Lama's formal request to Nehru government for asylum in India came via the United States. The request was originally sent by CIA-trained Tibetan radio operators travelling with the Tibetan leader's group as he moved from Lhasa and journeyed towards the Indian border. They transmitted the request to the United States, apparently through Okinawa. The CIA promptly sent the information to New Delhi, where it was quickly answered in a positive fashion. It is this Tibetan problem that drove a wedge between India and China and strained their relationship also. With all these shortcomings, India had been trying to set right the internal conditions. Employment has continued to grow in Indian agriculture, at a much slower rate than in industry and services, and there were modest growth rates of output and labour productivity. In 2004, nearly 60 per cent of total employment was still in agriculture. India developed a sustained agriculture growth, since Independence, with agricultural stagnation over the previous 70 years (Roy, 2007).

The share of exports in GDP in India is significantly below that of China where it has tripled in less than two decades to reach one-fifth of GDP. There is an explosive growth of high-tech component. Further, manufacturing will continue to play a central role in generating the exports required to finance the rapidly expanding import bill. Alessandrini *et. al.* (2007) note that India's exports are still specialised in goods with a low technological content, but there have been some modest improvements in this respect over the period of rapid growth, with pharmaceutical products. Rapid growth in Asia, especially in China and India, is transforming the world economy. This experience poses new challenges for the understanding of the process of transition and growth. There is ample evidence that the potential for rapid change and development is enormous. The comparison between India and China suggests that there are different patterns of growth and development as well as differences in the role of institutions and government. It is also the case that, especially in India, growth has been unbalanced. Not only are there enormous differences between sectors, most obviously between agriculture and industry and commerce, but also between states and regions (Bhaskar and Gupta, 2007).

India, at the dawn of its independence, could not initiate for the Southeast Asian security. However, India's importance for security politics of Southeast Asia has begun to grow. The debate, on the implications of India's rise for

Asian and global balance of power, centres around the new expectations and residual skepticism about the sustainability of India's recent impressive economic performance. If India can maintain this performance, India's political and military weight in Southeast Asia will undoubtedly improve. India's "Look East" policy launched in the mid-1990s is strongly believed to be a policy beneficial to the nations of Asia. The expectations on India's rise have also begun to infuse a new dynamism into India's relations with the powers of Asia namely China and Japan. Consequently, India is no longer in isolation either to the regional politics of Southeast Asia or to the great power system around it. From the mid-1950s, its economy turned inward and its foreign policy drew closer to the Soviet bloc and India is now becoming an important factor in the security calculus of Southeast Asia (Raja Mohan, 2008).

India and China in Asian Affairs

India's enthusiasm for participating in and shaping the regional political and security arrangements is relatively new. After its early disappointments in trying to build Asian unity and solidarity in the 1950s, India's political emphasis decisively turned global and multilateral. The leadership of the Non-Aligned Movement (NAM) gave India scope to articulate its larger aspirations. But the obsession with NAM inevitably diluted the inheritance from British Raj, which was at the heart of the imperial defence system in the entire Indian Ocean littoral. Independent India nursed the ambitions of sustaining the Raj legacy of regional security. Its early political activism in southern Africa, the Middle East and Southeast Asia, its large Army, and the plans to build an ambitious Navy all pointed to a strong Indian role in Asia. The notion that "Aden to Malacca" was India's sphere of influence, was deeply rooted among the post-independence foreign policy-makers in New Delhi. In fact, the foreign policy assertiveness of India, in the early Cold War years, generated deep suspicion in some Western quarters that India might emerge as the "successor of Japan's Asiatic imperialism". Later, these fears were considered as baseless.

The enduring consequences of the subcontinent's partition and the conflict with China over Tibet and the boundary compelled India to deal with conflicts within its own neighbourhood. India's insular socialist policies resulted not just in India's relative economic decline, but also witnessed the erosion of historic trade links with the neighbouring regions in Asia. With no economic basis, India's relations with all the major powers, including the United States, Europe, Japan, and China remained under-developed. As India drew closer to the Soviet Union, in order to manage the regional balance of power within the subcontinent, this association with Moscow increasingly became disconcerting to the countries which valued their traditional links with India. The Indian military, which had a long record of participating in wars beyond the subcontinent, was now bogged down in territorial defence. The foreign policy of non-alignment also meant that the Indian military shunned contact and cooperation with the outside world, including the Soviet Union. Although India's Third World activism meant taking positions on all global issues, these degenerated into mere posturing against one or both superpowers and the inability to come to the aid of friendly nations in conflict with their neighbours. Further, by its bold stand in support of Vietnamese intervention in Cambodia, India got alienated from all the great powers, other than the Soviet Union.

India's first regional initiative, in the post-Cold War period towards Southeast Asia, was the "Look East" policy. The urgent imperative was to be a part of the region's new economic dynamism and rebuild political relations with the rest of Asia. Among all the sub-regions of Asia and the Indian Ocean littoral, Southeast Asia promised to be the most attractive in terms of the political and diplomatic opportunities. In Central Asia, India was quick to reach out to the newly independent republics of the former Soviet Union. Yet its efforts to influence developments there actually were constrained by the lack of direct geographic access. The oil-rich Persian Gulf was now at the top of India's foreign policy agenda. But the overwhelming dominance of the United States in the Gulf and its extended conflicts with Iran and Iraq left little room for any major initiative there by India.

In contrast to all these regions, the greater coherence of ASEAN and the goodwill of countries like Singapore provided an opening for the sustained Indian diplomacy in the region. The steady expansion of economic ties provided a new basis for India's cooperation with the region. It was the admission of India as an institutional partner of ASEAN that allowed India to actively develop an all-encompassing engagement with the region. Prime Minister Manmohan Singh observed in 2006 that from the tentative sectoral dialogue partnership to a more affirmative nod to the membership of the East Asia Summit (EAS) process in 2005, India's Look East policy advanced steadily and became one of the most organised components of its external relations. This policy, it is believed, would bring about conditions to build up strong relations among the Asian countries. He further stated as follows:

> In 1992 our Government launched India's "Look East" policy. This was not merely an external economic policy; it was also a strategic shift in India's vision of the world and India's place in the evolving global economy. Most of all it was about reaching out to our civilisational Asian neighbours. The doubts about

India's internal stability, its capacity to emerge as an economic force, its geopolitical bind with Pakistan and China were deeply entrenched in Southeast Asia. Therefore, security partnership with India could only be considered as a distant prospect.

As India is reconnected with Southeast Asia, the security issues were not a priority for either New Delhi or ASEAN. While the ASEAN leaders were prepared to experiment on the prospects for a deeper economic relationship with India, they were intensely wary of a security entanglement with New Delhi. As they prepared to launch the ASEAN Regional Forum (ARF) in the early 1990s, the ASEAN leaders explicitly told India not to press its case for membership. And when New Delhi did push for it, it was rejected. ASEAN was concerned that India would bring the whole baggage of its difficult problems with Pakistan and China into ASEAN. While India was eventually admitted into the ARF in 1997, there was an explicit understanding that India would play a low-key role for the moment, and as its economic interaction with the region expanded, it would be possible to eventually consider wider political and security relationship. In India's own understanding of the history of its Look East policy, the first phase was focused exclusively on economic and institutional partnership. It was only in the second phase that began with the turn of the millennium that the security dimensions of the Look East policy came to the fore. As India's External Affairs Minister Yashwant Sinha pointed out in September 2003, the Look East policy began to move away from the exclusive focus on economic issues in phase one to a broader agenda that involves security cooperation, including joint operations to protect sea lanes and pooling of resources in the war against terror. The military contacts and joint exercises, that India launched with ASEAN States on a low-key basis in the early 1990s, are now expanding into full-fledged co-operation. This is a welcome development in the sphere of co-operation of the ASEAN States.

A central feature of India's new security engagement with the Southeast Asia was a steadfast naval diplomacy which was displayed in the early 1990s. Decades of military isolationism came to an end and India opened the service exchanges with the major powers and the regional States in the Indian Ocean littoral. India's preliminary naval interaction with the United States received considerable international attention and India devoted special attention to military engagement with the Southeast Asian nations. In 2005, the Indian Aircraft carrier, INS *Viraat*, arrived for the first time in the ports of the Southeast Asia, Singapore, Jakarta in Indonesia, and Klang in Malaysia. In the spring and summer of 2007, the Indian Navy sailed all the way up to Vladivostok and conducted a series of bilateral and multilateral exercises with a number of nations that included major powers like the United States, Japan, Russia, and China as well as regional States like Singapore, Vietnam, and the Philippines. India has also been keenly interested in supporting the efforts of coastal states of the Malacca Straits, including the conduct of bilateral naval patrols, to promote the security in this vital sea region. India's recent military diplomacy culminated in large-scale naval exercises with the United States, Japan, Australia, and Singapore in the Bay of Bengal. These exercises raised alarm about a potential "Asian NATO".

Beyond the expanded reach and scope of its naval diplomacy, India had from the early 1990s embarked on the wider and more institutionalised cooperation with the military establishments of the Southeast Asian nations. India and Malaysia signed a memorandum of agreement on defence co-operation in 1993 under which India began to train the air force personnel of Malaysia. Training of Singapore military personnel was also carried on steadily and it culminated in a more comprehensive arrangement in 2003, when the two countries signed a bilateral defence co-operation agreement. From that time onwards, India has given Singapore a more convenient and wider access to training facilities in India. Similarly, India and Indonesia too are reportedly discussing the prospects of jointly producing weapons and military equipments. Ideas about equity tie-ups, between the companies on both sides in the defence sector, have apparently been taken up for consideration. These proposals have emerged out of the pursuit of security cooperation arising from the defence cooperation agreement signed in 2001.

India's unfolding military diplomacy in Southeast Asia is due to basic political change. For nearly four decades, India had withdrawn into a shell of military isolationism that became the flip-side of its foreign policy of non-alignment. India then had begun to emphasize the virtues of offering security co-operation to the friendly neighbours in Asia and the Indian Ocean.

The dramatic rise of China, the slow but steady re-emergence of India, the reassertion of Japan, and the uncertainties in the policies of a power that had dominated the region for more than half a century — the United States — have compelled Southeast Asia to rethink its strategic environment and devise new approaches for managing the emerging challenges to its security.

As they grow and take up challenging new roles, it is inevitable that China, India and Japan will all loom larger on each other's radar screens. Under these conditions, the development of these countries in various spheres and their efforts and activities in international arena will have far reaching consequences. Since the end of the Cold War, India had developed diplomatic relations with all the great powers. India's bilateral relations with China, United States, and Japan are appreciably good since the middle of the twentieth century. India has proclaimed "strategic partnerships" of varying intensity with all the three powers. But it should be pointed out here that none of India's three great power relationships has arrived at a fruitful end and the benefits of the relationships are not up to the expected level.

As regards the ties, between India and China, are concerned, they are extraordinarily complex and are misunderstood both within the two nations. Neither the passionate debates within India about China nor the external impressions of Sinc-Indian relations conform with the real direction of Sino-Indian relations. In India, majority feel that China is a real threat to India and the other group of people are of the opinion that both China and India could join together to build up a strong Asia. As the two nations emerged on the world stage as significant powers, in the middle of the last century after a long period of relative decline, India and China did not find it easy to build good neighbourly relations. Even as they proclaimed high principles of friendship, the two countries have often been drifting towards inevitable conflicts.

Distrust over Tibet resulted in India the concluding of bilateral security treaties with Nepal, Bhutan, and Sikkim during 1949–50. As India drew closer to the Soviet Union amidst the Sino-Soviet conflict, China was wary of Indian policies which focus on balancing China. New Delhi in turn was very much concerned with the hostile policies of China, especially its support to Pakistan in its quarrels with India and the strengthening of Islamabad's strategic capabilities, including its nuclear and missile programmes.

This behaviour of mutual balancing has been partly mitigated in the recent years as India and China have worked hard to construct a more cooperative relationship. After a tentative rapprochement which began at the end of the Cold War, India and China have successfully deepened and broadened their relationship. Bilateral trade between the two countries has been greatly developed and is expected to earn more than 60 billion US Dollars by 2010. China is all set to become India's largest trading partner in a few years. The two countries embarked on a dialogue to resolve their long-standing political differences. In 2003, the two countries resolved their differences over the Sikkim's integration into India. They are also engaged in an intensive political exercise to find a fair and reasonable solution to their difficult boundary dispute. The interaction between the two societies has also been rapidly expanding. These positive trends, however, do not necessarily imply that the sources of competition between the two countries have been exhausted.

India and China have acquired greater economic and political power and influence and there is also a sense of competition between them across the broad front — from the maritime domain to the outer space. From Latin America to Siberia, and from southern Africa to Central Asia, China and India are locked in a global competition, and occasional cooperation to ensure the resource security. Pointing out the protection of their sea lines of communication, China and India are determined to expand naval power and ensure maritime presence far away from their shores. China and India might differ in their opinions on several issues and might get into conflicts on several matters. But India's relations with China will not become adversarial. The Sino-Indian relationship is likely to see the enduring elements of both rivalry and cooperation. The challenge before Beijing and New Delhi is to continuously expand their cooperation and develop a better mutual understanding and prevent any potential misreading of each other's intentions.

Further, the long-standing perception across the world that Southeast Asia forms one of the important theatres of conflict between India and China has gained some weight. This is rooted in the belief that in South Asia and Southeast Asia, the presumed spheres of influence of New Delhi and Beijing overlap. Beijing resents India's attempt to seek influence in Southeast Asia and similarly New Delhi tries to prevent China from seeking its legitimate interests in the subcontinent. In Southeast Asia, analysts date back this rivalry to the Afro-Asian conference at Bandung in Indonesia in 1955, when Chinese Premier Zhou Enlai upstaged Jawaharlal Nehru. India's cultivation of a special relationship with Vietnam in the 1970s and its support to Vietnamese intervention in Cambodia and opposition to China's war against Vietnam tended to confirm the fact of an enduring rivalry between India and China in Indochina. Since the early 1990s, the intense engagement of New Delhi and Beijing with the military rulers of Burma had been widely seen as a renewed manifestation of Sino-Indian rivalry.

India maintains a good relationship with Russia and at the same time it wants to have cordial ties with USA and China. India's main objective is to emerge as an indispensable element in Asian balance of power. India's emphasis is on simultaneous expansion of political and economic relations with all the great powers and avoidance of choosing sides between them. India feels that it is under no compulsion at the moment, from either Washington or Beijing, to choose one of them. But at the same time it is reasonable to expect that there will be a greater military and strategic content to Indo-U.S. relationship than the Sino-Indian ties. For example, the U.S. proposal to help India to modernise its armed forces, while maintaining the arms embargo against Beijing, clearly works in India's favour. This does not necessarily mean that India has to become a partner for the United States in Asia. The United States is aware that a stronger India, even outside the U.S. alliance system, will inevitably contribute to regional stability. In this connection, it should be pointed out here that India's principal objective is to ensure an enduring balance of power in Asia.

However, on certain issues, India has maintained its independent position for it believed that intervention will always lead to complications and conflicts. On the question of international intervention in Myanmar to promote democracy, India found itself on the same side as China. More important than the merits of the Indian position on Myanmar, it was a clear signal of India's independent positions on the regional issues. From the early 1990s, when India launched its Look East policy, its relationship with East Asia has come a long way. ASEAN's experimental economic engagement with India, after many disappointments, has begun to yield fruit. The expectations of India's robust economic performance and the prospect that it will emerge as one of the world's four largest economies, had created a sound basis for India's relations with ASEAN (Raja Mohan, 2008). With faster economic growth and scientific and technological developments it is inevitable that in India's military and strategic capabilities lie a great strength to the nation.

As India embarked on the purposeful "big power" diplomacy with the United States, China, and Japan, ASEAN's profound reservations about security cooperation with India have begun to melt. After a tentative start focused on military exchanges, the security cooperation between India and ASEAN countries had begun to broaden to include more substantive areas like training and future arms transfers. India's positive relations with all the major powers and ASEAN's own sense of new vulnerabilities have made New Delhi a potential partner. ASEAN countries recognised that the rise of India is a reality and they had little difficulty in inducting India into the EAS. Also, they are not very much perturbed over the relationship between India and China. It is believed that so long as India is seen as moving forward purposefully, it will remain a valuable partner for Southeast Asia.

Chinese media, like the *Beijing Review,* highlighted the problems between India and China (Deshpande, 1988). But problems of any kind can easily be tackled and solutions can also be given. China and India can move towards mutual co-operation with higher degrees of trust. The civil aviation agreement, science and technology co-operation agreement will certainly lead to good relations between the two. A concerted effort should be taken to bridge the differences. Each country writing Satanic Verses of the other will have to stop. It is a happy augury that one of the outcomes of the Rajiv Gandhi's visit has been the commitment on the part of India and China that they will try and solve the border disputes. These steps should be tried at the earliest, so as to develop good relations and lasting peace in the respective areas. Even the Chinese must have been pleasantly surprised at the foreign policy consensus in India. Also, it is possible and plausible to argue that a few Chinese leaders were paying their tributes to the remarkable reticence of Indian political parties, from the right to the left, on the ticklish question of the Tian Anmen incidents. The Chinese must have been thankful that although Tian Anmen (Gate of Heavenly Peace) has not been particularly peaceful still, there was heavenly peace in India on the Tian Anmen question (Deshpande, 1990).

Another important development in Sino-Indian relations is the statement by the Chinese foreign minister that China has no desire to mediate between India and Pakistan. They would welcome India and Pakistan to sort out their problems. China's attitude towards Pakistan is an irksome point in Sino-Indian relations and no country in Asia has been taking all out efforts in supporting India's genuine claims of territorial propriety. Sino-Indian relations have always got entangled in Pakistan-obsession. Even during the difficult times (from the perspective of Sino-Indian relations) of 1965 and 1971, the Chinese tried and kept Sino-Indian relations at the bilateral level. There was an effort to keep the Indians informed of the fact that the sound and fury emanating from Beijing was not to be accompanied by any action. In April 1971, Zhou Enlai had assured the Pakistan President Yahya Khan that China would always support Pakistan. A China expert writing in May 1971 had taken the view that Zhou Enlai's letter amounted to a signal to Rawalpindi (and to New Delhi if it chose to see it so) that China would not involve itself in a military operation south of the Himalayas. It only indicates that the Chinese have attempted to keep the Sino-Indian relationship as uncomplicated as possible. There has always been some respect in China for India's size and importance.

The other problem is that of the border. Indians still do not distinguish the fact between the officials' report of 1961 and Sino-Indian border problem. China's claims and plans over Mac Mahon line territorial solutions first proposed by Zhou Enlai in 1960 and later reiterated by Deng Xiaoping in the early eighties and India's less responsive attitude still continue and do not reach any final destination In the recent years, China has diffused and contained many conflicts by localising them.

More positively, the policy of decentralised development and regional autonomy has encouraged local initiatives and incentives (Bardhan, 2009). In addition, problems from nature torment the Chinese country. Yet, Chinese efforts, to keep the nation march towards great levels, had been a perennial activity.

India and China: Comparison

There are interesting contrasts in the style and content of governance in China and India. In China, there is more decisive policy initiative and execution than in India. This is not attributable to an authoritarian set-up. In general, collective action problems in goal formulation and policy enforcement are less severe in China than that in the conflict-ridden, extremely heterogeneous society of India where any major controversial decision is preceded by endless discussion and succeeded by loud agitation, breast-beating street antics, fistfights among the conflicting groups and damage to public and private property and ultimately and after some delay ended with the imperfect compromise. But, for the same reason, executive authority in India, though weak, is more legitimate. The same disorderly processes of fractious pluralistic democracy that make decisiveness on the part of the leadership difficult also make executive authority more legitimate in the eyes of the people. The Chinese leadership, conversely, has to derive popular legitimacy from the ensuring rapid economic growth and job expansion and also somewhat from advancing towards "harmonious" goals. Ethnicity-based dignity politics, group upliftment, and other sectarian issues that crowd the political agenda in India are less of an encumbrance. In spite of these internal and external problems and challenges, both countries with determination march towards their proposed goals of becoming super powers in Asia and the World.

Both China and India have done much better in the last two decades, in terms of economic growth. Each country's polity has shown remarkable resilience in its own way. However, the structural weaknesses in their governance mechanisms and the enormousness of the social and political uncertainties, that cloud the horizons for these two countries, should not be under-estimated. In both China and India, rates of growth have varied considerably since the early 1950s, more strikingly so in the case of China. China experienced its most rapid growth during 1952- 58, suffered reverses in the following several years and showed fairly rapid growth again following 1961 except for a minor dip during 1966-68. India showed more or less steady growth from 1950 to 1964, lost ground in 1965 and 1966, and moved ahead again from 1966 to 1971. Since then, India has met with further serious economic setbacks, attributable to very poor rainfalls in 1972 and 1974 and to sharp increases in world prices of oil, fertilizers and food grains. Official national income figures are not yet available. Yet, the 1972-74 period was one of the general economic stagnations for India. By contrast, China has been less vulnerable to poor weather and world price increases and appears to have experienced continued economic growth over the past few years. Thus, during the past decade, China's average annual growth has been greater and India's growth has been lower than their respective averages for the entire post-War period (Weisskopf, 1975).

In contrast with the Chinese experience, the pace of Indian land reform was glacial, and its impact largely restricted to zamindari abolition, with only minuscule redistribution of land (Matson and Seldon, 1992). The contrast in dynamics of rural poverty and inequality in India and China remains, despite the apparent convergence in the 1980s on household based agricultural production and significant state determination of market prices and terms of trade. The wider distribution of real income gains under the Chinese economic reforms was rooted in earlier institutional transformation, the asset leveling and infrastructural investment realised in the collective era. Mass abject poverty is reproduced in rural India by the same constellation of price and procurement policies and input subsidies that has secured national food self-sufficiency and significant agricultural growth in green revolution regions without redressing the growing class polarisation and regional concentration of the poor.

In a sharp contrast with the Chinese experience, the vision and base for Indian economic reforms in the 1980s remained firmly rooted in rationalising industrial policy. The year 1962 marks the war between China and India and low intensity proxy wars (Sushil Kumar, 2003). The Green Revolution has to a great extent created a self sufficient India. As per Ghandi's vision, rural areas have been receiving attention and are uplifted with welfare schemes. Relations with foreign countries are improved to a great extent so as to achieve mutual benefits by the passage of time. In all counts, India has been emerging as a power in the recent years and in this development China has also been in the forefront.

With such potentials, it is the responsibility of these two nations to lend a helping hand to the developing Southeast Asian countries for their self-sufficiency, welfare and growth related programmes. China and India are great nations right from ancient times and are known for their ancient civilisations and cultural heritage. As big brothers, they can also settle differences of all kinds among the countries of Southeast Asia to maintain the lasting peace in this region. If such an example is set by these two nations in Asia, it will be a model to the countries in other parts of the world.

Conclusion

Thus it is evident that India and China, as two great Asian powers, are marching steadfastly towards a greater progress in all spheres. But the developing nations of South and Southeast Asia are still confronted with various problems concerning food, health, human resources development, human rights and personal safety of citizens due to terrorist activities. Under such conditions "One Asia" concept will be a dream. For a safe and comfortable life of people and for general progress of nations, strong nations like India and China sinking their differences must come together to work for a prosperous and terrorism-free Asia. In the fields of science and technology, atomic energy, industry and agriculture, both should share their knowledge and expertise so as to get mutual benefits. They should also contribute to the development of other Asian nations which are also craving to march towards progress and prosperity. Also, India and China should follow the policy of "live and let live" so as to inspire the super-powers and other nations of the world to follow suit. Such role model activities will undoubtedly create a peaceful and congenial atmosphere for all the people of the world, to move together towards a better tomorrow.

References

Acharya Alka and Deshpande, G.P.(2003), "India-China Relations: The Territorial Imperative: Past and Present." *Economic and Political Weekly,* November 8. pp. 4728-30.

Alessandrini, M., Fattouh, B. and Scaramozzino, P. (2007). "The Changing Pattern of Foreign Trade Specialisation in Indian Manufacturing." Oxford *Review of Economic Policy,* 23 (2). pp. 270-91.

Bardhan Pranab (2009). "India and China: Governance Issues and Development." *The Journal of Asian Studies,* 68 (2). pp. 347-57.

Bhaskar, V. and Gupta Bishnupriya (2007). *Oxford Review of Economic Policy,* 23 (2). pp. 135-142.

Datt, G. and Ravallion, M. (2002). "Is India's Economic Growth Leaving the Poor Behind." *Journal of Economic Perspectives,* 16. pp. 89-108.

Deshpande, G.P. (1988). "India and China: Bringing out the Old." *Economic and Political Weekly,* 23 (52/53). pp. 2721-2722.

Deshpande, G.P. (1990). "India-China Ties without the Pakistani Entanglement." *Economic and Political Weekly.* 25 (14). pp. 701-702.

Dev, S.M. and Ravi, C. (2007). "Poverty and Inequality: All India and States, 1983-2005." *Economic and Political Weekly,* 10 February. pp. 509-21.

India Border Conflict, A Realist Approach." *Journal of Cold War Studies*, 8 (3). pp. 165-94.

Economic and Political Weekly, 27 (14). pp. 701-15.

Raja Mohan C. (2008). "India's Geopolitics and Southeast Asian Security," in Daljit Singh and Tin Maung Maung Than (eds.). *Southeast Asian Affairs.* Singapore: Institute of Southeast Asian Studies, pp. 43-690.

Roy, T. (2007). "A Delayed Revolution: Environment and Agrarian Change in India." *Oxford Review of Economic Policy,* 23 (2). pp. 239-50.

Sushil Kumar (2003). "Power Cycle Analysis of India, China and Pakistan in Regional and Global Politics." *International Political Science Review*, 24 (1). pp. 113-22.

The Hindu. "Chinese Incursion," 1.9.1959.

The Hindu. "China Accuses India," 5.9.1959.

Weisskopf Thomas E. (1975). "China and India: A comparative Survey of Performance in Economic Development." *Economic and Political Weekly*, 10 (5/7). pp. 175-94.

4

The Role of the North-East Frontier Agency in Sino-Indian Relations

Deepa Karthikeyan

Frontiers Vs Boundaries

The collapse of Imperial regimes in the Asian sphere was followed by the introduction of the modern nation-states as defined by the sspecific parameters of territory, population and sovereignty. This transition from the old to the new brought along with it the Western concept of a 'boundary', replacing the pre-modern Asian idea of a 'frontier'. Frontiers, as an idea, which pre-existed the emergence of modern nation-states in Asia, were not lines but areas or zones of transition between the state powers.[1] On the contrary, the introduction of statehood, in Asia, required 'boundaries' which unlike frontiers were specific markers that aimed at accurately defining and demarcating the territory of one state from that of the other.

The decision on where these 'boundaries' must be laid was based on the factors, ssuch as historical evidence, national sentiments, strategic concerns and practical difficulties of administration by both sides and were required to be agreed upon through negotiations between the abutting sovereigns. However, differences amongst the newly created member-states, on what entailed their area of jurisdiction often set in motion a new dynamic of conflict and co-operation.

The Republic of India and the People's Republic of China, that came into existence in the niddle of the twentieth century, were confronted by a similar problem of having to divide their historical frontiers in a manner consistent with the western definition of a state, i.e. in the words of Neville Maxwell the problem of 'converting their frontiers into boundaries'. This resulted in the evolution of a new territorial contest between the two regions, that more or less has remained unresolved till date.

Given the above context, this paper attempts to explore the causes for the protracted nature of the Sino-Indian border conflict with special emphasis on the role played by the territories along the Northeast. The first section takes a look at the various factors that led to the evolution of the boundary dispute with specific emphasis on historical details of current relevance. The second section attempts to identify the central role played by Tibet in the evolution of the Sino-Indian conflict and reiterates the strategic consequences of a 'China occupied Tibet' on the security of the Northeast. In section three, an attempt is made to outline the role of the Northeastern frontier region in the larger Sino-Indian context, with special emphasis on Sikkim and Bhutan. Section four attempts to bring out certain conflicting perspectives, relating to the Northeast, that must be investigated more closely while formulating a roadmap for the development of the region, within the larger Sino-Indian context.

Section I

Genesis of the Dispute

The geo-political conflict, that continues to harangue Sino-Indian relations in the twenty-first century, traces its roots to a long history of a perceived overlap in the Indian and Chinese spheres of influence. Explaining the influence of such a perceived overlap on the nationalist policies of these states, in the post-independent phase, John.W. Garver notes 'At the core of modern India's nationalist narrative is the notion that India is a great nation whose radiant influence moulded a wide swath of the world beyond its boundaries.........The historic stage on which India had played out this great creative role extended from the Himalayan Mountains in the North to the seas in the South, into Southeastern Asia on the East, to Persia in the West, and into Central Asia in the Northwest'. Similarly, explaining the Chinese sense of perceived greatness he states, 'China's nationalist narrative also postulates that throughout most of its history, China was a great nation and, unlike India, a powerful state whose influence extended over wide regions of Asia...... China's traditional sphere of influence included both Inner and Outer Mongolia, Xinjiang, Tibet, parts of Central Asia, the entire Himalayan Karakoram region including Hunza and Gilgit in northern Kashmir, Nepal, Bhutan, Sikkim in the central Himalayan region, the small Kingdoms of what later became India's Northeastern states, Burma, Bengal, Vietnam, Thailand and Sulu Island'.[2]

Interestingly, despite the presence of such a strong overlap in their perceived spheres of influence, the absence of the need for boundaries helped the two regions co-exist in peace. This status quo continued well into the later part of the nineteenth century, despite the intrusion of the British into the Asian space, on account of a history of limited British interest in the frontier zones except for the purpose of sustaining a buffer zone between India and Tibet, China and Russia to the North.[3]

However, in 1890, when China first asserted its claim over the Karakoram Range as their southern boundary in Sinkiang, the British began to view the frontier zones differently. The need to establish specific markers dividing British India from Tibet inspired a series of British expeditions into these mountainous terrains and culminated in the formulation of the 1914 text. The text, aimed to make Tibet a genuine buffer zone through the introduction of a second buffer into the Sino-Tibetan debates, similar to the one provided in the case of Mongolia and was proposed by Henry McMahon, a chief British delegate. The McMahon solution to the Sino-Indian situation proposed the division of the region into Outer Tibet (which would provide for a boundary between China and the British Indian frontier) and Inner Tibet (which would remain a part of China).[4]

The complexity of such a concept along with strong disagreements between China and Tibet, over the 'Inner Line', led to the rejection of the proposal by the Chinese. However, the Tibetans, on the contrary, had no qualms with the McMahon Line, and continued to conduct traditional Tibetan administration in those areas where it extended across the new boundary. Despite Chinese reservations, the British, on account of the presence of a 'friendly Tibet' in the North continued to lay the groundwork for control up to the McMahon Line. In fact, as late as 1947, the then British Governor of Assam went to the extent of concluding that Tawang was "undoubtedly British, (but) . . . controlled by Tibet".[5]

In 1947 India broke away from colonial bondage and emerged as an independent democratic republic inheriting from the British not just its new constitution but also the statist boundaries as laid down by British-India including the infamous McMahon line. On the other hand, in 1949 China witnessed a shift in its fundamental statist orientation from that of an Imperial one controlled by dynasties to a Communist state led by a very powerful government. Initially, the presence of an unresolved border along the frontier regions occupied very little space in the list of preferences as laid out by both these independent states. In so far as China was concerned, when the PRC was established in 1949, the Sino-Indian border dispute represented an important but small element of an immense task as they were simultaneously negotiating or renegotiating to achieve the agreed and accurately defined limits to sovereignty with about ten states, contiguous with China over tens of thousands of miles.[6] Similarly, India's energies in the first three years, after independence, were completely focused on Pakistan and on dealing with the herculean task of rehabilitating the refugees created by a bloody partition in 1947.

This complacence by both states on the question of a Sino-Indian boundary, however, was broken in the year 1951, with the Chinese invasion of Tibet. The military occupation of Tibet, a region that India not only holds ancient commercial and cultural ties with but also shares a long common border of 2115 Kilometers along the Himalayas, raised serious concerns for New Delhi. The strategic location of the region along with its long history of political autonomy and favourable ties with India made the liberation of Tibet from Chinese control a compelling political and strategic priority for India. On the contrary, Beijing viewed Tibet as an integral part of the Chinese state and saw Indian expressions of concern regarding Tibet to be a direct manifestation of Indian interference in China's internal affairs.[7] These differences between India and China on the status of Tibet and Indian apprehensions against an expansionist China brought to the forefront the need to re-visit the controversial boundary dispute and resolve the differences that persisted between the two states.

The frontier territories that find themselves at the heart of the border dispute between China and India are often categorised into three main sectors namely the western, middle and the eastern sectors. The territory contested in the western sector consists of the dry and desolate plateau of Aksai Chin that is approximately 38,000 square kilometers in area.[8] In the middle sector, an area of 2000 square kilometers and in the eastern sector, an area of about 90,000 square kilometers (roughly corresponding to the Indian state of Arunachal Pradesh) continues to remain disputed.

China's claims on the territories along the southern foothills of the Himalayas is based on the premise that these regions traditionally fell under Tibetan administration and by virtue of being the natural successor to the traditional Tibet region, China inherits the right to control and administer those regions. The counter-claim provided by the Indian leadership then and to a great extent now is that a well-defined boundary did exist along the crest line of the eastern Himalayas[9] and had been agreed to by the Tibetan government in the controversial Shimla conference. Thus, when a military highway was constructed in the disputed territory of Aksai Chin, by China, just West of Tibet in the 50's, these differences on the perception of Tibet between the two countries became sharper and were followed by a series of diplomatic exchanges and negotiations which tragically failed to resolve the border question and culminated in the 1962 Sino-Indian war.

The East-West Swap

The month long-war of 1962 witnessed the humiliating defeat of the ill-prepared Indian forces by the Chinese and culminated in an East-West swap. Under this new agreement, China implicitly agreed to abandon its claims on the territories lying along the southern slope in the eastern sector (which India perceives to be strategically important for the protection of its Northeastern states), while India in exchange agreed to abandon its claim on Aksai Chin (which China considers important for the effective control of Tibet).[10] In fact, this settlement was implicitly summarised by Chou En-lai when he asked India to adopt, towards the western sector, an attitude similar to China's attitude towards the eastern sector.[11]

However, the lack of effort in the translation of such a cautiously designed 'package deal' into a concrete agreement, binding on both the contending parties under principles of international law, left behind a foreign policy loophole. This became visible when Chinese negotiators pressed their claims in the eastern sector, south of the McMahon line in the sixth round of talks in 1985. In fact, China's Vice Foreign Minister Liu Shuqing went to the extent of saying that "the eastern sector is the biggest dispute and key to the overall solution" and added that if India was now willing to make certain concession in the East especially with respect to its Tawang region, China would certainly consider making a gesture in the West.[12] Such a direct reversal of Zhou Enlai's 1960 proposal must be understood in the light of how both China and India perceive Tibet.

Section II

Centrality of Tibet

While China has had a fairly successful record in terms of sealing boundary disputes, as illustrated in the case of Burma, Nepal, Pakistan,

Afghanistan, Mongolia, Korea, and Laos and to a great extent with both Russia and Vietnam, the protracted nature of the Sino-Indian boundary dispute can be re-traced to the presence of certain persisting difference between the two on one region, namely Tibet. Tibet has historically remained an ethnically distinct and politically independent region with only brief periods of foreign occupation.[13] Even as the British, in their efforts to thwart what Lord Curzon described as the "Russian Domination of Asia",[14] tried to develop China's suzerain control over the region, Tibet continued to enjoy a high level of autonomy with only limited Chinese administrative and military presence. In fact, a treaty, that was concluded as early as 821 AD between China and Tibet, stands as a testimony to the autonomous political status enjoyed by the region as a separate sovereign.

The 821 treaty that was signed between China and Tibet was a peace treaty that aimed to bring an end to almost two centuries of war between the two regions and read:

Both Tibet and China shall keep the country and frontiers of which they are now in possession. The whole region to the East of that being the country of great China and the whole region to the West being assuredly the country of great Tibet; from either side of the frontier there shall be no warfare, no hostile invasions, and no seizure of territory.[15]

Thus, in 1951, when China invaded Tibet, its actions were a blatant violation of a long history of Tibetan independence and a rejection of the region's traditional 'status quo'. The Chinese exercise of bringing Tibet under their sovereign control while invoked on claims of history and national sentiments, were actually based on clear geo-strategic calculations. Firstly, an independent Tibet, according to Chinese analysts, represented a strategic loophole, within the Chinese defence matrix, as it provided easy access into the interior regions of China such as Sichuan and Yunnan. This fuelled the common perception that an independent Tibet would become a base from which the imperialists could menace China's West,[16] thereby making the assimilation of Tibet into the Chinese state an immediate priority of the newly formed Communist Government. Secondly, when annexed, Tibet constituted almost 12.8 per cent of China's total land area and 40 per cent of China's total mineral resources. Tibet's copper deposits are potentially the largest in Asia and its Lithium deposits are potentially the largest in the world.[17] The presence of such a diverse resource base was and is extremely crucial to the ambitious industrialisation plans of China, thereby making the invasion of the region all the more attractive.

Finally, China was always cognisant of the geographical advantage that India enjoyed with respect to Tibet. The lines of transport between India and Central Tibet were substantially more convenient than that between China and Tibet. In fact, after the signing of the seventeen point agreement between the Dalai Lama and Beijing, central personnel dispatched to Lhasa travelled via India and thence up the Chumbi valley. Initially even the food delivered to the central government personnel in Lhasa had to be imported via the Indian port of Kolkata.[18] This geographic advantage along with a long history of favourable commercial and cultural connections between India and Tibet provided the former with a natural upper hand in terms of establishing strong political ties with the region. This was seen as being imminently dangerous to Chinese national security interests and made the inclusion of the region under the Sovereign control of the state all the more important. Thus, Chinese concerns with regard to Tibet influenced the formulation of China's policies on the boundary front to a great extent and also explains the reversal observed in the geo-political swap.

Section III

North-eastern Region in Sino-Indian Relations

The renewed Chinese claims on the territories in the eastern sector, along with the continued occupation of Tibet by China, presents New Delhi with a grave security situation in terms of protecting its territories. While Chinese presence in the Aksai Chin region does present India with certain serious security issues, the fallacy of providing undue and sometimes exaggerated attention to the western frontiers, by the Indian government, at the cost of protecting its Northeastern region continues to remain one of India's most serious administrative short-comings. In fact, this tendency to overlook the significance of the Northeastern region as an important security zone was expressed in a letter of November 7, 1950 by Sardar Vallabhai Patel to Jawaharlal Nehru. In the aftermath of the invasion of Tibet by the Chinese army, Patel, expressing concern about the grave dangers confronting India's Northeastern Region, states: "throughout history we (Indians) have seldom been worried about our North-East frontier. The Himalayas have been regarded as an impenetrable barrier against any threat from the North….. All along the Himalayas in the North and North-East, we have on our side of the frontier a population ethnologically and culturally not different from Tibetans and Mongoloids. The undefined state of the frontier and the existence on our side of a population with its affinities to the Tibetans or Chinese has all the elements of the potential trouble between China and ourselves…. While our western and North-western threat to security is still as prominent as before, a new threat has developed from the North and the Northeast. Thus, for the first time, after centuries, India's defence has to concentrate itself on two fronts simultaneously."

Despite these words of caution, the role and the significance of the Northeastern Region in the larger Sino-India context and at a more micro-level within the national context is one that continues to remain underestimated.

Role of Sikkim and Bhutan in Sino-Indian Relations

The administration of the Northeastern region has historically been a continual challenge for New Delhi. The presence of chronic instability in the region, on account of a rapid proliferation in the number of anti-statist groups, creates opportunities for China to exploit the political 'status quo' in the region to punish India for its supportive attitude towards the Dalai Lama. In fact, between 1962 and 1979, China actively supported and encouraged insurgencies in the Northeast through the provision of arms and military training to the anti-Indian rebels.[19] While such active support by the Chinese to the insurgencies in the Northeastern region has subsided substantially in the recent years, the possibility of future resumption of support, given the deteriorating relations between the two countries, is an important strategic concern.

Another important feature characterising the Northeast is the fact that the region remains connected to the Indian mainland through a narrow strip of land mockingly termed the 'Chicken's neck'. This corridor connecting India with the Northeast measures around twenty-five Kilometers at its narrowest point and lies South of the Chumbi Valley, a region often described as the single most important piece of real estate on the Sino-Indian frontier.[20] The Chumbi valley lies at the tri-junctions of India, China and Bhutan and continues to remain host to a large number of Chinese PLA bases. While historically, this valley provided for a natural commercial corridor between India and the Upper Brahmaputra valley, its occupation by the Chinese provides the communist state with an 'anvil' on which the Indian defences can be easily shattered, thereby proving to be the 'Achilles heel' in the Indian security system.

The presence of such a geo-strategic loophole along the eastern sector of the Himalayas, brings to the forefront the role played by the regions surrounding the Chumbi valley, namely Sikkim and Bhutan. The geographical proximity of both these regions to the Indian state complemented by anti-Chinese sentiments, driven by the fears of invasion, amongst the peoples of Bhutan and Sikkim, has helped them sustain a 'special' relationship with India.

This special status that India enjoys with respect to these two regions helps offset the strategic leverage that China holds through the occupation of the Chumbi valley. However, the actual extent of this advantage, created on account of friendly relations with the two regions, is greatly reduced on account of the poor road-network in these areas from the Indian side. For example, between Gangtok and the main pass into the Chumbi, Natu La, the few roads that were constructed remain narrow and steep, making movement of people and goods very difficult.

Troubled Waters

A crucial link between Northeastern India and China, which often escapes discussion, is that of water. The over emphasis on conventional threats to security has resulted in the marginalisation of one of the most natural trans-boundary linkages: Rivers. On account of its control over the Tibetan plateau, no country in Asia can influence the direction of the region's water future more than the Chinese state. The largest river systems in the Asian region originate in Tibet and supplies water to a raft of countries including China, India, Bangladesh, Myanmar, Bhutan, Nepal, Cambodia, Pakistan, Laos, Thailand and Vietnam which together constitute almost 47 percent of the global population.[21] However, the aggressive pursuit of a Chinese model of economic development, that sidelines concerns of environmental and human security at the altar of economic growth, has resulted not only in the reckless destruction of Tibet's fragile eco-system but continues to be one of the greatest security threats to India and especially the Northeast.

Diversion of rivers for large hydro projects and irrigation, including the ambitious South-North Water Transfer Project that aims to divert river waters cascading from the Tibetan highlands and the channeling of the Brahmaputra to feed China's parched Yellow river, reads as a suicide note to the North and Northeastern regions in India. As a lower riparian, India must accommodate this water reality while formulating its Sino-Indian policies keeping in mind the development of the Northeast.

Section IV

The Tibet Dilemma

Given the central role played by Tibet in the security of China's interior provinces, to expect China to accommodate anything on the lines of providing greater autonomy or even recognising the leadership of the Dalai Lama in the Tibetan region is one that is not only antithetical to its national interests but also fundamentally opposed to the basic Confucian philosophy of the Chinese, where power flows down from the state to its people. Given this premise, India must try and identify an approach that will enable her to maximise her returns in terms of securing her territory in the Northeastern frontier regions from the destabilising influences of China.

A first step in putting an end to the increasing number of violations by the Chinese across the Line of Actual Control (LAC) would probably involve having to resolve the boundary question in a manner consistent with India's security objectives. As of now, thirteen rounds of negotiations have been concluded, and the disputes in the eastern sector and the western sector have barely been touched upon. This extended impasse, however, seems to be in favour of the Chinese who seem to be utilising the time to add to their territory beyond the Line of Actual Control.[22] This makes the resolution of the boundary question an immediate strategic imperative and calls for the conversion of the LAC into the Line of Control (LOC). However, this is easier said than done as Chinese disagreements over the territories along the Himalayan region are strongly interlinked to their disagreements on Indian policies with respect to Tibet. Tibet will continue to remain a perennial link that provokes mutual suspicion in Sino-Indian relations.

As of now, despite the conclusion of nine rounds of talks, the Dalai Lama has maintained his principle of 'Genuine Autonomy' as a pre-condition to open negotiations between Tibet and China. The demand for genuine autonomy, as maintained by the Dalai Lama, demands that autonomy must be granted not only to present day Tibet (TAR) but also to greater Tibet, which includes the whole of Qinghai, the southern part of Gansu, the Western part of Sichuan and the North-western part of Yunnan. This demand for 'Genuine Autonomy' has become a controversial premise leading to continued hostility between the Dalai clique and China.[23] In this context, India may act as a catalyst to help both China and Tibet arrive at an acceptable formula for Tibetan autonomy within China on the lines of the 1954 agreement, by persuading the Dalai Lama to relax his pre-conditions to negotiations, so as to help improve Sino-Indian relations and in turn water down the impending security threat from the Chinese to the Northeastern states of India.

Conflicting Perspectives

The presence of the multiple factors, characterising the Northeast, that tends to contradict one another at different points in time, makes Northeast India a site where the real test of the Indian state lies. Given the above premise, an attempt is made to address some of primary concerns of the Northeastern region, within the larger Sino-Indian context. Here, two common and often conflicting perspectives of development are brought out. The first one is a strictly Military-led perspective where concerns regarding conventional threats, such as military aggression or terrorist infiltration drive development rationale. This perspective is more commonly held in policy and academic circles in India. The second one is a slightly more comprehensive yet an approach that is almost absent, and includes factoring in environmental, political, socio-cultural and certain other non-conventional threats to the region and its people. These perspectives while coincide sometimes, they are more than often seen to offset one another within the Indian context. One can illustrate the same by taking a closer look at the issues under each of these two perspectives.

'Military Perspective' to Development

As a response to the well-established Chinese fortifications on the other side of the Line of Actual control, former Indian Army Chief and current governor of Arunachal Pradesh General J.J. Singh recently announced that between 50,000 and 60,000 troops will be deployed along the LAC on top of future infrastructure and road development projects. In addition to the infantry placements, the Indian Air Force is also expected to open a newly refurbished airbase in Tezpur near Assam, with plans to increase the strength of the squadron to 18 aircraft, along with four nuclear-capable Sukhoi-30 MKI fighter jets.[24] However, while these measures are aimed to deter the Chinese from making any bold moves in Tawang, the actual impact of these measures on the development of the region is one that needs to be assessed yet on account of the poor infrastructure within the frontier regions. The infrastructural reality of the Northeastern region as controlled and administered by India, in fact, continues to paint a picture of apathy and negligence. The region continues to remain unconnected from inside and often finds its development process submerged in bureaucratic corruption, thereby making the region an attractive bait for the fulfillment of Chinese geo-strategic ambitions.

On the domestic front, the threat of a complete cut-off of the Northeastern region from the Indian mainland is accentuated by the large asymmetry between India and China in the nature and magnitude of infrastructural investments made by the two along the frontier regions. Given the tenuous nature of the terrain characterising the frontier areas lying between China and India, multiple and good roads connecting the region with the Chinese and Indian mainland becomes an absolute imperative to strengthen the defences of their respective countries. From the Chinese point of view, building motor roads into Tibet was a top order of business for the People's Republic of China. In fact, Mao's orders to the PLA, as it prepared to 'liberate' Tibet, was to 'advance while building roads'.[25]

The opening of these new roads via Qinghai, western Sichuan, and Aksai Chin into Tibet by China, has helped the state to overcome the geographical disadvantage that it previously suffered in terms of administering these regions. The development of very good roads on the Chinese side, connecting Tibet with Interior China, has also made the Chumbi valley almost irrelevant as a corridor for exchange of goods making China less dependent on the Indian Northeast for the transport of food and materials to Tibet. From the Indian side, while efforts such as the recent approval of a 1850 Km trans-Himalayan highway in Arunachal Pradesh along with the stationing of additional troops are being made, a lot more needs to be done in the area of infrastructure to effectively strengthen the security of the Northeast, especially along the frontier territories.

In the absence of such measures to develop the transport infrastructure of the region, any attempt, in increasing the strength of the armed forces would simply imply the demographic inundation of the region with military personnel, which would merely add to the discomfort of the communities living there.

'Non-Military Perspective' to Development

While these measures will enable India to directly tackle its security problems along the Northeastern frontier areas, any attempt to develop the region purely on the premise of military security in the region will set in motion a process that may prove to be antithetical, both to the interests of the people in the region in the short run and the interests of the nation in the long run. Thus, apart from evolving efficient measures to tackle issues of security, the center must undertake a more comprehensive approach to development in the region that goes beyond the parochial security driven one.

The Northeastern region is distinct from the Indian mainland both in terms of its history and racial constitution. The region is also very rich in biodiversity and consists of almost one-third of the total bio-diversity reserves of the country and, therefore, represents a fragile ecological zone that needs to be preserved. Given the above premise, any attempt, to merely emulate the Chinese model of development that sacrifices the environmental, social and cultural aspects of a region at the altar of national interest, would be very dangerous.

Sadly, despite being a democratic state, a similar process of lop-sided development that sacrifices the interests of the people for the development of the state is becoming increasingly visible. The construction of large dams, such as the Kameng (600 mw), Lower Subansiri (2000 mw), Upper, Middle and Lower Siang

(11,000 mw, 750 mw and 1700 mw respectively) and Ranganadi I and II (450 and 150 mw respectively)[26] in the Northeastern Frontier territories to bring 'development' in the region, does not take into consideration the environmental and social impacts of the same. The displacement of millions of people, complemented by lack of a fair compensation and rehabilitation process, is a very common affair in the Northeast in specific and in India in general.

Moreover, these projects are seldom designed to benefit the locals, who are often marginalised as 'uncivilised' or 'unequal'. For example, no power transmission lines were erected for supplying power to the towns of Doimukh, Nirjuli, Naharlagun and Itanagar, which are just located at a distance of eighteen to thirty kilometers from the power house, from the three units of Ranganadi hydel power projects commissioned in Arunachal Pradesh, while ironically power transmission lines were readied before the generation of power from the power house at Hoj to Malda in West Bengal. These unconcealed omissions of the people, in the Northeastern frontier regions the are slowly appearing for any one to see in the form of new insurgent groups, like Arunachal Dragon Force (ADF) and the National Socialist Council of Arunachal Pradesh (NSCA).

Thus, the mere building of new roads and dams, that only add to their misery and not their standard of living, is dangerous as it camouflages the real problems brewing inside with a superficial sense of prosperity and growth. This will in turn make the region an easy bait to Chinese geo-strategic ambitions. While making efforts to develop the region from within, India must also begin to investigate and discuss unconventional threats to security with China, such as the proposed diversion of the Tsang-po at Tibet. In fact, when China built the Shiquanhe dam over the Indus in 2004, India, was not even aware of the presence of such a dam over the Indus less than 100 Kilometers from the LAC in Ladakh at Demchong till late 2007.[28] The fact, that such a big project so close to our borders, had eluded detection is worrying and brings out the ignorance amongst the members of the Indian political establishment, when it comes to addressing un-conventional security threats.

This water-threat attains greater relevance in the light of the fact that China has not yet signed a single United Nations treaty on the responsibility of riparian states along with the fact that not even a single water sharing agreement has been signed yet by the two countries. This makes the need, to address this threat through the signing of bilateral water agreements with China, must, therefore, be made as big a priority as resolving the boundary dispute.

Conclusion

China and India while continue to lay claims on a long history of shared greatness, the two exhibit sharp divergences in their understanding of what entails a path of progress. In 1949 when the People's Republic of China came into existence it carried with it the traditions of a Confucian state that subscribed to a political system where power flowed down from state to the people instead of flowing up from the people to the state.[29] On the contrary, in 1947, India chose to travel along a democratic path. While drawing comparisons between the success stories of both these countries, one must keep in mind that India, despite all its shortcomings, continues to hold on to the unique distinction of having climbed up the ladder through a democratic process, where the state cannot simply trample over the lives of its people on the pretext of 'greater common good'.

However, despite this unique advantage that India holds, in the Asian region, democracy is often used as an excuse to substantiate the sluggish and often unequal progress seen in the state. This attitude, amongst the members of the political establishment, who continue to use 'democracy' as a convenient excuse to ignore the daunting task of development, is visible in the sad state of affairs that we now see along the frontier regions in specific and the Northeast in general.

Moreover, all developments in the Northeast, be it railways, roads or dams, are given a military colouring, which actually contributes to the distress of the communities living here rather than alleviating them. In fact, every development, that takes place on the Chinese side, is met with a whole lot of media anxiety with almost little or no action from the Indian side, except for the stationing of more troops along the Siliguri corridor. To avoid such a lop-sided process of 'Military–led' growth, New Delhi must address the social, political and economic concerns of its people, rather than merely using the region as a spring-board for the defence of the nation's geo-strategic space.

Thus, instead of merely getting apoplectic every time China develops Tibet, India must acknowledge the importance of its Northeastern frontier, both in the larger Sino-Indian context and within the national framework, and accordingly adopt policies that would enable the comprehensive development of the region, so that India can convert its distinction of being the largest democracy into a strength rather than a weakness.

References

1. Neville Maxwell, "Sino-Indian Border Dispute Reconsidered", *Economic and Political Weekly*, Vol. 34, No. 15 (April 10-16, 1999), pp. 905-918.

2. John W. Garver, *Protracted Contest: Sino-Indian Rivalry in the Twentieth Century*, (Seattle, Washington Press, 2001), pp.11-12.

3. Lieutenant Commander James Barnard Calvin, *The China-India Border War (1962)*, Published by the Marine Corps Command and Staff College, (April 1984) p.12.

4. *Ibid*, p. 21.

5. *Ibid*, p.24.

6. Neville Maxwell, "Sino-Indian Border Dispute", *Economic and Political Weekly*, N.1.

7. John W. Garver, *Protracted Contest:* ...., N. 2, p.32.

8. 15,800 square miles of this area was brought under Chinese control when the People's Liberation Army 'liberated' Tibet in 1951 and continues today under Chinese administration.

9. John W. Garver, *Protracted Contest:* ..., N.2, p.79.

10. *Ibid*, p.100.

11. Detailed coverage of Zhou's press conference and their implicit proposal of an East-West swap is in Maxwell, *India's China War*, pp.161-69.

12. John W. Garver, *Protracted Contest:* ...., pp.104-105.

13. The only other time that Tibet came under the complete control of Chinese was in the year 1720 when the region was occupied by the Chinese Emperor K'ang Hsi.

14. Rowland, John, *A History of Sino-Indian Relations*, (Princeton, New Jersey, 1967), p. xi.

15. N.N. Jha, "Dealing with the Dragon", *The Pioneer*, October 8, 2009.

16. John W. Garver, *Protracted Contest:*...., N.2, p.36.

17. *Ibid*, p.37.

18. *Ibid*, p.85.

19. For example in 1967, groups of Naga guerillas were trained by the Chinese at a camp near Tanzhong in southwestern Yunnan province. In fact in 1969 China even began supplying arms to the Mizo insurgency and trained Manipuri militants and went to the extent of setting up a co-ordination bureau to oversee the supply of arms, training and funding to the Northeastern insurgencies at Yunnan.

20. John W. Garver, *Protracted Contest: Sino-Indian Rivalry in the Twentieth Century*, (Seattle, Washington press, 2001) pp. 161-69.

21. Brahma Chellaney, "China Aims for Bigger Share of South Asia's Water Lifeline", *Japan Times*, June 26, 2007.

22. N.N. Jha , "Dealing with the Dragon", *The Pioneer*, October 8, 2009.

23. Prem Shankar Jha, "The Bull in China's Shop", *Tehelka* (New Delhi), Vol. 6, Issue 43, 31 October 2009, p. 26.

24. Damein Tomkins, "China-India Relation: An unresolved Border and 60,000 Troops deployed", *New Atlanticist*, June 23, 2003, at http://www.acus.org/new_atlanticis < accessed on 29/12/09>

25. John W. Garver, *Protracted Contest: ...*, p. 83.

26. Ramananda Wangkheirakpam and Smitu Kothari, "*Dams in the Northeast will also ruin Livelihoods*", *Down to Earth*, Vol.12, December 2003.

27. Pura Tado, "Peace Process in North-East India: The Arunachal Scenario", in Prasenjit Biswas and C. Joshua Thomas (ed.), *Peace in India's North-East: Meaning, Metaphor and Method*, (Regency, New Delhi, 2006), p. 456.

28. Romesh Bhattacharji, "Where is the Dam?", *Frontline*, November 21-December 4, 2009, Vol. 26, No 24, p.39.

29. Prem Shankar Jha, 'The Bull in China's Shop', N. 23, pp. 26-27.

5

BRIC: An Instrument for Building a Fair Global Economic and Political Architecture

A. Lakshmana Chetty

BRIC, representing a cluster of fastest growing emerging economies, namely, Brazil, Russia, India and China, is a compact co-operative mechanism. Even though the term, BRIC was coined in 2001 by the global chief economist at Wall Street Bank, Goldman Sachs, Jim o' Neill, who had cobbled together the names of the emerging nations to form an acronym, it was left to the former President of Russia, Vladimir Putin, "to cast the concept in flesh and blood" and also to project it as "an alternative forum to G-8".[1]

In realising their cherished ambition of emerging as the architects of a new global order, the BRIC nations pursued the path of consultation and consensus which yielded rich dividends. Existing power–holders, who had been disinclined to "share or lose power", have begun to recognise the need to listen to the voice of reason of the emerging nations. Enthused and encouraged by this positive trend, the BRIC Foreign Ministers held their first ever stand alone meeting in the Russian city of Yekaterinburg in May 2008 while the BRIC leaders held their first summit meeting in the same venue in June 2009.

This paper seeks to trace the origin and growth of the concept of BRIC, to analyse the factors that favoured the promotion of spirit of unity and understanding among its members which would lead to the institutionalisation of their meetings and interactions at the levels of the Foreign Ministers and the Heads of Government/State; and finally, to make a critical evaluation of the evolving grouping which has been hailed as the "guardian of the interests of developing countries".

Origin and Development of BRIC Concept

The BRIC becomes an acronym which refers to four rapidly developing economies — Brazil, Russia, India and China. Even though the BRIC concept was enunciated as early as in 2001, it had started attracting the attention of not only the BRIC nations, but the entire global community since 2003, when Goldman Sachs published its Global Economics paper No:99 entitled *Dreaming with BRICs : The Path to 2050* which is all about the rapidly growing economic clout of BRIC nations which triggered a shift in the global economic hierarchy. The paper starts with a startling forecast:

> Over the next 50 years, Brazil, Russia, India and China – the BRICs economies could become a much larger force in the world economy. If things go right, in less than 40 years, the BRICs economies together could be larger than the G6 in US dollar terms. By 2025 they could account for over half the size of the G6 (the US, the UK, Japan, Germany, France and Italy). Of the current G6, only the US and Japan may be among the six largest economies in US dollar terms in 2050.

The paper went on to say: "China could overtake Germany in the next four years, Japan by 2015 and the US by 2039. India's economy could be larger than all but the US and China in 30 years. Russia would overtake Germany, France, Italy and the UK." The paper further said that the size of Brazil's economy would overtake that of Italy by 2025 and that of France by 2036. These awe-inspiring projections have been reinforced by the revealing data about the collective achievement of the BRIC quartet in a brief spell. The BRIC nations together account for 25.9 per cent of the world's land mass, 42 per cent of the world's population, 14 per cent of Global Domestic Product (GDP) and 12.8 per cent of the Global trade volume.[2] It may be noted that Goldman Sachs made these projections prior to the financial storm which hastened the process of BRIC nations overtaking the rich nations. Ernst & Young ITEM club has predicted that the BRIC nations would account for 40 per cent of global economic growth between 2009 and 2020.[3]

BRIC is neither a bloc nor an organisation in the traditional sense. It is also not a club which stealthily harbours the ambition of ganging up on any country or countries. Though a small grouping numerically, BRIC is promising economically and politically and vows to emerge as an instrument for radically changing the economic and political landscape of the world. President of Brazil, Lula da Silva, noted:

> BRIC is more than a grouping of big countries, bundled together only by the size of their economics, the vastness of their natural resources and willingness to project their values and interests.
>
> We stand out because in the recent years our four economies have shown robust growth. Trade between us has risen 500 per cent since 2003. This helps explain why we now generate 65 per cent of world growth which makes us the main hope for a swift recovery from global recession.[4]

BRIC was originally an economic proposition. Nonetheless, the four rising powers of the world representing this trans-continental outfit sought to form some kind of "political club" with a view to converting their growing economic power into greater geopolitical clout. Underlining the need for political weight to achieve the desired results, President Lula said:

> For throughout my political career, going back to my experience as a Union organiser, I have learnt a basic lesson. To be effective, it is not enough to be right or to have justice on one's side. Nobody will speak up for the weak and vulnerable unless they themselves first join ranks. To speak out forcefully, to dialogue, but from a position of steadfast conviction backed by our political weight.[5]

Political cooperation was evident in the meetings of Foreign Ministers and the Senior Officials of the BRIC countries where they exchanged views on major international and regional issues of common concern. Former Foreign Secretary Shivshankar Menon has pointed out that there has been an "increasing congruence in our approach to international issues" and that "our bilateral relationships have steadily acquired depth and significance".[6] There is a growing perception among the watchers of the BRIC that its emergence as a "formalised geopolitical entity" would have profound long-term consequences for the global economy as well as public order".[7]

Strengths of the BRIC Countries

The strength of the BRIC nations lies in their shared perceptions of the prevailing global political and economic architecture. By opposing the existing unipolariy, they have emerged as staunch advocates of a multi-polar world. Deprecating the dominant role of 'unregulated free market' in globalisation, development and economic process, the emerging countries insisted on an inclusive kind of globalisation and proper growth coming into being. Backed up by their rising clout, the four major developing countries asked for the democratisation of international decision-making on vital issues, which should take cognisance of the changing global scenario.

The BRIC four cherished the ambition of utilising the BRIC forum to realise their strategic aspirations. While Russia wanted the BRIC "to play the role of a strategic counter weight to the U.S. and NATO", China perceives BRIC as a "useful platform" to get its own profile aggrandised as "a setter of global economic norms", India and Brazil harbour a grievance against the world which has denied them their due place at "either the political or economic high tables of the world order".[8]

The growing political clout of the BRIC nations serves as a factor in the development of the grouping as a formidable force. While two of the BRIC countries have been serving as permanent members of the UN Security Council, the other two remain strong contenders for the same. As Russia is a full-fledged member of the G-8, the other three enjoy the distinction of being members of the out-reach Five.[9]

Economic potential of the members is at the root of the popularity of BRIC. Natural resources abound in BRIC countries. Together, they produce 52 per cent of total coal, 21 per cent of oil and 24 per cent of natural gas. Russia and Brazil have emerged as potential suppliers of energy, thanks to their huge reserves of hydrocarbon and uranium. Russia is endowed with the largest gas reserves. It is the second largest oil exporter and the fourth largest uranium producer in the world.

In 2008, Brazil discovered huge offshore oil fields – estimated at 50-80 billion barrels of light crude – making it the "oil superpower of the future".[10] Brazil has also emerged as the world's first sustainable bio-fuels economy. It is also reckoned as the world's leading producer and exporter of ethanol which is an important source of renewable energy.[11] Like the other three members of BRIC, Brazil has strong capabilities in science and technology.

BRIC countries, led by China, would account for 65 per cent of basic metals output, 38 per cent of the world's chemicals, 30 per cent of vehicles and 28 per cent of electronics production by 2020.[12] It was forecast that BRIC would account for 40 per cent of global economic growth between 2009 and 2020. China would account for a quarter of this growth and would become the world's biggest economy in ppp terms by 2019. India's economic growth is expected to be the fastest among the BRIC nations over the next 30 to 50 years, thanks to its largest youngest population.[13] BRIC nations, credited with huge foreign reserves and robust incomes from energy and technology exports, have been able to weather the current global financial crisis with ease. BRIC nations hold a total of $ 3 trillion foreign reserves. China topped the list with $ 1.5 trillion foreign reserves, followed by Russia with $ 500 billion, India with $ 300 billion and Brazil with $ 200 billion.[14] As O'Neill has pointed out, the BRIC nations, far from being affected by the financial crisis of the West, were actually growing faster than the originally predicted. In an interview to an economic forum in St. Petersburg on June 8, 2008, O Neill observed : "Of the four BRIC countries, Russia, China and India have all grown on average 2 per cent more than we suggested. It is a hell of a lot, so they are now collectively 16 per cent of global GDP, so it is all happening a lot quicker".[15] The U.K. trade and investment report, titled "Survive and Prosper: Emerging markets in the global recession" prepared in collaboration with the Economist Intelligence Unit (EIU), was all praise for the continued high growth of India and China, especially as the emerging market economies have managed to outshine those of the developed countries in 2009. Vinod Thomas, Director-General and Senior Vice-President, Independent Evaluation Group at the World Bank, stated that "the global economy will shrink by about one per cent in 2009, followed by a growth of little less than three per cent in 2010, driven mostly by China, India and some other emerging economies".[16] An Indian analyst has pointed out that, but for India and China, "the emerging market economies would contract in 2009".[17]

Weaknesses of the BRIC Countries

The track record of the BRIC nations' relations with each other had been poor. Russia and China, though managed to resolve the long drawn bitter border conflict, were not free from the fears of "neighbourly transgressions". China and India bilateral relations have been plagued by the still-vexed border problem which remains unresolved even 47 years after a border war. BRIC members differ on questions like expansion of the UN Security Council. Russia and China chose to remain status quoists Permanent Members, while India and Brazil have been aspiring for a permanent membership.[18]

There were differences between the BRIC members in regard to GDP growth rates and external trade. India and China continued to register substantial growth rates even in 2009 when the global recession was at its peak. On the contrary, Brazil's economy posted a one per cent GDP decline while Russia was expected to suffer a deep fall by six per cent. While a steady growing internal consumer demand and state investment fuelled the development of China and India, both the export–oriented commodity–based economies of Russia and Brazil suffered.[19]

The BRIC four have not only starkly different economies but also obviously differing sorts of relationship with the United States which complicated the issue of their individual attempts to get united. A senior Kremlin economic adviser pointed out that the currency of each of the four had either been historically unstable or had not been easily convertible. Elaborating on this subject, Yevgeny G.Yasin, head of research at the Higher School of Economics in Moscow, observed: "Between the BRIC countries, there is really little in common. Each of them has its own destiny, its own special character, and it will be much more difficult for them to agree among themselves than separately with Western countries".[20] It was also pointed out that the four countries did not do much business with one another. In 2008, only two per cent of China's trade was with Russia though the two have been the next door neighbours.[21] Further, India, China and Brazil have been working together on the issue of climate change, while Russia remained nonchalant to the issue.[22]

O'Neill was well aware of the weaknesses of the BRIC countries when he propounded the BRIC concept in 2001. He was confident that the prospects of BRIC still looked bright because, in his view, weaknesses were negligibly less than the strengths of the four emerging economics. Holding a similar line, Arun Kumar Singh, a defense analyst, said that it is ironic that despite a major border dispute and an adversarial relationship with China, India-China trade continued to grow very impressively (as also India-China military exercises), while India-Russia trade, for all the excellent relations, was unfortunately limited to defense, energy and space exploration.[23]

Business Economist too Argued on the Same Line

> Each country has its differences, its positives and negatives. But the point of BRIC was of overcoming the many differences and

coming together to push forward larger issues of economic growth and development. They have a similar growth plan : to enlarge their middle class; create jobs for the poor; develop a technologically advanced economy and increase their political clout in the global arena.[24]

Road to BRIC Summit

The idea of holding a BRIC summit meeting was mooted in June 2007 by an active third world leader and the President of Brazil, Lula da Silva, who has been a vociferous critic of the prevailing world order and has played a critical role in bringing the emerging economies and the developed economies together to form the G-20 (dubbed as "the steering committee of the world economy"). Even though Lula's move did not immediately take shape, it did spur an interaction among the member countries at ministerial and other levels. Further, the Finance Ministers and Central Bank Governors of BRIC nations met in November 2008 and again in March 2009 – ahead of the G-20 summits held in the US and the UK respectively – to tackle the global crisis-exuding confidence and as the Russian Prime Minister Vladimir Putin has put it, BRIC would be "the locomotive of the world economy in coming years".[25]

By taking a joint stand on the global crisis, the BRIC four secured a greater voice for emerging economies. For instance, BRIC leaders played a crucial role in reworking the US-drafted G-20 communiqué issued in Washington in November 2008. As the Russian Deputy Foreign Minister Dimitry Pankin has pointed out, while the initial draft "made no mention of the need to give the emerging nations a bigger say in the international financial institutions", the final communiqué stated that the emerging and developing economies "should have a greater voice and representation" and called for an urgent expansion of the Financial Stability Forum (FSM) – the global economic policy powerhouse which till then was a bastion of the G-8 – to give "a broader membership of emerging economies". This facilitated the BRIC members' joining the FSM board.[26]

First Stand Alone BRIC Foreign Ministers Meet

The respective Foreign Ministers of the BRIC used to meet on the sidelines of the UN General Assembly to discuss the prospects of mutual cooperation. They also directed their Ambassadors and other ranking officials at international bodies to interact with each other as frequently as possible, especially on the issues including trade, energy, environment and finance. Even though the BRIC

Foreign Ministers earlier held informal meetings at the UN, their meeting in the Russian city of Yekaterinburg on May 16, 2008, assumed significance because it was their first formal independent meeting designed to give major push to their quadrilateral initiative. Yekaterinburg was specifically chosen as a venue because by virtue of straddling "the geographic border between Europe and Asia in the Ural maintains", it underscored "Russia's dual European and Asian identity".[27]

On top of the agenda were economics and cooperation at multilateral fora. *The China Daily* argued that the formal agenda was not so significant as Kremlin's political achievement in hosting a high profile gathering of four nations with huge resources. It also described the meeting as a response to the signals from Washington that Russia was no longer welcome in the capacity of a member of the G-8 industrialised nations. It may be recalled that in March 2008, John McCain, the Republican US presidential candidate, had called for Russia's expulsion from the G-8 in favour of offering the same place either to Brazil or to India, maintaining that Russia lacked democratic credentials. Christopher Granville, an American analyst, having seen in the Russian move an attempt to sideline the U.S., remarked that the chief motive of Russia in hosting the meeting was to demonstrate that "political clubs can be formed with or without the participation of the United States".[28] Even though different views were advanced regarding the Russian initiative to host the meeting of the Foreign Ministers of BRIC, one cannot deny the fact that the move was designed to display Russia's growing international stature.

The BRIC leaders discussed a wide range of global issues including strategic security, threat of militarisation of space, trans-border crimes and international terrorism, global economic meltdown, food security and climate change. Meeting hardly two months before the G-8 summit in Japan, the BRIC nations sent across the message that they rejected Western unilateralism and welcomed a new world order. "Building a more democratic international system founded on the rule of law and multilateralism is an imperative of our time," the BRIC four Foreign Ministers declared in a joint communiqué.[29] Emphasizing the need for a fair and equal interaction between the developed and the developing nations, the BRIC four noted: "Sustainable development of global economy in the long-term as well as finding solutions to the acute global problems of our time, such as poverty, hunger and diseases are only possible if due account is taken of the interests of all nations and within a just global economic system."

The BRIC Foreign Ministers called for resolving disputes through "political and diplomatic efforts" and for adopting "a cooperative approach to international security" that would serve as a factor in "the concerns of all and address them in a spirit of dialogue and understanding". In an open challenge to the US, the BRIC nations gave a call for "multilateral efforts to prevent an arms race in the outer space".

In an upbeat mood, the BRIC Foreign Ministers in Yekaterinburg vowed to turn the group into a powerful instrument to transform the world for the better. Russia's Foreign Minister Sergey Lavrov said: "We are the world's fastest growing economies. We have many common interests in the globalised world and share many views on how to build a more democratic, fair and stable world".[30] Exuding the Yekaterinburg spirit, Brazil's Foreign Minister Celso Amorim declared: "We are changing the way the world order is organised".[31]

The one and only issue on which there was divergence of opinion was that, while Russia proposed to express support for the bids by India and Brazil for U.N. Security Council seats, China opposed the move. Nonetheless, a compromise formula was finally worked out, but it did not make any reference to the Security Council: "The Ministers of Russia and China reiterated that their countries attach importance to the status of India and Brazil in international affairs, and understand and support India's and Brazil's aspirations to play a greater role in the United Nations." This meant that China has back tracked on its earlier support for India's membership of the Security Council during a bilateral summit in Beijing. Visibly upset, EAM Pranab Mukherjee noted wryly that the developing countries were not represented in the Security Council even as most decisions there affected them. He emphasized that any restructuring of the Council must include developing countries.[32] Foreign Minister of Brazil went a step further to warn, that unless the Council was reformed, the UN risked being sidelined by other organizations and forums.[33]

However, as a Russian analyst has pointed out, this discontent note did not shake the four nations' resolve to institutionalise BRIC as a political and economic forum. The Foreign Ministers agreed to meet again on the margins of the 63rd U.N. General Assembly in September 2008 and to hold their next stand-alone meeting in India in the following year.[34]

The interactions at various levels within the framework of BRIC enabled the four nations "to coordinate and cooperate with each other to build synergy between them". These meetings also helped BRIC to draw global attention and to secure international acknowledgement of the potentials of the grouping to emerge as a "veritable power house and a strong bargaining bloc". The impressive showing of the quad prompted China's Ambassador to India, Zhang Yan, to justifiably claim that BRIC had already become the buzzword around the world.[35]

Informal Meetings of Top Leaders of BRIC

Toeing the line of their Foreign Ministers and Finance Ministers, the top leaders of the BRIC nations met on the sidelines of the international forums such as G-8 and G-20. In June 2008, they met in Hokkaido, Japan, by way of attending G-8 summit, and issued their own declaration on climate change. In November 2008, they met at the first G-20 summit in Washington to assess the impact of the financial crisis. Again in April 2009, they had met to attend G-20 summit's second meeting in London only to conclude that the global downturn was much "more severe" than what they had anticipated in Washington in November 2008. A cursory glance at some of the important decisions of the London summit, would reveal that the coordinated stand of the BRIC four had largely influenced the decisions taken at the G-20 summit in London.

Believing that "prosperity is indivisible, that growth, to be sustained, has to be shared; and that our global plan for recovery must bare at its heart the needs and jobs of hard-working families, not just in developed countries but in emerging markets and the poorest countries of the world too," the leaders of the G-20 pledged to:

1. "restore confidence, growth, and jobs;
2. repair the financial system to restore lending;
3. strengthen financial regulation to rebuild trust;
4. fund and reform our international financial institutions to overcome this crisis and prevent future ones;
5. promote global trade and investment and reject protectionism, to underpin prosperity; and
6. build an inclusive, green, and sustainable recovery".[36]

Summit Meeting of the BRIC Leaders

Feeling the urgency of giving an effect to the decisions taken at London summit, the BRIC nations decided to hold a summit meeting. In fact, the proposal for a top level BRIC meeting was first made by the Brazilian President Lula as far back as in 2007.

There were various other factors that influenced the decision to hold a summit meeting. The inspiring forecast of Goldman Sachs Report of 2003 that the BRIC nations "look likely to be tomorrow's giants," enthralled not only the governments of the BRIC four but also their intelligentsia, academics and other opinion-makers, a fact that in turn led to the BRIC summit.[37] BRIC leaders felt that the summit level interaction would serve the twin purposes of sending signal to the global community as well as to all stakeholders in the BRIC countries themselves that their political leadership lent utmost importance to the new grouping.[38] The summit meeting would also serve the purpose of notifying the world that the grouping's "political interactions would help to alter the shape of the international financial system and the global economy that it underpins."[39] America's declining economic power came in handy for the BRIC four who were fired by "the zeal to demonstrate a growing willingness to coordinate their efforts as they sought to counter US global domination and forge a bigger role for themselves."[40]

Proceedings of the Summit

The BRIC summit meeting was held on June 16, 2009, in Yekaterinburg, where the BRIC Foreign Ministers had gathered for their first stand-alone meeting in the previous year. The BRIC summit came on the heels of the SCO summit which was also hosted by Russia in the same venue earlier on the same day and was attended by three of the BRIC countries (India, China and Russia) and chiefly focused on the SCO themes of regional security and sustainable development. The world, which was in the thick of the severest financial crisis, naturally entertained high hopes about the BRIC summit especially as its participants have ardently started advocating the reform of global financial order. The summit leaders themselves were in an optimistic mood. Russia's deputy Prime Minister Sergei Ivanov said ahead of the summit, that the BRIC nations would become "the locomotive to pull the global economy out of the current crisis."[41] In an interview to *The Hindu* on the eve of the summit, the President of Brazil, Lula, said emphatically: "Our meeting celebrates more than just the first BRICs summit. It marks a major turning point in how our countries engage in a world undergoing profound change. We will seal a commitment to help provide fresh answers to old problems and to offer bold leadership in the face of inertia and indecision."[42]

At their historic first ever summit, the BRIC leaders exchanged views on a wide array of issues. However, their major focus was on the issue of global financial and economic crisis and its implications for the world economy, even though the leaders discussed various other issues such as food and energy security, climate change, protectionism, international terrorism and reform of the UN. At the end of the summit, the BRIC leaders issued a 16-point joint statement embodying their decisions.

Salient Features of 16-Piont Joint Statement

At the outset, the summit leaders gave a call for the reform of multilateral financial institutions in accordance with the roadmap and the time-table provided by the G-20 Summit in London, in April, 2009. In a direct attack on the Western domination of the Bretton Woods institutions including the IMF and the World Bank, the BRIC leaders called for a reform of international financial institutions to reflect the changes in the global economic scenario:

> We are committed to advance the reform of international financial institutions, so as to reflect changes in the world economy. The emerging and developing economies must have greater voice and representation in international financial institutions, and their heads and senior leadership should be appointed through an open, transparent, and merit-based selection process.[43]

The BRIC nations demanded that the reform of financial and economic architecture should ensure "democratic and transparent decision-making and implementation process at the international financial organisations". This meant that the IMF should be restructured and made more democratic so as to reflect the current global economic order rather than what existed at the time of its inception in 1945. The IMF's system of quotas should be reformed to enable the developing countries, including the BRIC nations, get greater share. BRIC leaders objected to the operation of IMF on the grounds that it suit the interests of some countries only. On the eve of the BRIC summit, Russian President Medvedev categorically stated: "What we need are financial institutions of a completely new type where particular political issues and motives, and particular countries will not dominate."[44] It may be noted, Jim O'Neill also underlined the need for accelerating the process of augmenting the association of the developing countries including the BRIC nations saying, that "the world doesn't want a separate club just looking after the growing countries the same as it doesn't need an old club looking after the declining – it needs a better club involving them both".[45]

The BRIC members made a "veiled attack" on the dollar: "We also believe there is a strong need for a stable, predictable and more diversified international monetary system." Even though there were periodic complaints from the global community over the years about the weakening dollar, the criticisms from the BRIC countries were more frequent and more acerbic. Led by China, they even proposed a supranational currency to replace the dollar. In March 2009, the Prime Minister of China, Wen Jiabao, expressed grave concern about the US budget deficits triggering inflation and weakening of the dollar which would hurt China's $ I trillion investment in American government debt.[46] As Russia believed that the US exercised a dominance in global affairs that exceeded its diminishing power, the President of Russia Medvedev, emphasized the need for the reserve currencies in addition to the dollar to stabilise the world financial system.[47] Brazil's Minister for Strategic Affairs too expressed similar sentiments: "The world economy should not remain entangled, so directly and unnecessarily in the vicissitudes of a single great world power. The developing countries should not have to see painfully accumulated hard currency reserves fall under the shadow of major devaluations."[48]

Even though China, Russia and Brazil were united in their demand for a robust challenge to American dollar, perceiving it as "hegemonic international reserve currency," they were reconciled to, what the Russian Finance Minister Aleksei L. Kurdin said, the fact that the world was not yet ready for resorting to another reserve currency.[49] Further, the consensus on the future of the greenback was ruled out, given China's dependence on exports and enormous holdings of the dollar dominated assets. In March 2009, China had US Treasuries worth $ 767.9 billion, Brazil $ 126.6 billon and Russia $ 138.4 billon. Therefore, depreciation of their dollar assets was the last thing they wanted. The Chinese leaders preferred the status quo to liquidated state.[50] However, Russia, China and Brazil—convinced of the need to limit the use of the dollar in their bilateral trades by taking recourse to their respective local currency—agreed to conduct their trade transactions in Russian roubles, Chinese yuan and Brazilian reals.[51] Presenting the general view of the BRIC nations at the summit on the issue of the dollar, Prime Minister Manmohan Singh stated: "It was agreed that these are highly complex issues, replacing the dollar by other currencies—with other currencies, national currencies or an SDR—and it was felt that this matter requires further examination by our finance ministers and governors of Central banks".[52]

The summit participants voiced their opposition to "protectionism" which meant putting an end to the multi-billon dollar Western agricultural subsidies that tend to distort to global markets. They looked forward to a "comprehensive and balanced" outcome of the WTO'S Doha Development Round. Commerce Minister Anand Sharma criticised subsidies doled out by the EU, the US and Canada to farmers, saying they denied a level playing field to growers in the developing countries. Therefore, he urged the developed countries "to make deep cuts in the subsidies—a minimum of 70 per cent".[53]

The BRIC four called for "coordination and cooperation" in the sphere of energy "including amongst producers and consumers of energy and transit states". The summit leaders "strongly condemned terrorism in all its forms and manifestations and reiterated that there can be no justification for any act of terrorism anywhere or for whatever reasons".

The BRIC quartet reiterated "the importance we attach to the status of India and Brazil in international affairs, and understand and support their aspirations to play a greater role in the UN". This meant that there was absolutely no change in the stand of China which continued to oppose India's bid for permanent membership of the UN Security Council. In addition to the BRIC Foreign Ministers' meeting in May 2008, the summit remained divided on the issue of expansion of the UN Security Council, thus sending the message to the world community that the BRIC was lacking in cohesion. India and Brazil – which have been arguing that a dynamic global political and security order demand the urgent reform of the UN Security Council which was put in place over six decades ago – remained disappointed. The BRIC leaders also failed to arrive at any decision either on establishing a more permanent international entity for the BRIC forum or on holding summits in future on a regular basis or on the expansion of the grouping. However, a temporary secretariat was established by Russia, the first country to chair the BRIC, so as to coordinate the work of the group and to hold the meeting. Even though the summit leaders failed to reach a consensus on the institutionalisation of summit meetings, the communiqué of the BRIC leaders stated: "Russia, India and China welcome the kind invitation of Brazil to host the next BRIC summit in 2010." When Russia favoured an annual summit format and China opposed the same, Manmohan Singh himself "came up with a flexible solution: the summits will be 'periodic', allowing for annual or less frequent meetings."[54] In any case, the summit made a fine gesture to the Brazilian President Lula who "was keen to host the next summit in 2010" before his term as president came to an end.

With regard to the expansion of the BRIC, Prime Minister Singh said that he did not wish the grouping to become a "talk shop." However, he maintained that it was too early to confer on BRIC, a concrete structure or to explore the possibilities of its expansion. To quote him: "It is the first meeting of the group at the summit level. This is an evolving situation, not one-time operation. We are meeting next year to take stock."[55]

BRIC Leaders' Joint Statement on Global Food Security

The BRIC leaders issued a separate declaration for food security[56] expressing their concern for people suffering from hunger and malnutrition. A report prepared by International Food Policy Research Institute (IFPRI) for the World Bank and Asian Development Bank said that twenty-five million more children would go hungry by the middle of this century as the climate change would lead to food shortages and soaring prices for staples such as rice, wheat, Maize and Soya beans.[57] The BRIC four, therefore, provided a "road-map" for global food security which was threatened by "the fluctuations of global food prices coupled with the global financial crisis". While blaming the developed countries-whose protectionist policies adversely affected the agricultural production in the developed world—for food crisis, they urged the advanced countries to "provide financial and technology support for developing countries in the field of food production capacity". The BRIC leaders underlined the need for "establishing a just and reasonable international trade regime for agricultural products, and giving farmers from developing countries incentives to engage in agricultural production".

Role of BRIC in Pittsburgh Meeting of Group-20 (G-20)

The G-20, comprising Argentina, Australia, Brazil, Canada, China, France, Russia, Saudi Arabia, South Africa, Korea, Turkey, the UK and the US besides the EU and the WB and IMF, was formally launched on September 25, 1999 in Washington D.C, with a view to facilitating the discussion and study and the review of policy issues among industrialised countries and emerging markets so as to promote international financial stability.[58] However, the G-20 meetings held in London in April 2009, and in Pittsburgh (U.S) in September 2009 respectively, assumed significance because of the uniquely important work they turned out. The London meeting was held at a time when the global economy was confronted by the greatest challenge in many decades. However, member nations "agreed to do everything necessary to ensure recovery, to repair our financial systems and to maintain the global flow of capital". [59] The "forceful response" from the G-20 stemmed the tide of "the dangerous, sharp decline in global activity" and stabilised financial markets.[60]

On September 24-25, 2009, the G-20 met in Pittsburgh "in the midst of a critical transition from crisis to recovery to turn the page on an era of irresponsibility and to adopt a set of prices, regulations and reforms to meet the needs of the 21st century global economy".[61] The momentous decisions taken and the solemn promises made by the member nations, turned the meeting into an historic one. Incidentally, the outcome of the meeting was quite pleasing to the BRIC nations (all of which happen to be the members of the G-20) because most of the issues they raised earlier at their summit in June 2009, were addressed at Pittsburgh.

Of the several issues on which, as Prime Minister Singh has pointed out, "genuine forward movement had taken place", the most important was the designation of the G-20 as "premier forum" for the future discussion of international economic issues. This meant that the G-8, which was founded in 1975 as the premier world economic grouping and was dominated by the developed countries of the West, would be superseded by the G-20. Diplomats said that henceforth, the G-8 would primarily focus on geopolitical issues.[62] Premier Singh hailed the move thus: "G-20 will henceforth be the premier forum for international economic issues. This is an important development broadening the governing structure."[63] The Indian press was all agog at this historic decision. *The New Indian Express* commented: "For some years now, there has been a view that India and China would be included in an expanded G-8. The decision to make G-20 the top economic forum brings the two Asian giants to the high table...."[64]

Another far-reaching step by the G-20 was to enhance the quota for the developing countries in the IMF by five per cent. By effecting a five per cent shift in the IMF quota share – on the basis of which voting rights were allocated – from overrepresented countries to dynamic emerging markets and developing countries which hitherto were underrepresented, the G-20 had met the demand of the BRIC nations for "greater voice and representation in international financial institutions" to emerging and developing economies. It also marked "the emergence of Asia, led by India and China, as key to world economic management".[65] Elaborating on the shift in the IMF quota share, Premier Singh said: "As of now, the developing countries' quota is about 43 per cent. The four BRIC countries had suggested a balancing to the extent of 7 per cent, in which case the developing countries would have more than 50 per cent or nearly that. But this was not acceptable to the West which have been enjoying a majority quota share."[66]

Yet another significant decision at Pittsburgh related to protectionism needs mention here. The communiqué of Pittsburgh said: " We will fight protectionism." The G-20 "while actively rejecting protectionist measures", supported "open trade and investment" so as to "advance global prosperity and growth stability."[67] It may be recalled that one of the issues against which BRIC four spoke with one voice at Yekaterinburg was the "protectionist measures being imposed by the US and other European countries." Prime Minister Singh along with the leaders of China, Brazil and South Africa, resisted at Pittsburgh the move by the US and the European nations to put up tariff and non-tariff barriers to block market access to exports. Prime Minister Singh said: "We reject protectionism of all forms on the economic and trade fronts. We have evidence of creeping protectionism in many European countries and the US."[68]

The G-20 also completed the "emergency financing plan" of the IMF by mobilising $ 500 billion "to a renewed and expanded IMF New Arrangements to Borrow (NAB)". BRIC nations had pledged to contribute $ 70 billion additionally to the IMF, by coming forward to buy credit notes against the gold reserves, the IMF held.[69]

With the setting in motion of the process of passing the baton from the developed world to the emerging nations, the G-20 recognised the need to reconstruct the Boards of global financial institutions such as IMF and World Bank so as to make them more broad-based by enhancing staff diversity and by appointing "heads and senior leadership of all institutions through" an open, transparent and merit-based process. These reform measures were expected not only to make these financial bodies more democratic but also to meet the aspirations of the dynamic emerging markets and developing countries, including the BRIC countries. Credit largely goes to the BRIC nations for facilitating the forward movement at long last, in addressing the agenda of the internal reform of the IMF and the World Bank, which would enable them to play a significantly enhanced role in the twin tasks of global economic development and global poverty alleviation which constitute the "core mission" of the development banks.

Besides refurbishing the IMF, the G-20 entrusted the IMF with the task of conducting a regular "peer review" of the macroeconomic and regulatory regime of the individual countries. The significance of this move lies in the fact that the developed as well as the developing countries would be subjected to international scrutiny. Heretofore, only the developing nations were required to be reviewed. Prime Minister Singh hailed the setting up of a mechanism for peer review as a "positive development." Pointing out the unique feature of the peer review, Premier Singh said: "As far as our domestic policy is concerned, the IMF already reviews it... so I don't see what more can be done as far as Indian policy is concerned. But the policies of major advanced countries within the framework of review by G-20 will give us on opportunity to pick holes in the functioning of their economies."[70]

Conclusion

To begin with, BRIC has been primarily an economic concept, although the evolving global order offered enough space for it to embrace the political role by espousing "a new equitable world order with a fully democratic representation of communities". The global financial crisis, while exposing the severely flawed economic management of the advanced countries, facilitated the BRIC nations' riding on the crest of their dazzling economic successes and made them feel fortified and assertive. Having been disenchanted with the rigid "aristocracy of the Western countries", quite a few expected BRIC to become an effective engine of the world economy. The BRIC summit too indicated that their expectations would not be belied. An array of stimulus packages to counter the slump—yielded quite a crop of good results contributing significantly to the global economic stability—which not only enhanced the credibility of the BRIC four, but also reinforced their due claim for an enhanced role befitting their economic stature in building a fair global economic and political architecture. The G-20 summits held in London and at Pittsburgh respectively within a span of six months culminated in reshaping the global financial structure in such a way that the BRIC nations were ensured a greater say in the global issues of economic and political relevance.

Thus, the efforts of the BRIC four to advance the global prosperity and growth stability, were duly rewarded. While the G-20 supplanted the G-8 as the premier body concerning global economic issues, the BRIC nations eclipsed the developed nations and emerged as the world's new political and economic centres of gravity. No wonder, after their splendid accomplishments at Pittsburgh, the BRIC four are able to find themselves on the crest of a wave. And the thrill of their legitimate pride: stemming from their successes, continues under its own momentum.

References

1. Vladimir Radyuhin, "A forum to counter G-8's supremacy". *The Hindu*, May 29, 2008.
2. "China expects consensus on financial system reform at BRIC." Summit,http:/ english.peopledaily.com cn/90001/90776/ 90884/6675623.html
3. "The Rise of BRIC," *Business Economics*, (Kolkata), May 1-15, 2009, p. 31.
4. *The Hindu*. June 16, 2009.
5. *Ibid.*
6. *Strategic Digest*, June 2009, p. 537.

7. http:// www.globaleconomiccrisis.com/blog/archives/ 427.
8. Satish Kumar, "BRIC : Axis of Prosperity," *Deccan Chronicle*, June 15, 2009.
9. *Ibid.*
10. Vice-Admiral (Rtd.) Arun Kumar Singh, "No military alliances," *Ibid*, June 26, 2009.
11. *Ibid.*
12. *Business Economics*, N. 3 p. 33.
13. *Ibid.*
14. http://www.thaindian.com/newsreportal/unicategorized/brics—Yekaterinburg —summit–100198683.html
15. *The Hindu*, June 6, 2008.
16. *Ibid*, October 14, 2009.
17. K.T. Jagannathan, "Emerging Markets outshine developed economies," *Ibid*, September 22, 2009.
18. Kumar, N. 8.
19. Oleg Mityayev, "BRIC countries catch up and overtake G.7," *The Hindu*, June16, 2009.
20. "Emerging economic powers meet in Russia". *New York Times*, June 16, 2009.
21. *Ibid.*
22. *The Hindu*, May 15, 2009.
23. Singh, N.10.
24. *Business Economics*, N. 3 p. 35.
25. *The Hindu*, October, 25, 2008.
26. *Ibid*, November 18, 2008.
27. Radyuhin, N. 1.
28. http://www.chinadaily.com.cn /china/ 2009/sco/ 2009-06 /11/content 8272918. htm
29. For text of "The Joint Communiqué of the Meeting of the Foreign Ministers of the People's Republic of China, the Russian Federation, the Republic of India and the

Federation of Brazil" issued on May 16, 2008, see http://ie.chinaembassy. org/eng/ newsPress/t456502htm. For a good account of the meeting of Foreign Ministers of BRIC quartet. See *The Hindu*, May17, 2008.

30. Radyuhin, N.1.
31. *Ibid.*
32. *The Hindu,* May 17, 2008.
33. *Ibid.*
34. Redyuhin, N.1.
35. *The New Indian Express*, May 14, 2009.
36. For text of the Joint Statement "The Global Plan for Recovery and Reform." 2 April, 2009", Issued by the Leaders of Group of Twenty, see *http:// www.londonsummit.gov.uk/resources/en/PDF/final-communique.* Also see Prime Minister Manmohan Singh's remarks on the decisions of the G-20 Summit in London in *Strategic Digest*, July 2009, pp 662-63.
37. Editorial, "Image boosting the BRIC way". *The New Indian Express*, June 30, 2009.
38. Staish Kumar. N.8
39. *The Hindu*, June 16, 2009.
40. *The Deccan Chronicle*, June 15, 2009.
41. *The New Indian Express*, June 15, 2009.
42. *The Hindu*, June 16, 2009.
43. For the Joint Statement of the BRIC leaders issued at the end of their meeting on June 16, 2009. See *Strategic Digest*, July 2009, pp. 663-65.
44. *New York Times*, June 16, 2009.
45. *The Deccan Chronicle*, June 9, 2008.
46. "Emerging Economic Powers meet in Russia," N. 20.
47. *Ibid.*
48. *Ibid.*
49. *Ibid.* Also see for a related comment, Editorial "The dollar's fall," *The Hindu,* October 16, 2009.

50. *New York Times*, June 16, 2009.
51. *Ibid.*
52. *The Hindu*, June 16, 2009.
53. *Ibid*, December 9, 2009.
54. *Ibid*, June 17, 2009.
55. *Ibid*, June 18, 2009
56. For text of BRIC leaders' Joint Statement on Global Food Security see *Strategic Digest*, July 2009, pp. 668-09.
57. Suzane Goldberg, "25 million more children will go hungry by 2050." *The Hindu*, October 1, 2009.
58. See Sonu Trivedi, *A Handbook of International Organizations* (New Delhi, 2005). pp. 160-63.
59. *Leaders' Statement: The Pittsburgh Summit*, September 24-25, 2009. http://www.pittsuburghsummit.gov/mediacenter/129639.htm
60. *Ibid.*
61. *Ibid.*
62. *The Deccan Chronicle*, September 26, 2009. For a good analysis of the decisions of Pittsburgh. See C.R.L. Narasimhan "Primacy given to G-2O in global recovery task." *The Hindu*, October 5, 2009.
63. *The Deccan Chronicle*, September, 2009.
64. *The New Indian Express*, September 26, 2009.
65. *The Deccan Chronicle*, September 27, 2009.
66. *The Hindu*, September 27, 2009.
67. Leaders' Statement….. n. 59
68. *The Deccan Chronicle*, September 27, 2009.
69. *Ibid.*
70. *The Hindu*, September 27, 2009.

6

China Factor in India and Vietnam Relations

L.R. Mohan Kumar Reddy

India and Vietnam are strategically located in Asia and they are growing economic and military giants in their respective zones of South Asia and South-east Asia. Geo-strategic importance influenced India to evince keen interest in promoting its relations with Vietnam in the region and *vice versa*. The emergence of communist China in 1949 bordering both India and Vietnam added another dimension to India and Vietnam cooperation. Vietnam's strategic significance lies in terms of its geographical size, configuration and vicinal location in the regional frame work of Indochina States vis-à-vis China and Southeast Asia. The cooperation between India and Vietnam, particularly against the background of Look East Policy towards South-east Asia, constituted an important dimension in India and Vietnam relations.

India always desires stable, independent and nonaligned character of the Indochina region, which comprises the states of Vietnam, Cambodia and Laos, for its own security. The power which dominates Indochina could threaten security of India also. This was proved during the Second World War when Japan occupied Indochina and threatened India's northeastern frontier through Burma[1] (present Myanmar). Both India and Vietnam share disputed borders and have been subjected to military aggression by China. Vietnam is performing the role of checkmate against southward expansion of China, thus ensuring safety of other countries of Southeast Asia/strategy which is vital for the security of India also. Above all, the collapse of the Soviet Union and the desire of China to emerge as Super power also made India and Vietnam to be cautious in its security which can be ensured among other things strengthening cooperation.

As India is a major military power in Asia, Vietnam expects India to play an useful and constructive role in the promotion of peace and stability in South-east Asia as China is posing a major challenge to the region. Given the growing indifference of the USA and Japan's reluctance to play any military role, perhaps only India along with Vietnam can counterbalance China and act as psychological restraint. The fact generates a degree of commonality of interests in the foreign policy agendas of India and Vietnam towards China with regard to Southeast Asia.[2] India saw a strategic reason to consolidate its relations with Hanoi regime through the cold war years. The China factor, through the cold war to the current context of post-cold war era, loomed large in connecting the bilateral equations. Indira Gandhi, Prime Minister of India, realised that if India were to become a permanent power in Southeast Asia, it would have to prevent a Chinese advance into Southeast Asia—a strong anti-Chinese Indochina could guard the flank of the Indian sphere of influence in South Asia. Both were concerned with checking southern advance of Chinese power.[3]

After the collapse of the Soviet Union and the end of cold war, India began to revive its ties under Look East Policy with Southeast Asian countries including Vietnam. The expansion of ASEAN to include Vietnam has also enhanced relations with ASEAN. India also integrated into ASEAN from the sectoral dialogue partner in 1993 to summit states in 2002. Meanwhile, India was also part of ASEAN's Regional forum (ARF) during 1996. The ARF was set up in 1994 as a regional security dialogue platform. The entry into ARF put India on a par with the Western nations and China vis-à-vis Southeast Asian Regional security and economic and political arrangement. India believes that Vietnam's integration into ASEAN helped strategic environment in Southeast Asia in favour of India. As India moved closer to ASEAN by its Look East policy, Vietnam maintained good political and strategic relations with India.

China has been one of the most important factors in the overall evolution of India's foreign and security policies. China factor has been critical in guiding India's ties with the Southeast Asian countries including Vietnam. A strong Vietnam is an asset to both India and ASEAN to check Chinese hegemonism. The changing international security environment presents a picture of where Russia which earlier stood by India and Vietnam for strategic needs, today engaged in building up military might helping projection capabilities of China threat perception common to India and Vietnam. In such circumstances, India and Vietnam worked together in building strategic partnership based on the convergence of interests, while making all the efforts keeping China peacefully engaged in Asia-Pacific.[4]

In the past, there was cold war divide between Indochina countries and ASEAN-6 for a very long time. China factor gradually moved India towards Vietnam, a dominant country in Indochina. India's increasing solidarity with Vietnam following its estrangement with China found expression in India's recognition of Vietnam installed Heng Samrin government in Cambodia. The attitude of India was partly guided by the larger policy of containing China's influence among the Indochina countries of Southeast Asia. During 1979, to show India's solidarity with Vietnam, Vajpayee, foreign Minister of India cut short his maiden visit to China as China attacked Vietnam while he was still on China's soil. When the Cambodian crisis was continuing, India along with Vietnam and former Soviet Union were trying to undermine the Chinese role in Southeast Asia which was seen as a sole factor guiding India's Southeast Asian Policy at that time.[5] Though never stated officially, the common factor that has cemented India and Vietnam ties is that of China. China launched punitive military attack on both India (1962) and Vietnam (1979). China's perceived strategic concerns regarding India and Vietnam forced China to create strategic pressure points to destabilise these countries. In the case of India, China created Pakistan threat (Nuclear and missile threat) and in case of Vietnam, it posed proxy military challenges in Kampuchea, besides direct force on both land and sea borders.[6]

The Defence Minister of India, George Fernades, when he visited Hanoi in March 2000 said that India must firm up strategic ties with key ASEAN and Asia Pacific countries including Vietnam. He added that neglect of Vietnam would be at New Delhi's "own peril".[7] Both India and Vietnam have good reasons for China's figuring in their respective threat perceptions because of previous record of China's aggression on both India and Vietnam, and China's unsettled border disputes with both the countries. India and Vietnam, therefore, have a natural strategic congruence with regard how to restrain China from aggressive actions in the future, while engaging it diplomatically. India's strategic and national security interests demand that Vietnam emerges as a strong state. Relatively, India is better placed to contribute towards this aim in all fields – defence, political cooperation, economic and technical assistance.[8]

The China factor weighs heavily and figures prominently in the calculus of both India and Vietnam. Indian Defence Minister George Fernades was accurate when in 1999 he described China as a "major threat" to India. Indian Prime Minister Atal Behari Vajpayee had also in 1998 mentioned the Chinese threat as an impulse for India's nuclear weaponisation.[9] Recently a Vietnamese foreign ministry official had remarked "we don't trust China".[10] In other words, Vietnam is suspicious of China and fearful of Chinese intensions.

India has had strategic understanding with Vietnam. Vietnam is in the process of reducing its military personnel quantitatively replacing with new equipment. But its military equipment almost supplied by the former Soviet Union is outdated especially MIG 21 fighter aircraft. The Vietnamese navy is also not strong. Given its claims for the islands in the South China Sea, both the Air force and Navy should receive attention in Vietnam. Vietnam is not in a position to replace its MIG-21 aircrafts or build a credible Navy. Therefore, India stepped in defence cooperation in Vietnam.

The most significant defence pact was signed in March 2000 during Defence Minister George Fernades' visit to Hanoi, the first such visit by an Indian Defence Minister to Vietnam. The wide ranging defence agreement paved the way for greater military-to-military cooperation, sale of advanced military light helicopters, assistance in repairs, overhaul of Hanoi's mainstay MIG fighters and raising the level of military contacts between the two countries. The defence cooperation agreement signed at the conclusion of visit of the Defence Minister George Fernades to Hanoi also provides for the framework for periodical talks between the Defence Ministers of the two countries and cooperation between Indian Coast Guard and Vietnamese Sea Police in combating growing menace of piracy in the eastern seas.[11] Bilateral agreement was reached on Joint naval training to combat piracy, jungle warfare and counter insurgency training, repair of MIG Aircrafts, pilot training and assistance on small and medium arms production. India also agreed to help Vietnam defence industry extending technical know-how through Indian Defence Research and Development Organisation (DRDO).[12] Fernades described the agreement as the "most significant".[13] India's strategic aim is to assist Vietnam in building armed forces which are militarily strong and self reliant. Given India's well developed defence capabilities including army equipment production and training facilities at competitive cost, Vietnam could find close convergence in this vital field.

To curb China's growing military influence in Southeast Asia, the Indian Navy has conducted joint exercises with Vietnam along with Singapore, Japan, South Korea, Indonesia and Malaysian navies to ensure the safety of the strategic water ways in the region such as Straights of Malacca and Kra

Isthumas. In this context, India's Look East Policy launched in 1991 primarily due to economic concerns, has now taken an added security dimension.[14] The joint exercises carried out by the navies of India and Vietnam for nearly a decade, among others, opened new possibilities for cooperation in anti-piracy, disaster relief, rescue operations and security of sea lanes.[15]

The defense pact signed in March 2000 provided added impetus to the maritime cooperation between India and Vietnam. During the visit of the Defence Minister of India to Vietnam in 2000, a fresh protocol was signed on defence cooperation which incorporated joint exercises by the navies of India and Vietnam and also by the coast guards of both the countries. The defence pact signed with Vietnam soon symbolised by an Indian navy Flotilla exercising with Vietnam Naval Vessels in the South China Sea. China was thus warned that Beijing can not do exactly as it pleases in India's backyard.[16] India had deliberately conducted high profile joint naval exercises in the South China Sea probably to indicate to Beijing that New Delhi had the ability to impinge on China's traditional strategic area.[17] Considering Vietnam's security problems in the South China Sea, India's affirmation of help boosted Vietnam's confidence.

China views India's Southeast Asian diplomacy could complicate Chinese-ASEAN relations, as growing Indian –ASEAN naval cooperation impinge on Chinese maritime interests and make a final resolution of territorial disputes in the South China Sea even more difficult. Indian-Vietnamese-Japanese defence cooperation under the aegis of the USA is also viewed with suspicion given China's unresolved territorial issues with each country. As China and India already have intractable territorial dispute, mutual suspicions and the potential for rivalry is added by the emerging India-USA-Australia Cooperation.

Both India and China formed separate sub-regional arrangements for the Mekong basin countries. Both the countries formed their respective Mekong groups in quick succession. China initiated "Agreement on Commercial Navigation on Lancang Mekong river" in April 2000 and India initiated Mekong Ganga Cooperation in November of the same year.[18] In November 2000, India signed along with Cambodia, Laos, Myanmar, Thailand and Vietnam, the "Vientiane Declaration" at Laos named Mekong Ganga Cooperation (MGC). This new six-nations-sub-regional forum deals with tourism, human resources, culture and transportation. Transportation assumes greater importance as signatories agreed to develop transport network which includes "East West

Corridor" and "Asian Highway".[19] India and China thus are interlocked in a competitive game in the Mekong region. Both have joined separate regional groups and act independent of each other in devising strategies of cooperation with the countries of the region.

With an eye on China's growing influence in Southeast Asia, India has created the intriguing model of regional cooperation that plays on historical relations and cultural ties between India and Southeast Asia. More important, MGC laid out on ambitious agenda that will serve to advance India's security agenda in the region. India's attempt to establish sustained ties with Mekong riparian states, due to geographical proximity and strategic reasons, again reactivated Look East Policy from a different dimension of politico-strategic partnership with Indochina states including Vietnam.

The signing of MGC further accelerated the development of bilateral relations between India and Vietnam. By taking the advantage of Myanmar as a "gateway" to Southeast Asia, New Delhi believes to convert North east region of India from a security burden to region of economic prosperity. Moreover, by improving the road route between India and Myanmar, via Northeast, New Delhi will eventually connect a section of Asian Highway. When completed, this entire Asian Highway project route will link Vietnam.[20]

Omission of India and China from their respective groupings signaled the mutual divergent paths, the two Asian giants were charting in the same region. Politics is the determinant of Sino-India leadership in these two groups. China's exclusion from the MGC is seen as India's answer to Beijing's opposition to the enlargement with Mekong countries.

In a strictly competitive sense, it could be an exaggerated perception. The fact that China, the country of the origin of Mekong river was excluded from the MGC, one might entertain the suspicion that project was intended for increasing India's influence in the region. India's entry into the Mekong region is no way inviting rivalry between India and China. Further, China also welcomed the initiative setting aside misgivings if any.[21]

However, in the post-Cold War period, the foreign relations of India and China on one hand and those of Vietnam and China on the other hand moved dynamically towards a better understanding as never before. 1990s witnessed an unprecedented goodwill gestures by India and China, Vietnam and China and India and Vietnam which had the impact on the stability, security and economic development of South, Southeast and East Asia. Yet, there is a continuation of mistrust and misunderstanding of these nations. If these Asian giants, India, China and Vietnam tread the path of friendship and cooperation, they can make immense contribution to the peace and progress of the region. China's role in providing peace in the region also depends on its relations with Vietnam. The progress achieved in the normalisation of relations should not be undermined by the unsolved issues. The geographical proximity facilitates promotion of cultural exchanges, technology transfer and trade and all the three can derive mutual benefits. Warmer relations among these nations would herald a new era in Asia-Pacific.

References

1. Mohammed Ayub, *India and Southeast Asia: Indian Perception and Policies*, (London, 1990), p. 8.
2. Yogendra Singh, *Indo-Vietnam Relations: The Road Ahead*, (Institute of Peace and Conflict, New Delhi), Special Report, No. 40, April 2007, pp. 1-5.
3. John W Garver, "Chinese-Indian Rivalry in Indochina." *Asian Survey*, Vol. 27, No. 11, November 1987, p. 958.
4. K. Raja Reddy, "India, Vietnam and Asia-Pacific." *Proceedings of the Indian Association of Asia Pacific Studies*, (Sambalpur, 2004).
5. For details see, Hemen Ray, *China's Vietnam War*, (New Delhi, 1983).
6. Swaran Singh, "China factor in India's ties with Southeast Asia," in Frederic Grare and Amitabh Mattoo (eds.). *India and ASEAN, The Politics of Look East Policy*, (New Delhi, 2001), pp.191-203.
7. Statement of George Fernandes, *Vietnam*, (Embassy of Vietnam, New Delhi). April 2000.
8. Prakash Nanda, *Rediscovery of Asia: Evolution of India's Look East Policy*, (New Delhi, 2003), p.389.
9. J N Dixit, *Across Border : 50 years of India*, (New Delhi, 1988), p. 408.
10. S. Prasamrajan, "'Ahoy Hanoi': With India and Vietnam Reviving Old Bonds," *India Today*, 20 November 2000, p. 50.
11. http://www.tribune.india.com/2000/20329/world.html.
12. Tridib Chakraborti, "From National Reconstruction to Market Economy : Space and Time Analysis of India's Look East Policy," in P V Rao (ed.) *India and ASEAN: Partners at Summit*. (New Delhi, 2008), p. 328.

13. *The Hindu*, 29 March 2000.

14. C.S. Kuppuswamy, "India's Policy: Looking Eastwards." *South Asian Analysis Group* (India), No, 151, 29 April 2002.

15. Sudhir Devare, *India and Southeast Asia: Towards Security Convergence* (Singapore, 2006), p. 56.

16. Bharat Karnad, "Counter poise to China: India as a Geo-strategic Fulcrum." *The Times of India*, 6 September 2000, p. 4.

17. Waheguru Siddu and Co-authors, *China and India: Cooperation and Conflict*, (Boulder, 2003), p. 58.

18. P.V. Rao, "Sub-regional Cooperation," in K. Raja Reddy (ed.) *India and ASEAN: Foreign Policy Dimensions for the 21st Century,* (New Delhi, 2005), p.163.

19. *Ibid.*, p. 166.

20. Tridib Chakraborti, "Explaining the Penumbra of Look East Policy." In K. Raja Reddy (ed.), *India and ASEAN*, N.18, p. 66.

21. Amit Baruah, "Looking East", *Frontline*, 8 December 2000, pp. 49-50.

7

Weighing India-China Relations in the 21st Century: An Analytical and Comparative Assessment under the NDA and UPA Governments

Mohor Chakraborty

Introduction

India's relations with China are comparable to a flowing stream, which in its course, flows steadily, having faced boulders and stumbling blocks. In order to find an answer to the sensitive question as to what the boulders are that have impeded the smooth flow of bilateral relations, one needs to introspect by delving deep into the chronology of Sino-Indian ties and their impact on the psyche of their peoples. Indubitably then, we come across a mental catharsis that has impeded the smooth flow of the stream, springing directly in the aftermath of the 1962 Border War. The lineage of the shock, that Jawaharlal Nehru was unable to absorb, was tackled judiciously and pragmatically by his grandson, Rajiv Gandhi, further cemented by his 1988 China visit. The rest, as we all know, is history. The question, which now arises, is whether the intrinsic mental block has been removed, either partially, or fully. It is evident, by following the graph of Sino-Indian relations through the finale of the cold war and into the post-cold war era that the dividing curtain has opened, as both countries have embarked upon their individual missions of carving out a niche for themselves in global politics in general and Asian politics in particular. In this light, the paper purports to highlight as well as to make a comparative analysis of Sino-Indian ties under the two coalition governments in India and an attempt will also be made to discuss under whose tenure the relations developed either for the better or for worse.

With the fall of the former Soviet Union, a new global order has come into existence, based on the precepts of globalisation and liberalisation. This novel situation placed most of the developing countries in a serious dilemma, to cope with which, India and China initiated a number of economic reforms. India, under the leadership of P. V. Narasimha Rao announced its New Economic Policy in July 1991 and simultaneously unveiled the process of economic coordination with the countries of Southeast Asia, through its "Look East" policy. As a natural extension of this policy, Indian policy-makers realised that China had an advantage in Southeast Asia as a corollary of its strategic ubiquity in the region, which made it imperative for New Delhi to take Beijing into account for playing a more effective role with reference to its "Look East" policy. Likewise, the Chinese leadership wanted to establish its benign image and portray an image soft in nature, especially among the countries with which it had bitter memories of the past. Moreover, China considered India an emerging and prominent global player first, due to its vibrant democracy, expeditiously growing economy, nuclear weapon status, and a modernised conventional armed force. Secondly, China preferred to have peace on its borders and concentrate on building up its economic and military prowess, to keep abreast of the larger spectrum of global trade and commerce in the era of interdependent and inclusive globalisation, for which India offered a perfect landscape, with a huge middle-class population and sprawling market. Finally, China perceived the upgradation of Japan's maritime defence capacities and the growing influence of the United States (US) – the sole super power – as sources of potential instability and threat, not only to itself, but also to the entire Asia Pacific region.

Under such a backdrop, while it may be assumed that the vicissitudes of the New World Order have led to some degree of recession of the mental block; several other factors have come up in the trajectory of Sino-Indian bilateral relational development. The focal point of the paper is to analyse the nature and substance of Sino-Indian relations during the two stable coalition governmental tenures in India, viz., National Democratic Alliance (NDA) and the first phase of United Progressive Alliance (UPA-I), in the post-cold war years. Since 1977, in Indian political process, coalition politics has remained an integral part in its federal structure due to the emergence of different regional parties. This resulted in the establishment of a number of coalition governments from 1977 onwards, where several important personalities, who hitherto held the portfolios of Foreign Minister and Finance Minister, became Prime Minister in the later years. Knowing fully well the mindset of these personalities, their policies as the Heads of the Government were clearly reflected in their policy-making in the later years. Since the paper concentrates on the two coalition governments which are different in nature, it shall not make a thorough review of their earlier policies, but would focus exclusively on the overall attitude of the NDA and UPA-I governments towards China in different situations in the post-cold war years. Over the spectrum of the NDA tenure (1998-2004) on the one hand, and the administration of UPA-I (2004 - May 2009) on the other, it is evident that common denominators – globalisation, liberalisation and economic interdependence, which have necessitated the enhanced economic, political and strategic cooperation; India's quest for nuclear power status and energy security; China's cozying up Pakistan, Myanmar and Maldives; and regional cooperation – have laid out the pace of Sino-Indian relations. In dealing with the relational kaleidoscope through the tenure of the NDA and UPA-I governments, these common denominators have been interspersed by another factor – United States – and its diplomatic endeavour to drive a wedge between India and China, in order to maintain its prominence in the Asia Pacific region.

The first NDA Government was elected to office in 1998, following the 12th Lok Sabha elections and the fall of I.K. Gujral's Congress administration. The NDA was a conglomeration of 32 right-wing, centrist and regional parties, led by the veteran leader of the Bharatiya Janata Party (BJP), Atal Bihari Vajpayee as the Prime Minister. On 17 April 1999, Vajpayee lost a confidence vote in the Lok Sabha and consequently tendered the resignation of his coalition government. As General Elections had previously been held in 1998, those of October 1999 (13th Lok Sabha elections) were the third in 40 months. Resultantly, Vajpayee was sworn in once again as Prime Minister on 13 October 1999. The NDA government's foreign policy agenda was an integral part of its larger effort of building the nation's capabilities through economic development, strengthening social well-being and quality of life, and of protecting India's sovereignty, territorial integrity and security, not only in its defence and economic aspects, but also in the widest sense of the terms. For this, its concerns and interactions went well beyond South Asia to include other neighbours and countries immediately adjoining this region – India's "extended neighbourhood", and the wider world. With respect to China, the NDA administration sought to have cordial relations, based on the Five Principles of Peaceful Co-existence (Panchsheel) and commitment to the process of dialogue to resolve outstanding differences, aimed at a further development of friendly, cooperative, good-neighbourly and mutually beneficial relationship.

With the end of the tenure of the NDA government, the 14th Lok Sabha elections were held in India in May 2004, which brought another coalition government at the Centre – United Progressive Alliance (UPA) – with Dr. Manmohan Singh as the Prime Minister. This post-poll alliance brought together political parties that either allied with the Congress in various states, or were willing to support a Congress-led national government. Although the UPA did not enjoy a clear majority on its own, it managed to complete its five-year term from 2004 to May 2009 by securing outside support from the Left Front, Samajwadi Party and the Bahujan Samaj Party. The foreign policy of this government was embellished by a distinct continuity with that of its immediate predecessor, particularly with respect to India's relations with her significant neighbours. In fact, the process of establishing better ties with Beijing, which had been initiated by the Vajpayee administration, was raised to a new and more concrete level by Dr. Singh. While the conduct of its foreign relations was also founded on the precepts of the Panchsheel, pragmatism and pursuit of national interest, its nature was forward-looking and optimally responsive to the various challenges and opportunities of the international order. With respect to China, the government aspired to sustain the positive spirit of bilateral ties, in order to carry forward the legacy of the NDA. Besides, the UPA administration was resolute in maintaining its pledge to the process of dialogue to resolve outstanding differences and build a long-term, constructive and cooperative relationship with China, marked by continuity, consolidation, and sustained momentum of high-level dialogue.

Sino-Indian Relations under the NDA and UPA-I Governments based on Determinants

1. Globalisation, Liberalisation and Economic Interdependence

The development of the relations between India and China has been influenced by the phenomena of globalisation, liberalisation and economic interdependence – the hallmark of the New World Order. The process of globalisation made it starkly evident that the benefits of a favourable global economic environment did not accrue automatically to any country and the remarkable differences persisted in the degrees of success that different countries had in taking advantage of the opportunities for strengthening their economic edge and performance. Although globalisation has enormously contributed to overall international prosperity, the uneven performance and the uneven distribution of rewards across the countries and regions are linked to the phenomena of globalisation, liberalisation and economic interdependence, resulting in rapid integration of economies worldwide, through trade, financial flows, technology spillovers, information networks and cultural cross-currents. The fact that the qualitative intensification of globalisation, economic interaction and China's entry into the World Trade Organisation (WTO) in 2001 as its offshoot, has provided a positive momentum and forward direction in Sino-Indian relations, evidently demonstrated by the survey of bilateral trade figures (as shown in the tables below) during the two distinct periods of NDA and UPA-I governments.

From Tables 1 and 2, it is evident that the total export from India to China during the NDA tenure (figures calculated from 1998-1999 to 2003-2004) was US$ 7,678 million approximately, while it graduated to approximately US$ 37,621 million during the UPA-I administration (figures calculated from 2004-2005 to 2008-2009: April-December). On the other hand, while the total volume of import by India from China during the NDA tenure was US$ 12,761 million approximately, the corresponding amount in the successive UPA-I era shot up to US$ 86,696 million approximately. Apart from the bilateral trade computation, an appraisal of Sino-Indian high-level exchanges under the two coalition governments clearly reveals that the number of these visits during the NDA had surpassed those under the UPA-I counterpart. This can be attributed to the latter's obsession and preoccupation with Washington, particularly in the run-up to the signing of the Nuclear Deal. A chronological study of the high-level exchanges between the two sides carves the ascending graph of the bilateral relations under the NDA regime, that were flagged off when Jaswant Singh, Prime Minister Vajpayee's Special Emissary, held a meeting with the then Chinese Foreign Minister, Tang Jiaxuan, on the sidelines of the ASEAN Regional Forum (ARF) – Annual Meeting in Manila in July 1998. This marked the first thaw in their ties following the embittered Pokhran experience. Moreover, the Indian President, K.R. Narayanan's momentous China visit in May 2000 to mark the completion of 50 years of Sino-Indian diplomatic ties, ushered in a new era in politico-diplomatic coordination between Beijing and New Delhi. This visit helped in creating an affable atmosphere underlining the "historical necessity" and contemporary advantage of developing bilateral

Table 1: India's Trade with China under the NDA Government (in US$ Million)

Year (April-March)	*Export*	*Import*	*Total Trade*	*Balance Trade*
1998-1999	427	1,096	1,523	669
1999-2000	539	1,282	1,821	743
2000-2001	831	1,502	2,333	671
2001-2002	951	2,036	2,987	1,085
2002-2003	1,975	2,792	4,767	817
2003-2004	2,955	4,053	7,008	1,098
Total	7,678	12,761	20,439	5,083

Table 2: India's Trade with China under the UPA-I Government (in US$ Million)

Year (April-March)	*Export*	*Import*	*Total Trade*	*Balance Trade*
2004-2005	5,615	7,097	12,712	1,482
2005-2006	6,759	10,868	17,627	4,109
2006-2007	8,287	17,447	25,734	9,160
2007-2008	10,834	27,115	37,949	16,281
2008-2009*	6,126	24,169	30,295	18,043
Total	37,621	86,696	124,317	49,075

*Upto December 2008.

Source: Compiled by the author from http://www.indianembassy.org/indusrel/trade.htm and http://www.commerce.nic.in/eidb/icnt.asp

amity. Subsequently, as Sino-Indian relations started improving under Vajpayee's pragmatism, the five-day India visit of the Chinese Premier, Zhu Rongji in January 2002 provided a transformed dimension to politico-economic geniality between the two neighbours, particularly since Zhu deeply impressed the Indian business community and underscored the scope for trade and investment in China in the sectors like Information Technology (IT), services and engineering, among others. It was as a result of this visit that India and China agreed to fix the bilateral trade target at US$ 10 billion by 2005. Within a span of two years, in June 2003, Vajpayee visited China and this sojourn assumed immense significance since the leaders of the two countries pledged to solve the border problem by appointing special envoys/representatives for negotiating the issue.

On the other hand, the UPA-I saw the Chinese Premier, Wen Jiabao's highly successful visit to India in April 2005, in the context of which, the host Prime Minister, Dr. Manmohan Singh concurred with his guest to celebrate the year 2006 as the "China-India Friendship Year". This visit ushered in a new lease of life in Sino-Indian ties, specifically when both countries declared the establishment of strategic partnership for forwarding regional peace and prosperity. The momentum of bilateral ties was further boosted when the Chinese President, Hu Jintao visited India in November 2006 – a decade after his predecessor, Jiang Zemin had toured India. During this visit, President Hu acknowledged that India-China relations had maintained its thrust of all-round development, bolstered by "mutual political trust, expanded cooperation, broadened friendship and cooperation in international and regional affairs". Since the visit of the Chinese President, both the countries have endeavoured to enhance the shared association and successfully chart the course of strategic and cooperative partnership.

2. India's Quest for Nuclear Power Status and Energy Security

An important achievement of the NDA administration was India's proclamation of nuclear weapon status, following the Pokhran-II episode in May 1998, of which, China was very critical. In fact, Beijing accused New Delhi of pursuing hegemonic designs. As the immediate fallout of India's Pokhran explosion, a number of events complicated the regional situation. First, Pakistan followed suit and made the regional environment even more volatile in nature. Secondly, Beijing's animosity, directed at New Delhi's justification of its nuclear tests by demonising China, was further compounded when Vajpayee wrote a letter to the then US President, Bill Clinton citing the threat from China and Pakistan. Thirdly, the fact that the then Defence Minister of India, George Fernandes, pointed out China as the number one threat to Indian security, put India on a wrong footing vis-à-vis China. Ironically enough, China's post-Pokhran nuclear policy took a 180 degree turn – while it had hitherto criticised the Non Proliferation Treaty (NPT) and the global non-proliferation regime as a 'construct' of Great Power hegemony, after the Pokhran tests, when Vajpayee reiterated the proposal of signing a no-first use of nuclear weapons treaty with Beijing, it remained indifferent to the proposal and insisted on New Delhi signing the NPT and Comprehensive Test Ban Treaty (CTBT) unconditionally. In this context, a spokesman of the Chinese Foreign Ministry said: "The most urgent task for India is to implement the United Nations-Security Council (UNSC) resolution, abandon its nuclear programme and accede to NPT and CTBT as soon as possible." Such a statement clearly revealed that China, which had earlier turned down India's proposal of signing the no first-use accord on the ground that India was not a nuclear power, in the post-1998 situation, refused to recognise India's status. The Pokhran-II experiment demonstrated that India was poised for developing a deterrence strategy, thereby challenging China's capabilities in the South Asian region. The Indian nuclear tests also belied China's perception that India would not take any strategic initiative to guarantee its long-term interests from potentialities of conflict or competition vis-à-vis China, thus allowing it to continue its dual policy of striving towards the achievement of normal relations with India, while simultaneously increasing its defence entente with Pakistan. The fact that China failed to reach a common ground with India in relation to big powers and on cardinal international issues like the NPT and CTBT laid bare its insincerity on nuclear non-proliferation. Thus, in the immediate post-Pokhran milieu, China's relations with India reached a nadir, as it had been forced to acknowledge India's proven capabilities and was compelled to treat it as a major competitor on nuclear matters in the Asia Pacific region. It may be mentioned at this juncture, that China's approach to the 1999 Kargil conflict had brightened the prospects of Sino-Indian rapprochement. In fact, China, in the backdrop of the Kargil War had strongly affirmed the significance of preserving the Line of Control between India and Pakistan. Notwithstanding the efforts by the then Prime Minister of Pakistan, Nawaz Sharif to persuade Beijing otherwise, the latter refused to support Islamabad and invited the Indian Minister of External Affairs, Jaswant Singh to visit China during that time. However, unlike Washington, Beijing refrained from open criticism of Islamabad on the one hand and notably indeed, kept the pace of Sino-Indian border and bilateral confidence-building measures (CBMs) intact, on the other. In sum, the Pokhran explosion strained China's relations with India and it took a considerable time for the ties to look up.

While the Pokhran blasts prepared the promenade for a serious de-escalation in India's relations with China during the NDA period, the UPA era bore testimony to the heating up of bilateral relations owing to India's scramble for energy resources and the signing of the controversial Indo-US Civilian Nuclear Agreement, also known as the Indo-US Nuclear Deal. The Deal was finally operationalised between India and US on 10 October 2008, after being signed by the Minister of External Affairs of the UPA-I government, Pranab Mukherjee and his counterpart, Secretary of State (during the administration of President George W. Bush) Condoleezza Rice, in Washington. Among the Asian countries, India and China, with their respective huge populations and corresponding high energy demands, have an enhanced stake in the 'great game' of oil politics, prompted by their increase in energy imports and the forging of new client-supplier relations with the major energy-exporting and other non-Asian energy-importing nations of the world. Against this background, buoyed by high economic growth rates and learning from its experiences and contemporary developments, India has been rubbing shoulders with China in different parts of Asia, Africa and Latin America. On its part, China has been scouting for energy resources world-wide, besides outbidding the Indian firms in Bangladesh, Cambodia, Iran, Kazakhstan, Myanmar and Sri Lanka. Moreover, China's state-owned oil companies have outwitted their Indian complements in securing oil deals in several resource-rich countries, since they have been able to draw on generous credit lines, military and diplomatic support from Beijing. Although, New Delhi and Beijing have signed an Energy Cooperation Pact in 2006, their association in this sector has been contingent on certain stringent conditions, put forward by the latter, such as the one, which obliges Indian oil companies to willingly play the role of a junior partner to China's state-owned oil conglomerates. China's insatiable stalk for energy security has spawned maritime rivalry with India, exacerbated by its knitting of a "string of pearls" along the nautical choke points in the South China Sea, the Malacca Straits, the Indian Ocean and the Strait of Hormuz, through its search for and access to naval bases in Bangladesh, Cambodia, Myanmar and Sri Lanka – in India's vicinity. Any Chinese attempt to control events in India's geographic vicinity "would doubtless meet with Indian countermeasures; whereas the Chinese recognise that India's energy needs, that resemble China's own, could impel New Delhi into zero-sum competition at sea". Moreover, India's construed cooperation with China in the countries like Colombia, Iran, Myanmar, Russia, Sudan, Syria and Venezuela have the potential of embittering New Delhi's ties with Washington. This becomes increasingly significant in the aftermath of the Indo-US Civilian Nuclear Deal that has virtually re-scribed the rules of the global nuclear regime by emphasizing New Delhi's credentials as a responsible nuclear state, pending the integration with international nuclear order. The nuclear reconciliation between the global nuclear order on the one hand, and New Delhi on the other, has irked Beijing not only since it put India at par with China by conferring it rights commensurate with the latter in the nuclear domain, especially the right to have a nuclear arsenal and access to civilian nuclear technology, but has also provided India access to advanced conventional weaponry and dual-use technologies from the West, denied to China as a result of an arms embargo dating back to the Tiananmen Square massacre of 1989. Alluding to such concerns, on 2 March 2006, Qin Gang, Chinese Foreign Ministry spokesman argued that:

> India should sign the NPT and also dismantle its nuclear weapons....China hopes that concerned countries developing cooperation in peaceful nuclear uses will pay attention to these

efforts. The cooperation should conform to the rules of international non-proliferation mechanisms.

In the same vein, the *Peoples' Daily* reported in June 2008 that:

> The US has explicitly proposed in the agreement that it would hamper or intervene in the development of India's military nuclear plan, which will also help the country achieve its goals to be a nuclear power.

Actually, some Chinese strategic analysts have likened the Indo-US Nuclear Deal to US' strategic tilt towards China, evinced by President Richard Nixon in 1971, in order to contain the then common Soviet threat. Alleging that the Nuclear Deal has 'destabilising' and 'negative implications' for China's future, some analysts in China have issued a caveat to the Beijing leadership that it "should not take India lightly any longer". Almost concurrently, the Chinese media commentators have resumed their critique of US' 'hegemonic ideas of drawing India near, as a tool for its global strategic pattern', while accusing India of becoming Washington's monitoring station to gather intelligence on China. Expressing serious reservations about this Indo-US tactical convergence, *The Renmin Ribao* commented that:

> The US-India nuclear agreement has strong symbolic significance for India in achieving its dream of a powerful nation. In fact, the purpose of the US to sign civilian nuclear energy cooperation agreement with India is to enclose India into its global partners' camp, so as to balance the forces of Asia. This fits in exactly with India's wishes.

China has been extremely sensitive to India's overtures in the backdrop of the latter's signing the Nuclear Deal with US, perceiving it as a catalyst of shift in the South Asian balance of power. Thus, Beijing's attempts at strengthening its strategic presence in Bangladesh, Maldives, Myanmar, Nepal, Pakistan and Sri Lanka, should be viewed as its well-mediated architecture to checkmate India's burgeoning prominence, both in the regional and international spheres.

3. China's Cozying up Pakistan, Myanmar and Maldives

Among the countries of South and Southeast Asia, Pakistan, Myanmar and Maldives are strategically important regional players. Like US, China has viewed Pakistan as a springboard to Central and West Asian resource-rich nations, aimed at outsmarting India's reach to oil resources there. China's 'indirect strategy' of containing India through neighbouring proxies, like Pakistan and Myanmar, by the transfer of conventional arms, small arms and the alleged supply of nuclear designs, components, materials, facilities and technology has caused serious concern in its ties with India. The fact that US has turned a blind eye to this unholy entente since the dawn of the NDA administration, has seriously disturbed policy-makers in New Delhi. It was testified by US Nuclear Expert, Gary Milohllin before a Congress Committee in July 1998 that Washington had given the green signal to China to sell missile technology to Pakistan and Iran. In addition, in 1998, President Clinton backtracked on his professed acknowledgement in 1994 that the Kashmir issue could not serve as a reason for Pakistan's suspected nuclear armament agenda, when he said: "We made it clear to Pakistan Government that we respect its own determination of its national security needs".

Moreover, the US Deputy Assistant Secretary of State for Non-Proliferation, Robert Einhorn said in May 1998, a few days before the Pokhran Test: "Pakistan of course is a friend of US and we wish to have good relations with Pakistan. We also recognise China as a good friend of Pakistan and we do not intend to interfere in anyway with their close relationship."

Therefore, the 1998 Indian nuclear tests, which had opened up the possibilities of India becoming a major player in the international scene, came as a rude shock to Sino-US strategic content and was an assertion of India's independent policy, defying nuclear weapon powers at a sensitive time when CTBT was being implemented.

Under the UPA-I government, among other factors, Beijing's emphasis on the increasing instability and terrorist perpetration from Islamabad did not converge with New Delhi's considerations and this was clearly underlined when Prime Minister, Manmohan Singh, in his address to the Combined Commanders' Conference in October 2005, said:

> We cannot also ignore the strategic cooperation that Pakistan secured from China in many ways. We cannot rule out the desire of some countries [read, China] to keep us engaged in low-intensity conflict with some of our neighbours as a means of getting India bogged down in a low equilibrium.

With respect to Myanmar, it may be pointed out, that not only is it a strategic possession for its rich energy resources in the Asian region, but is the only Southeast Asian country which shares a land border with India and is a member of ASEAN, Bay of Bengal Initiative for Multi-Sectoral Technical and Economic Cooperation (BIMSTEC) and the Mekong Ganga Cooperation (MGC). China has harboured friendly ties with the repressive Junta since it came to power in Yangon in 1988, with the principal objective of utilising its facilities for keeping a tab on India's naval activities. Moreover, Beijing has also taken advantage of New Delhi's reticence towards the anti-democratic regime in Myanmar, taking cognisance of Washington's anti-Yangon rhetoric. Therefore, it has become pertinent for New Delhi to sustain the long-tem positive relational dynamics with Myanmar, initiated by the Vajpayee administration and continued in right earnest by Dr. Manmohan Singh, since it is not only important for maintaining regional stability, but also for the sake of holding peace in its northeastern fringes by preventing cross-border movement of insurgents, refugees and contraband items, so that India's internal security, territorial integrity and sovereignty are upheld in letter and spirit. Besides, it is deemed to mention in this context that, Maldives – a tiny island-nation in the Indian Ocean – is gaining prominence as a prime military and politically strategic location, stalked by both India and China. Although Maldives has pursued a pro-India policy, it is not ready to alienate China. As a matter of fact, Beijing and Maldives have signed an agreement way back in 2001, allowing China to establish a naval base in Marao for the purpose of countering the rise of Indian and American naval forces in the region, in lieu of Chinese support to its ailing economy. Thus, the Sino-Indian endeavour to make their individual presence felt in the South Asian and Indian Ocean Rim regions will have an important bearing on Maldives in the near future. As Mohan Malik points out, the same structural changes that are increasing the proximity between India and US are also raising the possibility of a slow, but steady enhancement in the tempo of the competitive trends between the two Asian neighbours – India and China. While emphasizing the crucial roles played by New Delhi, Beijing and Washington in the New Global Order, Malik contends: "Strained US-China relations would make India the pivotal power in the US-China-India triangle but tense India-China relations would put the US in a pivotal position."

Axiomatically, the US factor is destined to play a momentous role in Sino-Indian future relations.

4. Regional Cooperation

The process of globalisation has boosted the institutionalisation of regionalism and sub-regional organisations, particularly underscored by India's deeper integration with the Association for Southeast Asian Nations (ASEAN), as it graduated from a Full Dialogue Partner (in 1995) to ARF member (in 1996) and further as Summit-level Partner (in 2002) and East Asia Summit (EAS) Partner (in 2005). At the sub-regional level, India's active involvement in the organisations like BIMSTEC and MGC has been China's cause for disquiet. The Sino-Indian rivalry for one-upmanship is incessantly played out in regional multilateral fora, where each seeks advantage over the other. On its part, China gained entry into the South Asian regional scenario as an observer of South Asian Association for Regional Cooperation (SAARC) at the 13th SAARC Summit, held in Dhaka in November 2005, with the motive of "diluting India's hold in the region as a major economic power". A clear divide in opinion between India and Pakistan, pertaining to the Association's decision to include China within its fold, was demonstrated by the then Indian Foreign Secretary, Shyam Saran's initial reluctance to induct China unless it signed a Memorandum of Understanding (MoU) for being associated with SAARC. However, India's reservations vis-à-vis China's inclusion in SAARC were counterpoised by the enthusiastic preference for it, exhibited by Bangladesh, Nepal and Pakistan – three other pro-China SAARC member-states. Evidently then, on the one side of the spectrum, as India carves its footprints on the Southeast and East Asian soils through its coveted membership and involvement with regional and sub-regional organisations, China is not far behind in making its ambitious forays into South Asia, on the other end.

Besides these, there are a plethora of issues – like terrorism, non-traditional security threats, and commonality of views in the WTO negotiations and other multilateral fora – on which India and China have raised their concerted voices and expressed deep concern in the interest of the Third World countries. However, the development of Sino-Indian ties has been scarred by occasional irritants, especially with reference to India's bid in the United Nations-Security Council, confrontation in the areas of naval deployment in Indian Ocean and Bay of Bengal regions, unresolved border dispute, issue of Tibet, claiming of Arunachal Pradesh by China, competition for soft-power supremacy in Asia and the scare-mongering attitude of the Indian and Chinese media alike by painting inaccurate pictures of the conditions along the India-China border, among others. Despite some recent optimistic developments in India's bilateral ties with China, mutual relations remain "fragile, and as vulnerable as ever to sudden deterioration as a result of misperceptions, unrealistic expectations, accidents, and eruption of unresolved issues".

Conclusion

In the final analysis, we encounter the question as to under which coalition government in India have Sino-Indian relations been better and more promising – the NDA or UPA-I? In answering this, one needs to take cognisance of the domestic and foreign policy determinants that have conditioned bilateral relations between New Delhi and Beijing. Overall, if one can compare India's relations with China under the two governments, the perception remains that the NDA government exhibited more pragmatism and China-focus. The lack of China-focus by the UPA-I government is primarily attributable to the domestic strains of coalition politics that it countenanced, while giving final shape to the Nuclear Deal with US. However, mere computation of high-level exchanges and bilateral trade only provides the tangible elements of the mutual calculus and ignores the immeasurable and intangible determinants, like the nature of international politics, relational dynamics with neighbouring countries, the imperative of seeking newer avenues of cooperation and the psyche of the populations and measure of erosion of the mental block that the people of the two countries have harboured against each other, since the Border War of 1962. Consider the fact that if the year 1999 – when China refused to support Pakistan's anti-Indian stance during the height of the Kargil War – had been announced as the China-India Friendship Year instead of the year 2006 – a year fortunately not blemished by wars in the South Asian neighbourhood – would the balance have tilted in favour of the NDA regime, rather than its successor administration? Or, why did it take a macabre 9/11 to bring India and China under a single grand coalition against Al Qaeda terror, when pragmatically, the home-grown constraints and experiences of terrorism and low intensity conflicts within the national boundaries of India and China alike, should have voluntarily rosetted them in their fight against terrorism, without US acting as the global super cop? These are some observations that may be left to you to ponder over, while my humble submission is that rather than working out a balance sheet of Sino-Indian relations in black and white, the grey areas in their ties should also be accounted for, since it is difficult, if not impossible, to configure bilateral relations in a straitjacket.

References

1. Atal Bihari Vajpayee was sworn in as the Prime Minister of India in March 1998.

2. *Annual Report: 1998-1999*, Ministry of External Affairs, Government of India, New Delhi, 1999, pp. 3-7.

3. *Annual Report:2004-2005*, Ministry of External Affairs, Government of India, New Delhi, 2005, p. i-v.

4. *World Economic Outlook: Globalization – Opportunities and Challenges*, International Monetary Fund. Washington D.C., May 1997, p. 3.

5. Compiled by the author from http://www.commerce.nic.in/eidb/icnt.asp

6. For details, see http://www.commerce.nic.in/eidb/icnt.asp
7. K. Raja Reddy, "India and China Rapprochement: Cautious Moves", in Y. Yagama Reddy (ed.), *Emerging India in Asia Pacific*, New Century Publications, New Delhi, 2007, p. 209.
8. *The Peoples' Daily*, 30 November 2006.
9. *The Indian Express*, 24 May 1998.
10. *The Hindu*, 14 August 1998.
11. J.N. Dixit, "China-US Equation", *The Hindu*, 10 July 1998.
12. V. B. Menon, "India-China Relations: Critical Issues", Rajen Harshe and K.M. Seethi (eds.), *Engaging with the World: Critical Reflections on India's Foreign Policy*, Orient Blackswan, New Delhi, 2009, p. 169.
13. Swaran Singh, "India-China Relations Coming to a Full Circle", in N.K. Jha (ed.), *India's Foreign Policy in a Changing World*, South Asian Publishers, New Delhi, 2000, p. 142.
14. James Holmes, "China's Energy Consumption and Opportunities for US-China Cooperation", http;//www.uscc.gov/hearings/2007hearings/ written_testimonies/ 07_06_14_holmes_ statement.pdf, accessed on 2 September 2009.
15. The Nuclear Deal has created a one-time exception for India to keep its nuclear weapons without signing the Nuclear Non-Proliferation Treaty. It has thus resulted in an exception to Washington's prohibition of nuclear assistance to India by amending Section 123 of the Atomic Energy Act of 1954.
16. Mohan Malik, "India and China: As China Rises, India Stirs", in Harsh V. Pant (ed.), *Indian Foreign Policy in a Unipolar World*, Routledge, New Delhi, 2009, p. 179.
17. http://www.chinaembassy.org/03_02_2006.html, accessed on 2 September, 2009.
18. *The Peoples' Daily*, 20 June 2008.
19. Praful Bidwai, "Ties with China Sour as Alliance with US Grows", *Inter Press Service*, 6 July 2007.
20. *The China Daily*, 7 June 2007.
21. *The Renmin Ribao,* 10 August 2007.
22. *The Hindu*, 9 July 1998.
23. *The Hindu*, 2 May 1998.

24. *The Indian Express*, 8 May 1998.
25. *Manmohan Singh's Address to the Combined Commanders' Conference*, 20 October 2005, at http://www.mea.nic.in/speeches, accessed on 4 September 2009.
26. Satheesan Kumaaran, "Maldives and Geo-Politics of India and Sri Lanka", *The Sri Lanka Guardian*, 30 August 2009, at http://www.srilankaguardian. org, accessed on 4 September 2009.
27. Mohan Malik, "India and China: As China Rises, India Stirs", **N.16**, pp. 189-191.
28. Bruce Loudon, "India, China in Clash at Summit", *Australian*, 4 April 2007, p. 7.
29. Tridib Chakraborti, "SAARC Expands its Wings: Insinuations in the New Global Order", *World Focus*, Vol. 29, No. 5, May 2008, pp. 204-05.
30. Mohan Malik, "India and China: As China Rises, India Stirs", **N.16**, p. 190

8

Sino-Indian Ties Towards Forging a Viable Partnership

P. Munirathnam Reddy

Introduction

Military preparedness and economic prowess are considered the crucial elements of national power for a nation to be reckoned with as a major power in the international system. India and China are gearing up themselves to attain such status in the near future. Never in the history, until the Second World War, did they experience any dispute over the territorial issue. Independent India and Communist China locked up in dispute over the territorial boundary in 1962 and skirmishes again in 1965 and 1967. India has also unresolved territorial dispute with yet another immediate neighbour, Pakistan which has clandestinely moved close to China. Besides wars between India and Pakistan in 1965, 1971 and 1998, it continuously encouraged cross-border infiltration and transnational terrorism to weaken India. Of late in 1970s, India and China were set to normalise their relations and realised to cultivate economic and cultural relations as priority while keeping territorial dispute to be resolved through negotiations.

Historical Cultural Relations between India and China: The Role of China Bhavan

The Chinese Communist Party's organ 'Global Times' on 18 September 2009 chose 60 foreigners who shaped modern China in connection with the 60th anniversary of People's Republic of China, in which two glorious Indian personalities Gurudev Rabindranath Tagore the only poet listed as 11 and Pandit Jawaharlal Nehru were listed 19.[1] Tagore works have been widely translated in Chinese and these works are available in Chinese major libraries. Nehru and China's Foreign Minister Zhou Enlai were the main architects of the 'Hindi-Chini bhai bhai' concept that released a wave of brotherly feeling across the two nations. Jawaharlal's association with Rabindranath Tagore and Tan Yun Shan of Visvabharathi, Santiniketan had developed great admiration towards China and Chinese culture which prompted him to visit China in 1938 and again as Prime Minister in 1954.

The Nobel Laureate Rabindranath Tagore visited China on the invitation of the great Chinese scholar Liang Qichao of Beijing Lecture Association in 1924. Rabindranath Tagore's visit to China had been considered a great event in Chinese cultural history. Tagore had awakened the dormant conscience of the Chinese nation which had been intoxicated and doped by the modern splendours and glories of materialistic West for over a hundred years.[2] An American scholar Stephen Hay criticized Tagore's visit to China that he played a role of a prophet rather than a poet. According to him, Tagore propagated an ideal of orient, an ideal of One Asia and the cause of spiritualism against the materialism of the West.[3] It was this visit of Tagore that had given a momentous impetus to the new national movements awakening China.[4] The Chinese poets Hsu Chih-mo and Dr.Hu Shih and other friends of them in China formed the 'Crescent Moon Society' just to commemorate Tagore's historical visit to China in 1924 and translated Tagore's works into Chinese language. Tan Yun-Shan, the close associate of Rabindranath Tagore, inspired by Tagore came to India in 1927 and made India his home (Santiniketan). Tan Yun-Shan formed 'Sino-Indian Cultural Society' under the noble inspiration of Tagore, raised money and collected great many Buddhist books from China. Rabindranath Tagore inaugurated China Bhavan, the Study Centre for China, mainly aimed at fostering India-China relations in Visvabharathi University, Santinikethan, in 1937 and entrusted the organisation of China Bhavan to the Chinese scholar Professor Tan Yun Shan. China had conferred on Rabindranath Tagore a Chinese name called 'Chu Chen-Tan'.[5] 'Chu' was the old Chinese name for India, also called 'Tieu-Chu' meaning heavenly kingdom. 'Chen-Tan' was the old name for China. He was the symbol of unity and combination of India and China. Tan Yun Shan,with his scholarly works and his association with Chinese Chiang Kai Shek and Indian stalwarts (Tagore, Gandhi and Nehru) reconnected China and India for a closer and strong cultural relations. He was described as the modern Xuan Zang of China.[6]

China Bhavan has inspired many scholars and their researches contributed to retrace the pathways of cultural relations between India and China which Tagore exhorted in China: to reopen the channel of communication that was overgrown with weeds of oblivion, its lines can still be traced.[7] Tan Yun-Shan, P.C. Bagchi and other scholars researched the cultural connections that Buddhist India had with China and its cultural influence over 2000 years. According to Indian records, Emperor Ashoka sent a number of Buddhist monks to China and the Chinese records revealed that the Chinese Emperor Qin (whose tomb in Xian is inhabited by the Terrakotta army) imprisoned and executed the Indian monks in Xian in 3rd century B.C.[8] It is widely believed and acknowledged that Indian Buddhist missionaries Dharmaraksha and Kasyapa Matanga founded 'White Horse' monastery in the Chinese capital Beijing in 65 A.D.[9] Mahayana Buddhism firmly entrenched into Chinese society along with Confucianism and Taoism of China. Some dynasties of China patronised Buddhist religion, Buddhist monks and scholars from India. Some Chinese scholars and Buddhist pilgrims venturing perilous journey to India visited prominent places of Buddhism, learned the Sanskrit language, collected Buddhist scriptures and carried to China. Records of both the countries acknowledge an increasing number of travelling monks – 24 Indian scholars travelling to China in the year 67 A.D. and some 187 Chinese monks making the trip to India in the year 265 A.D.[10] through trade routes. Gunavarma, Kumara Jiva and Bodhidharma were considered the prominent Indian Buddhist monks who made China their home. Bodhidharma, the Pallava Prince from Southern India turned Buddhist monk, was credited with introducing the Chan (Dhyan) Buddhism and Indian martial arts into China in 5th century A.D. Bodhidharma was claimed to be the ancestor of Shaolin martial arts.[11] Fa Xian, Xuan Zhang (Hsuen-Tsang) and I-Ching were the prominent Chinese Buddhist scholars who visited India in search of Buddhist sacred scriptures. It is said that when Fa Xian (399-414 A.D) left China for India, Kumarajiva told him, 'when you go to India do not only study religious texts and philosophy of the land but try to learn the customs and manners of the people of India'.[12] Xuan Zang, the noted Chinese scholar (629-644 A.D), who spent most of his time at the University of Nalanda studying Buddhist theology and collecting and translating the sacred scriptures, was believed to have been accompanied by Sun Wukong, the monkey King[13] (Hanuman) during his perilous journey to India and back to China. I-Ching, the Buddhist scholar who came to India in the second half of the 7th Century (672 A.D) through sea route, stayed for six months in Sri Vijayan empire, an out-post of Buddhist India in Southeast Asia, studied at

Nalanda spending more than a decade and finally returned to China in 689 A.D. by spending another 4 years at Srivijian Empire translating Sanskrit Buddhist scriptures into Chinese.[14]

Dr. Dwarakanath Santharam Kotnis: A Bridge between Modern China and India

Jawaharlal Nehru was greatly impressed by the spirit of the Young Chinese who came to participate in 'Anti-Imperialist Conference' held in Brussels in 1927 and was attracted towards the Chinese Communist Movement which fought for the liberation of China. Indian National Congress under the leadership of Jawaharlal Nehru organised many rallies in India in favour of the Chinese liberation movement. The communist leaders Zhu De and Mao Zedong thanked Nehru through letters for the support given to their national movement[15] and Nehru himself visited China in 1938 to show India's solidarity with the liberation movement of China. In return, Generalissimo Chiang Kai-Shek visited India in February 1942 to consolidate ties with Indian National Congress. On the request of the Communist General Zhu De, the Indian National Congress had dispatched a voluntary medical team consisting of five doctors to assist the China Defense League, during the Japanese Invasion of China in 1938. All except Dr. D.S. Kotnis returned to India after serving 5 years. Dr. Kotnis, a young doctor from Sholapur (Maharashtra) who joined the Eighth Route Army led by Mao Zedong in 1939, was eventually appointed as Director of the Dr. Bethune International Peace Hospital built by the Mao Zedong army on the plains of North China. Kotnis married Guo Quiglan, a Chinese Nurse and Co-worker in the Hospital in 1941. They had a 3 month son named Yinhua (meaning India and China) when Kotnis died of severe struck of Epilepsy in 1942. The Communist leaders Zhou Enlai, Zhu De and Mao Zedong paid rich tributes to Dr. Kotnis for what he had done for thousands of wounded soldiers. Dr. Kotnis has been regarded as a symbol of Sino-Indian friendship and collaboration. Both China (1982 and 1992) and India (1993) have honoured him by releasing stamps and produced films on him. Dr. Kotnis together with the Canadian Dr. Bethune was commemorated in the Marty's Memorial Park in Shijia Zhuang, Northern China. The Chinese State leaders whenever visited India, made it a point to pay their respects by visiting Dr. Kotnis relatives in Mumbai. President Hu Jintao of People's Republic of China during his official visit to India in November 2006 met Dr. Kotnis relatives and presented an Album documenting Dr. Kotnis life in China and described him as 'a bridge between China and India'.[16]

Relations between Independent India and China

On October 1, 1949 the People's Liberation Army defeated the Kuomintang (Nationalist Party) of China in a civil war and established the People's Republic of China (PRC). On August 15, 1947, India became an independent dominion under British Commonwealth and became a federal, democratic republic after its constitution came into effect on January 26, 1950. India was the 16th state to establish diplomatic relations with the People's Republic of China and did it so on April 1, 1950. Mao Zedang viewed Tibet as an integral part of China and saw Indian concern over it as a manifestation of the Indian Government in the internal affairs of China. To avoid antagonising the People's Republic of China, Nehru informed Chinese leaders that India had neither political nor territorial ambitions, nor did it seek special privileges in Tibet, but that traditional trading rights must continue.

Panchasheel Agreement and After

In April 1954, India and the PRC signed an eight-year agreement on Tibet that set forth the basis of their relationship in the form of Five principles of peaceful coexistence (Panchsheel). The following are the principles:

(1) Mutual respect for each other's territorial integrity and sovereignty

(2) Mutual non-aggression

(3) Mutual non-interference in each other's internal affairs

(4) Equality and mutual benefit

(5) Peaceful coexistence

By this agreement India recognised China's complete control over Tibet (i.e. suzerainty and sovereignty). In this agreement India voluntarily gave up its military, communication and postal and other rights which India had inherited from the British in accordance with the Anglo-Tibetan Treaty of 1904. By surrendering these rights, it was very strange; India didn't demand any reciprocal concessions from China in the context of the '*Hindi-Chini bhai bhai*' spirit of 1950s. Nehru sought security in peace and trusted China's friendly gestures in April 1954. This was basically a cultural and trade pact between China and India streamlining their bilateral cultural and trade operations in Tibet. Article III of the Trade and Inter-course between Tibet region of China and India (The Panchsheel Agreement) enunciated the cultural significance of the Agreement that : (1) Pilgrims from India of Lamaist, Hindu and Buddhist faiths may visit Kang Rimpoche (Kailash) and Mavam Tse (Manasarowar) in the Tibet region of China in accordance with custom, (2) Pilgrims from the Tibet region of China of Lamaist and Buddhist faiths may visit Banaras, Saranath, Gaya and Sanchi in India in accordance with custom and (3) Pilgrims customarily visiting Lhasa may continue to do so in accordance with custom.[17]

Defending this Agreement in Indian Parliament, Nehru said, 'It was the recognition of existing situation there. Historical and practical considerations necessitated the step'.[18] When visited China in November 1954, Nehru received an extraordinarily cordial welcome everywhere in China and Nehru mentioned that this welcome represented something more than political exigency. It was almost an emotional upheaval representing the basic urges of the people for friendship with India. The Chinese premier Zhou Enlai paid a return visit to India in 1958.

Dalai Lama in India and Sino-Indian Conflict

Dalai Lama's arrival in India in 1959 was perhaps the one most important factor that changed the entire spirit of Sino-Indian relations. Prime Minister Zhou En-lai who during his earlier visit to New Delhi had assured Jawaharlal Nehru of his support in China's recognising the Mac Mahon Line as the Sino-Indian border, he however, wrote to Nehru later, saying that China had never recognised the Mac Mahon Line after Dalai Lama, spiritual and temporal head of the Tibetan people, sought sanctuary in Dhramasala, Himachal Pradesh, in March 1959, and thousands of Tibetan refugees settled in north-western India, particularly Himachal Pradesh. The People's Republic of China accused India of expansionism and imperialism in Tibet and throughout the Himalayan region. China claimed 104,000 sq. km of territory over which India's maps showed clear sovereignty and demanded 'rectification' of the entire border.[19] China-India relations gradually deteriorated and after the lapse of 1954 Panchsheel Agreement in 1962, China resorted to war and bounced on unprepared India over boundary dispute and seized 38,000 sq. km. of Kashmir Indian territory in October 1962, presently known as China occupied Kashmir (Aksai Chin) and declared unilateral cease fire. It further claimed 90,000 sq. km. of Arunachal Pradesh, the integral state of India (earlier known as North Eastern Frontier Agency (NEFA) as their territory. Zhou Enlai proposed that China relinquish its claim to most of India's northeast in exchange for India's abandonment of its claim to Aksai Chin.[20] The Indian government, constrained by domestic public opinion, rejected the idea of a settlement based on uncompensated loss of territory as being humiliating and unequal. Diplomatic relations between India and China were severed. India-China relations, freezed for over one and a half decades, were restarted only in 1976 by resuming the diplomatic channels. In the meantime, two more border skirmishes between China and India witnessed in 1965 and 1967.

Revival of Sino Indian Relations in 1976

The Indian Prime Minister Smt. Indira Gandhi initiated the revival of diplomatic relations between India and China in 1976 after India acquiring nuclear capabilities by conducting nuclear tests at Pokran (1975) and absorption of Sikkim (1975) as an integral state of India. Dr. K.R. Narayan was appointed as the Ambassador to China and he presented credentials in Beijing on 24 July 1976 and his counterpart Chen Zhao Yuan, the Chinese Ambassador to India presented his credentials in New Delhi on 20 September 1976, thus the first step to normalise the relations between the two nations inaugurated after the Sino-Indian conflict of 1962. The successive Prime Minister Morarji Desai used the services of Dr. Subramanyam Swamy (Union Law Minister) for further normalisation of relations with China and facilitating Indian Foreign Minister Atal Bihari Vajpayee's visit to China in 1979. Again in pursuance of Sri P.V. Narasimha Rao, the Foreign Minister of Smt. Indira Gandhi cabinet, Dr. Subramanyam Swamy paid an un-official visit to China in 1981, met the Chinese President Deng Xiaoping and paved the way for the reciprocal visit of Chinese Foreign Minister Huang Hua to India in 1981. President Deng Xiaoping also conceded Dr. Subramanya Swamy's demand, then pending for 3 years, for reopening the Kailash – Manasarovar route in Tibet for Hindu pilgrims.[21]

Huang Hua's visit to India initiated Sino-Indian border talks in 1981 and also paved the way for reopening the route of Kailash – Manasarovar, the mythological home of the Hindu pantheon, in Tibet for Hindu pilgrims and since then Hindu pilgrims in batches have continued to visit Kailash-Manasarovar without any hitch till today. In this improved bilateral understanding, the two sides explicitly agreed to maintain tranquility on the border issue. Border talks for peaceful negotiations thus revived facilitated cooperation in their bilateral trade which resulted in signing a 'trade agreement' in 1984, bestowing each other the Most Favoured Nation (MFN) status.

Prime Minister Rajiv Gandhi's visit in 1988: An Impetus to Sino-Indian Relations

After Indira Gandhi's assassination in 1984, China stiffened its position on the border and the border talks in 1986-87 achieved nothing. This period witnessed the two countries' military encounter in the Sumdorang Valley of the Tawang tract (Arunachal Pradesh) on the eastern sector of the border. China's construction of a military post and helicopter pad in the area in 1985 winter season and India's grant of statehood to Arunachal Pradesh, in February 1987, caused a hitch in the relations of both the countries and even they deployed new troops to the area, raising tensions and fears of a new border war. The professionalism exhibited by the Indian armed forces in tackling the Sumdorang crisis in 1986 amazed the Chinese side and it quickly realised that the 1962 could not be repeated. After a week of tense movements, both sides mutually agreed to withdraw their forces to their respective territories.

Prime Minister Rajiv Gandhi's historic visit to China in December 1988 was considered a milestone in the history of Sino-Indian bilateral relations. By meeting the Chinese President Deng Xiaoping, Rajiv Gandhi paved the way for a new approach to the Sino-Indian border issue by dropping India's earlier policy stance of asking for settlement of the border as a pre-condition for any improvement in relations in other fields. India not only agreed to describe Tibet as an integral part of China but also expressed concern over anti-Chinese activities by some Tibetan elements in India. In the light of the eight rounds of Sino-Indian border talks (1981-1987), India conceded that the Sino-Indian border was, in parts under marketed and in parts disputed and at least during the interim, accepted China's long-standing demand for the maintenance of tranquility on the Line of Actual Control (LAC). Both the countries decided to resolve the border question through peaceful negotiations based on mutual interest and acceptable to the peoples of both the countries and decided to form Joint Working Group (JWG) to be led by the Indian Foreign Secretary and the Chinese Vice-minister of Foreign Affairs with specialists on both sides mainly drawn from military and related organisations. Rajiv Gandhi also signed bilateral agreements on Science and Technology Cooperation, on civil aviation to establish direct air links and on cultural exchanges. The two sides also agreed to hold annual diplomatic consultations between Foreign Ministers and to set up a Joint Ministerial Committee on economic and scientific cooperation. JWG meetings on border issue were initiated in July 1989 (first round) and the high level visits of Defence Ministers (Sharad Pawar, 1992 and Chi Haotian, 1994) and Chiefs of Defence Forces (Vice-Chief of China's People's Liberation Army, Lt.General Xu Huizi (1993) and India's reciprocal visits of General B.C. Joshi, Chief of Army Staff (1994) and Admiral V.S. Shekhawat, Chief of Naval Staff (1996) have contributed to evolve, taking into consideration of the spirit of Panchsheel Agreement of 1954, two more Agreements (No war pacts), one on the 'Maintenance of Peace and Tranquility along the Line of Actual Control in the India-China Border Areas' at the time of Prime Minister P.V. Narsimha Rao's visit to China in 1993 and the other on 'Confidence Building Measures in the Military Field along the Line of Actual Control in the India-China Border Areas' at the time of Chinese President Jiang Zemin's visit to India in 1996.[22]

The official visits of Indian President R.Venkataraman (1992) and Vice-President K.R. Narayanan (1994) further consolidated India-China relations. Person to person and institution to institution contacts were established between the two countries such as, Institute for Defence Studies and Analyses, United Services Institution of India, Centre for Policy Research and Rajiv Gandhi Foundation from Indian side and China Institute for

Contemporary International Relations, China Association for Friendly International Contact, Fudan University etc. from Chinese side have been increasingly formalised. Similarly, Xinhua, People's Dai and Beijing Review have their accredited correspondents in India and India's Press Trust of India has a resident reporter in Beijing. The Agreements on the exchange of scholars between the Indian Council for Social Science Research and Chinese Academy of Social Sciences (1992) and Radio and Television Cooperation (1993) have broadly contributed to expanding mutual awareness. The Festival of China was organised in India in 1992 and Festival of India was held in China in April 1994. The Communist Party of China established direct links with the Indian National Congress and the Bharatiya Janata Party apart from Communist Party of India (Marxists). Direct flights between New Delhi and Beijing and telecom links between various cities of the two countries have been inaugurated. Contacts have also been evolved between various NGO's like trade unions and women organisations. The high point in India-China Cooperation was that China assisted India by supplying the much needed 'Heavy Water'[23] (supposed to be used in nuclear and missile programmes) at a very crucial stage when India's attempts failed to procure it even from Russia and USA, the friendly allies of India. Another important factor that one can gauge in friendly relations of the nations is the quantum of bilateral trade conducted. Though compared to their size and total foreign trade, the volume of Sino-Indian bilateral trade remained very small until 1980's but substantially increased in the early part of 1990s with the opening of border posts – Garbyang (February 1991) followed by Gunji (1992) in Uttar Pradesh and later Shipkila (1994) in Himachal Pradesh. In 1994, India became China's largest trading partner in South Asia overtaking China's long-standing close friend and ally Pakistan. Chinese President Jiang Zemins' visit to India in 1996 considered to be another high point in Indo-China relations as his visit of border left to the negotiations of expert groups of both countries on the firm scientific foundation and mutual acceptance. However, Sino-Indian relations hit a low point in 1998 following India's nuclear tests in May (Pokran II). Indian Defence Minister George Fernandes declared that "China is India's number one threat", hinting that "India developed nuclear weapons in defence against China's nuclear arsenel".[24] Relations between India and China remained strained until the end of the decade.

Priority to Economic Engagement and Enhanced Cultural Relations

Gradual re-engagement of Indian and Chinese diplomacy at the dawn of new millennium made Indian President K.R. Narayanan's visit possible to

China in 2000. Chinese Premier Zhu Rongji visited India in 2002 with a focus on economic issues. During the reciprocal visit of Indian Prime Minister Atal Bihari Vajpayee to China in 2003, China officially recognised Indian sovereignty over Sikkim. The two countries signed the Memorandum of Understanding on the reciprocal establishment of Cultural Centres in each capital and to facilitate their establishment. The two governments have also signed the Executive programme of the cultural exchanges and co-operation between China and India in arts and culture, education, social sciences, mass media, youth affairs, sports. In 2004, the two countries agreed to open up the Nathula and Jelepla passes in Sikkim which would mutually benefit both the countries. The Sino-Indian bilateral trade surpassed the US$ 10 billion mark for the first time. Chinese Premier Wen Jiabao visited India in 2005 and stated in Bangalore (the IT hub of India) that the increased Sino-Indian Cooperation in high-tech industries, the co-operation is just like two pagodas (temples), one hardware and one software combined, we can take the leadership position in the world.[25] The high level visit of the premier also yielded several agreements to deepen political, cultural and economic ties between the two countries. At the signing the agreement on the political parameters and guiding principles for the settlement of the India-China boundary question, the two countries reiterated their commitment to make joint efforts to maintain peace and tranquility in the border areas in accordance with the Agreements of 1993 and 1996. The two countries further agreed to promote the cooperation in the spheres of education, science and technology, health care, information, tourism, youth exchanges, agriculture, dairy development, sports and other fields on the basis of mutual benefit and reciprocity. The countries decided to establish an India-China Steering Committee on Scientific and Technological Cooperation chaired by their Ministers for Science and Technology. The two countries accepted the report of the India-China Joint Study Group (JSG) on comprehensive trade and Economic Cooperation prepared by Dr. Rakesh Mohan, Secretary (Economic Affairs), India and Mr. An Min, Vice-Minister, Minister of Commerce, China and recommended its expeditious implementation to remove impediments and to facilitate enhanced economic engagement between India and China by referring to the Ministerial-level India-China Joint Economic Group (JEG) for implementation. The two countries also signed a Memorandum to carry forward India-China Buddhist cultural links, with India and China jointly constructing an Indian style Buddhist temple in the International Garden of the Luoyang White Horse Temple.[26] The Memorandum envisages that India would provide the Buddha Idol and other accompanying materials including the main architectural design of the temple project, its blue print, materials used for the temple and the landscape planning. The Chinese side will provide 2,666.67 sq.m. of land for constructing the temple. The following year in November 2006, the Chinese President Hu Jintao visited India and strengthened the bilateral relationship to new heights. Both countries signed as many as 13 protocols/ MOUs/Agreements which include the establishment of additional Consulate – General in Guang Zhou (China) and Kolkata (India), cooperation between the Ministry of External Affairs (India) and the Ministry of Foreign Affairs (China), promotion and protection of Investments, export of iron ore from India, cooperation in agricultural research, cooperation in the field of education, cooperation between Indian Institute of Public Administration (IIPA) and Central Committee of the Communist Party of China (CPS) on the issues of common interest such as rural development, agriculture, poverty alleviation, public administration, public policy, role of government in a market economy and role of planning commissions, cooperation and development in forestry related fields of economy, manufacturing, processing and Science and Technology, cooperation in the Conservation of Cultural Heritage and prevention of theft, clandestine excavation and illicit import and export of cultural property.[27] As a result of the frequent visits of Indian and Chinese officials from the governments and trade organisations instilled confidence that led to the enhanced cooperation in the rapid increase of bilateral trade. It may be an apprehension a few years ago, that the Indian industry had a fear of being swamped by the Chinese imports but, however, later assessments showed that India enjoyed a positive balance of trade with China. The size of the Sino-Indian economy has been steadily growing and expanding. In 2008, China became India's largest trading partner and the bilateral trade between the two countries touched US $ 51.8 billion.[28] India has emerged as the 7th largest export market of China and the 10th largest trade partner. The targets of bilateral trade set by the Prime Ministers of the two countries during the visit of Premier Wen Jiabao to India in 2005 as US $ 20 billion by 2008 and US $ 30 billion by 2010 were met ahead of the deadline. The target fixed during president Hu Jintao's visit to India in 2006 to increase the bilateral trade to US $ 40 billion by 2010 was achieved in early 2008. In 2008, the target was again revised to US $ 60 billion by 2010 during the maiden visit of Prime Minister of India Dr. Manmohan Singh, to China in January 2008.[29]

China is also gradually becoming the destination for higher education to Indian students, next only to USA, UK and Australia. Easy admission system, affordable fees and high standards of facilities and quality education attracted

Indian students and their number rose from 230 in 2004 to over 6000 all over China in 2008. The dominant choice of the students has been medicine (MBBS) and the next preference goes to Chinese language learning.[30]

The visit of Prime Minister Dr. Manmohan Singh to China in January 2008 is another milestone in the bilateral relations between India and China. While addressing at the Chinese Academy of Social Sciences (CASS) in Beijing on 15 January 2008, Dr. Manmohan Singh expressed that he was very confident about the role India and China would play in transforming Asia and the World. Referring to the Chinese Premier Wen Jiabao's visit to India in 2005, he stated that India and China had established the strategic and Co-operative partnership and prosperity and agreed to resolve the border issue on a set of principles. Later, the two Premiers issued a joint agreement, "A shared vision for the 21st Century of the People's Republic of China and the Republic of India," on 14 January 2008 to promote the building of a harmonious world of durable peace and common prosperity through developing the strategic and cooperative partnership for peace and prosperity between the two countries. Further, the two leaders reiterated that China-India friendship and common development will have a positive influence on the future of the international system; the two sides also believed that in the new century Panchsheel, the five principles of peaceful co-existence, should continue to constitute the basic guiding principles for good relations between all countries and for creating the conditions for realising peace and progress of human kind. An international system founded on these principles will be fair, rational, equal and mutually beneficial, will promote durable peace and common prosperity, create equal opportunities and eliminate poverty and discrimination".[31]

It is the right time to recall the statement of Deng Xiaoping, President of Republic of China during his discussion with the visiting Prime Minister of India, Rajiv Gandhi, on 21 December 1998 that "China and India share a common responsibility to mankind" and the joint agreement on 14 January 2008 of the two Premiers Wen Jiabao and Dr. Manmohan Singh reflected as 'A shared vision of 21st Century", taking the bilateral relations to the higher plane to international responsibility.

Conclusion

Cultural relations and cultural diplomacy are considered an important component in International relations to maintain peace and enhanced cooperation and development among the nations. Traditional cultural linkages between India and China are very strong and there were occasions when both the countries normalised their strained bilateral relation by resuming and reminding historical cultural ties as a last resort. They even helped in keeping the boundary issue to the peaceful negotiations by the joint working groups. Commitment to Panchsheel and greater economic cooperation between India and China gradually becomes priority. As the bilateral relations improved, the trade between two countries improved in leaps and bounds from 1.2 billion in 1996 to 13.8 billion in 2004 to 51.8 billion in 2008 and is expected to reach 60 billion in 2010. China has more than 50% Buddhist population and many places of Buddhist importance whereas India was once considered a heavenly Kingdom by Chinese Buddhists. Facilities to Buddhist tourism between the two countries, if provided, have an enormous potential for bilateral income as well as a source of promotion of cultural relations. Chinese language learning and Chinese studies in India and Indian studies in China promote bilateral cultural understanding for peaceful coexistence and mutual benefit in economic, scientific and IT sectors. India has the reputation of good teachers abroad with an advantage of English being the language of instruction in their career building whereas the Chinese face handicap in getting opportunities abroad because of lack of English language skills. The Chinese government now is encouraging English learning as a tool for their expanding opportunities. India has to grab this opportunity in China to train the Chinese students and revive the good old tradition of Indian scholars visiting China, now with a different purpose. The teacher-student relationship would go a long way to further strengthen Sino-Indian relations and it becomes India's invisible capital in China.

References

1. www.timesofindia.indiatimes.com/world/China/Nhru-Tagore-amongforeigners-who-shaped-modern-China/articleshow/5027793.cms(18September2009) also see www. Zeenews.com/news564858.html (18 September 2009).

2. Tan Yun-Shan, "My Devotion to Rabindranath Tagore", In Tan Chung (ed.), *In the Footsteps of Xuanzang: Tan Yun-Shan and India* (Book Chapter, 32), Indira Gandhi National Centre for the Arts: New Delhi, 1999). At www.ignca.nic.ks_ 40htm

3. Lata Iyer, *Rabindranath Tagore's Visit to China, Mirror of Tomorrow*, (15 June 2009). At www.mirroroftomorrow.org/blog/_archieves/2009/6/15/4222239.htm

4. Tan Yuan-Shan, N.2.

5. *Ibid.*

6. Haraprasad Ray, "Tan Yun-Shan: The Pioneer of (Sino-Indian) Studies and Cultural Bridge between India and China" In Tan Chung (ed.), *In the Footsteps of Xuanzang:*

Tan Yun-Shan and India (Book Chapter, 28), Indira Gandhi National Centre for the Arts: New Delhi, 1999). At www.ignca.nic.ks_ 40htm

7. Gurudev Rabindranath Tagore, "Indian Savants' Observations on China." in Tan Chung (ed.), (Book Chapter-5), Indira Gandhi National Centre for Arts, New Delhi, 1998, www.ignca.nic.in/ks41009.htm

8. Chris Devonshire-Ellis, *India as China's Mentor*, at www.2point6billion.com/news/2009/09/india-as-china%c2%80%99s-mentor-224.9/23/2009

9. P.C. Bagchi, *India and China (A Thousand Years of Cultural Relations)*, Philosophical Library: New York, 1951, p.7.

10. *Ibid.*

11. www.en.wikipedia.org/wiki/Bodhidharma, retrieved 31 August and 24 September 2009.

12. Speech by Shri K.R. Narayanan, President of India, at the *Birth Centenary Celebrations of Professor Tan Yun Shan* at Santhiniketan, Visva-Bharati, 7 November 1998, Press Information Bureau, Govt. of India: New Delhi).

13. www.en.wikipedia.org/wiki/SunWukong. Retrieved 24 September 2009.

14. www.bookrags.com/printfriendly/?p=gale&u=i-ching-ued

15. Vice-President K.R. Narayan (speech) at Fudan University, Shanghai (27 October 1994), Tan Chung (ed.), *Across the Himalayan Gap*, (Book Chapter-3), Indira Gandhi National Centre for Arts, New Delhi,1998, at www.ignca.nic.in/ks_41007.htm

16. *The Sunday Tribune*, 17 December 2006, at www.tribuneindia. com/2006/20061217/spectrum/main6.htm

17. Swaran Singh, "Three Agreements and Five Principles between India and China" in Tan Chung (ed.), *Across the Himalayan Gap*, (Book Chapter-56), Indira Gandhi National Centre for Arts, New Delhi, 1998, at www.ignca.nic.in/ks-41062.htm

18. *Ibid.*

19. www.en.wikipedia.org/wiki/Sino-Indian_relations

20. Swaran Singh, "Building Security and Confidence with China in Tan Chung (ed.), *Across the Himalayan Gap*, (Book Chapter 57 Part I), Indira Gandhi National Centre for Arts, New Delhi, 1998,at www.ignca.nic.in/ks-41063.htm

21. Subramanian Swamy, "Myth and Reality in India-China relations", *The Hindu*, (opinion-Lead), 17 September 2009.
22. Swaran Singh, N. 20.
23. *Ibid.*
24. www.en.wikipedia.org/wiki//Sino-Indian_relations, retrived 4 August 2009.
25. *Ibid.*
26. Visit of Chinese Premier to India, "Joint Statement of the Republic of India and the People's Republic of China," *The Hindu*, 11 April 2005.
27. *India-China Protocol Agreement Documents*, Ministry of External Affairs, Govt. of India: New Delhi), www.jansamachar.net/prof.phb3?num=6298& long, retrieved 26 September 2009.
28. www.indiachina.org/trade_statistics.htm
29. www.in.china-embassy.org/eng/sbygd/fwzg/t400614.htm, retrieved 30 September 2009.
30. www.indiaedunews.net/In.Focus/January_2008/Indian_students_flock_to_China_for_higher_studies_3236/ and also see www.rediff.com/news/2004/oct/18specl.htm
31. http://in.china-embassy.org/eng/ssygd/fwzg/t145970.htm, retrieved 30 September 2009.

APPENDIX

Bold Initiatives, 1976-2008

1976 April 15: Foreign Minister, Y.B. Chavan, announced in the Parliament that China and India had decided to restore their diplomatic relations at the Ambassadorial level.

1979 February: During Foreign Minister Atal Behari Bajpai's visit to Beijing, China (a) for the first time acknowledged that there was a border dispute; and (b) assured to no longer support rebels in India's northeast region.

1980 June: Deng Xiaoping (a) revived Zhou En-lai's package proposal of 1960 China offered to recognise McMahon Line in the east for India's abandonment of claims to the Aksai Chin in the western sector; and (b) softened their support to Pakistan on Kashmir describing it as a bilateral issue between India and Pakistan.

1981 June: Foreign Minister Huang Hua during his visit to New Delhi announced that China would be opening two sacred sites of Mansoravar and Kailash to the Indian pilgrims. This visit also paved the way for beginning of first Sino-Indian border talks which had eight rounds between 1981 and 1987.

1983 April: China's resumption of party-to-party ties between Communist Party of India (Marxist) which was later extended to the Congress Party and Bhartiya Janata Party as well.

1984 February: The two sides signed a protocol granting each other most favoured nation status.

1988 December: During Prime Minister Rajiv Gandhi's visit to Beijing, three agreements were signed on: (a) cooperation in the field of science and technology; (b) granting reciprocal over flights rights and; (c) two year cultural exchanges.

1991 February: On February 2, the two signed an agreement for the resumption of border trade and on February 6 signed an agreement opening Garbyang (Uttar Pradesh) as first border port. More points were later opened at Gunji (Uttar Pradesh) in 1992 and Shipki La (Himachal Pradesh) in 1994.

1991 December: During Premier Li Peng visit to New Delhi, the two sides signed five documents: (i) on Mutual Establishment of Consulate Generals in Bombay and Shanghai; (ii) on Consular Affairs; (iii) the Memorandum on Restoring Border Trade; (iv) the Protocol on Bilateral Trade for 1992; (v) the MoU on Scientific and Technological Cooperation for Peaceful Use of Outer Space.

1993 September: The visiting Prime Minister Narasimha Rao to Beijing and his Chinese counterpart Premier Li Peng signed (i) the famous CBMs agreement, and (ii) agreement on cooperation in Radio and Television.

1994 May: India Festival, the first such foreign show in China, had 130 strong groups traveling to 16 cities in 51 days. It was in response to the Chinese cultural festival in India during 1992.

1995 August: The Joint Working Group (JWG) in its 8th meeting in New Delhi agreed to disengage troops from two posts from each side in the Wangdong tract which is the first Asian example of disarmament.

1996 October: The JWG agreed to open two more points (Dichy and Lepulekh) for annual meetings between the military commanders from the two sides.

1996 November: During President Jiang Zemin's visit to New Delhi, the two signed four agreements: (i) on extending the CBMs to the military field, (ii) on combating smuggling of narcotics and arms, (iii) on maintenance of Indian Consulate in Hong Kong after July 1997, and (iv) on maritime shipping.

2003 June: Prime Minister Vajpayee visited China signed MOU on the reciprocal establishment of cultural centres in each other country's capitals and also signed the executive programme of cultural exchanges between the governments of China and India for the years 2003-05.

2005 April: Premier Wen Jiabao visited India and on the occasion India and China signed as many as twelve agreements/protocols/MOUs. They include: political parameters and guiding principles for the settlement of boundary question, MOU on Civil Aviation, Protocol of phyto-sanitary requirements for the export of grapes, bitter gourds from India to China. MOU on cooperation between Indian Council of World Affairs and Chinese People's Institute of Foreign Affairs, MOU on Film Cooperation Commission, MOU on the construction of Indian style Buddhist temple on the western side of White Horse Temple in Luoyang, China.

2006 November: Chinese President Hu Jintao visited India. On this occasion, as many as 13 Agreements / Protocols / MOUs have been signed between India and China. They include: Reciprocal establishment of Consulates General at Guangzhou and Kolkata, cooperation between MEA India and MFA China Agreement for the promotion and protection of investments: Export of rice from India to China, MOU between ICAR and Chinese Academy of Agricultural Sciences (CAAS) for cooperation in Agricultural research, exchange programme in the field of Education, Forestry Cooperation, MOU on Cooperation in the conservation of Cultural Heritage and Agreement on preventing Theft, Illicit import and export of Cultural Heritage, etc.

2008 January: Prime Minister Manmohan Singh paid a visit to China. Both the premiers Manmohan Singh and Wen Jiabao released a joint communiqué: "A Shared Vision for 21st Century of China and India"(?). The two sides were convinced that it was time to look to the future in building a relationship of friendship and trust, based on equality, common development and belief in Panchsheel. The two sides welcomed the positive facets of economic globalisation and condemned the source of terrorism in all forms. Finally, the two sides remain firmly committed to resolve outstanding differences, including on the border question through peaceful negotiations. The two sides also recognised that both China and India bear a significant historical responsibility to ensure comprehensive, balanced and sustainable economic and social development of the two countries and to promote peace and development in Asia and the world as a whole.

Source: Swaran Singh, "Building Confidence with China" in Tan Chung (ed.). *Across the Himalayan Gap*, 1998 (Book Chapter 57 Part 2, Appendix and Table-4: Bold Initiatives: 1976-1996, Indira Gandhi National Centre for Arts, New Delhi, 1998. The events from 2003 to 2008 are the author's additions to the above Appendix.

9

China Factor in India– Japan Relations

Nalini Kant Jha* and *Subhash Shukla

Introduction

The 21st century is being termed as the Asian century with China, India and Japan being the major powers in Asia. China and Japan are neighbouring countries separated by a narrow strip of water. China and India are neighbours facing each other across the mountains. China, Japan and India are all big countries each with a population exceeding a hundred million. Their GDPs are $1.4 trillion, $4.3 trillion and $0.5 trillion, respectively. For this reason, the three countries can be called the three giants in Asia.

However, the mutual economic security and strategic interests of India and Japan bring them together in a bid to contain the common threat of China, in order to build a triangular balance of power in Asia between these three countries. Whereas, strategic relationship which India and Japan enjoy with the U.S., it could possibly lead to a trilateral relationship between them and which, in turn, might establish a quadrangular balance of power in this continent.

This research paper traces the reasons behind the growing security and economic relationship between India and Japan as well as why China is the common factor in bringing them together as well as why it is the common inhibiting factor in establishing a full-fledged open trilateral security relationship between India, Japan and the U.S.A. or establishing a quadrilateral security relationship between India, Japan, the U.S.A. and Australia.

China as a Mutual Security Threat

Ever since India's independence, the dynamics of cold war politics had clouded the Indo-Japanese relations. Japan was a part of the Western alliance led by the United States. India adopted a neutral stand towards the cold war by adopting the path of nonalignment, that is, equidistance from both the superpowers the U.S. and U.S.S.R. China was part of the Communist bloc till 1969. However, after the Sino-Soviet split, there was a Sino-U.S. rapprochement, but India and Japan did not enjoy cordial and harmonious relations even during the Cold War with China. With the end of the Cold War and the opening up of the Indian economy to the world, Indo–Japanese relations, gradually, started to improve, but the nuclear tests by India in 1998 again jolted their relationship which tended to improve after India raised the threat of a nuclear China along with a nuclear Pakistan to its security in the South Asian region.

While Japan is constrained by its World War II legacy to acquire the full range of military capability befitting an independent economic power, the Japanese see China as rapidly acquiring a power projection capability and modernising its military forces, including a missile build-up that puts all of Japan within its range. Signs of increasing nationalism and allegedly growing assertiveness in Chinese policies have also disturbed Tokyo. The speculation, that the U.S. may reduce its military presence in the Asia–Pacific region, further heightens Japanese security concerns. A large segment of Japanese society feels that Japan should amend its constitution and develop militarily to become a normal power. According to Japanese Defense Agency, the number of incursions by the Chinese naval vessels into Japan's EEZ and territorial waters has increased manifold. China's territorial claims, to the Senkaku Islands in the East China Sea, conflict with Japan's claims over them. Tokyo wants a maritime boundary halfway between the country's two coastlines but Beijing argues for a demarcation in line with the natural extension of the continental shelf, thus claiming territorial waters that almost reach the Japanese island of Okinawa, which is a military base for the stationing of U.S. troops. A nuclear North Korea enjoying close strategic and security relations with China also poses a threat to the Japanese.

Similarly, India has territorial disputes with China, and the two countries fought a border war in 1962. In terms of India's security and threat perceptions,

China is the biggest adversary. It was the China threat factor along with the Sino-US – Pak axis that forced India to have a security agreement with the U.S.S.R. in 1971. In 1998, India used the 'Chinese threat' to go ahead with its nuclear tests. India perceives China's acquisition of naval facilities in Myanmar as a naval threat and at the same time Chinese help for developing port facilities at Bandar Abbas in Iran, Gawadar in Pakistan, Chittagong in Bangladesh and Hambantota in Sri Lanka is also viewed by India with great anxiety. China's close military and security relations with Pakistan, its growing influence in Myanmar and in Nepal poses great threat to India.

Japan and India also have the potential to assist each other with their foreign policy objectives – notably, Japan's concern over North Korea's nuclear weapons program and India's concern over the numerous conflict-prone and impoverished states along its periphery. Japan's engagement with South Asia and India's with North East Asia will, therefore, assist in checking the growing influence of China in their immediate neighbourhood.

Finally, the rise of China is clearly a factor in growing cooperation between New Delhi and Tokyo. China's growing emphasis on both its naval power projection capabilities and ballistic missile and space based weapons capabilities has implications for both Japan and India. Both of them have expressed ambitions in joining the space race and in expanding naval operations beyond their immediate neighbourhood. China's anti-satellite weapons test on January11, 2007, is likely to accelerate the space race in Asia with Japan and India both playing catch up with China.

China has also expressed ambitions to expand its blue water naval capabilities to protect its growing oil imports through the Indian Ocean and Strait of Malacca, through which 80 per cent of its oil imports transit. China's attempt to secure Sea lines of Communication along the Indian Ocean through building up its blue water naval capabilities and its "string of pearls" strategy to develop port facilities, as mentioned above, in Pakistan, Bangladesh, Sri Lanka, Iran and Myanmar, has fuelled fears in India over China's encroachment into its backyard as part of a wider Chinese policy to encircle India. The worry of India is that the Chinese may turn these facilities into forward bases that could threaten the Indian homeland and use them to nudge local states into supporting Chinese policies that undercut Indian security.

China's naval ambitions have also brought it into confrontation with Japan in the East China Sea where, as mentioned earlier, both states are engaged in a maritime territorial dispute over the Senkaku/Diaoyu islands and three oil and gas fields, where Japan regards the median line as the boundary of its Exclusive Economic zone, while China claims jurisdiction over the entire continental shelf. The incursion of a Chinese nuclear powered submarine into Japanese waters off the Okinawa Islands in November 2004 and a Chinese naval destroyer taking aim at a Japanese P3-C surveillance aircraft near the disputed waters in September 2005 have demonstrated China's naval posturing in the region.

China's growing interests in securing chokepoints and constructing ports along strategic waterways, also, has implications for the international community given that 50,000 ships comprising 40 percent of world trade and half of world trade in oil and natural gas transit through the Malacca Strait while 40 percent of the world's oil trade transit the Strait of Hormuz. Notably, more than 50 per cent of India's trade passes through the Strait of Malacca while more than 80 per cent of Japan's oil imports transit the Strait. Beijing's intention, to build its own aircraft carrier, demonstrates its ambitions in expanding its blue water naval capabilities.

Given India's and Japan's shared concerns over China's space program and naval power capabilities, both states may decide to develop a joint approach to check China's growing military influence in the region. Cooperation between the navies of Australia, India, Japan and the United States following the Asian Tsunami in December 2004 illustrates the potential for cooperation between India and Japan. The Indian Navy, the world's fifth largest, has set up a Far Eastern Naval Command facility off Port Blair on the Andaman Islands to increase its presence in the Strait of Malacca and possibly monitor Chinese naval activities in the region.

It is this common concern over China's military growth, supported by a strong economy that provides a common ground for security cooperation between India and Japan.

Steps taken to counter the Chinese Threat

During the Japanese Prime Minister Mori's visit to India in August 2000, he stated that looking to the 21st century, Japan wanted to build a multifaceted cooperative relationship with India in a wide range of fields, terming this relationship as the 'Global Partnership between Japan and India in the 21st century'. The two sides expressed a desire to institutionalise a dialogue between the ministries of defence and foreign affairs for coordinated actions on security and foreign policy related issues, like the security of sea-lanes, joint naval exercises to combat piracy and disaster management.

Before Manmohan Singh became the Prime Minister in May 2004, there used to be a talk of a strategic triangular relationship, involving India, Japan and China, which was in fact initiated by the then Japanese Ambassador to India, Mr. Yasukini Enoki. While Chinese authorities refrained from commenting on this idea, it evoked interest in some sections of the Chinese academic circles. In an article, Mr. Feng Zhaokui, Research Fellow at the Japan Research Institute of the Chinese Academy of Social Sciences, has stated: "Among China, Japan and India there should not be the kind of thinking of pulling another over to one's side so as to contain the other or joining hands with a superpower in the regions outside Asia to contain or even encircle one of the three countries. China, Japan and India–each lay great emphasis on the importance of relations with the United States. In the meantime, they should attach great importance to the mutual relations with one another rather than letting oneself becoming a pawn of a superpower outside Asia in containing one of the countries within the region."

However, after Manmohan Singh's visit to U S.A. in July 2005 when India and the U.S. signed an agreement on cooperation in the field of civilian nuclear energy, India developed sudden silence on any idea of a triangular relationship with China and Japan and instead it started showing interest in a quadrangular relationship involving India, Japan, the U.S. and Australia.

Thereafter, during Prime Minister Manmohan Singh's visit to Japan in December 2006 he stated that Japan and India were natural partners as the largest and developed democracies of Asia, with a mutual stake in each other's progress and prosperity. He said that the decision to establish a Strategic and Global Partnership between India and Japan would impart stronger political, economic and strategic dimensions to bilateral relations, serve long term interests of both countries, enhance all-round cooperation and contribute greater regional peace and stability.

Hence, Japan supported the Indo- U.S. civilian nuclear deal and helped India get the nuclear waiver from the 45 members Nuclear Suppliers Group (NSG) along with the U.S., which was initially opposed by the Chinese. While China does not view, with increasing concern, the growing strategic relations between the two countries in the form of joint exercises, Beijing suspects that there is an anti China backdrop to the Indo-US civilian nuclear deal. The Chinese suspicion is that this agreement was the US *quid pro quo* to India agreeing to a strategic cooperation to containing the Chinese naval power in the Bay of Bengal and the Indian Ocean region. Manmohan Singh's visit to Japan in 2006 caused concern in China that tended to see an American nudge behind the sustained attempts since 2005 to bring India and Japan closer together. The Chinese did not see it as a natural corollary of India's Look East policy, instead they see it as an American attempt to contain China.

India and Japan signed a declaration on security cooperation on 22nd October 2008 and both of them asserted that their partnership would be "an essential pillar for the future architecture of the region". Though the security declaration largely contains elements like joint exercises, disaster management and counter terrorism which figure in Indian agreements with many countries, what is likely to raise eyebrows around Asia is the fact that Japan considers India so crucial to its strategic calculus that it is the third country after United states of America and Australia with which India has signed such a document. It appears that India also seems to have picked Japan as its important partner for the task of fashioning the political and security dimensions of Asia's emerging institutional structure.

Like Japan's agreements with the U.S. and Australia, the shared commitment of India and Japan to democracy, open society, human rights and the rule of law is fore grounded, though the scope of security cooperation envisaged is far less than Tokyo's military alliance driven arrangements with Washington and Canberra. Terrorism, piracy and non-proliferation are covered but there is no reference in the Indo-Japan text about the new security challenges and threats referred to in the Japan-Australia agreement – a code phrase for the rise of China.

However, after the signing of the declaration on security cooperation, Indian Prime Minister Manmohan Singh told a gathering of Japanese and Indian businessmen that the increase in India's bilateral trade with China in the past one year alone is more than the whole of India's total trade with China. This statistical data was not intended to minimise the importance the strategic and global partnership with Japan but to drive home the point that India was not going to allow its ties with Tokyo to affect its ties with Beijing. It is, however, true that the political and security cooperation was the second leg of the bilateral relationship; but the first leg of economic cooperation, between the two countries, was yet to realise the full potential, though Japan provides 30 per cent of India's foreign aid and is, even in this period of global economic turmoil, committing more than $ 4 bn. to the Delhi–Mumbai freight and industrial corridor.

Mutual Economic Relations and China

There is an economic angle to India's relations with Japan that relates to India's expectations of a major role by Japanese investors in developing the infrastructure in India. Despite the remarkable improvement in its economic performance over the last few years with an average GDP growth rate of 8 per cent, it will not be able to catch up with the Chinese economy in the near and medium unless and until it is able to improve its infrastructure and ensure the availability of energy. For this to happen, it is estimated that Japan would have to contribute the major share of the investment required for the improvement of India's infrastructure. The efforts of the Government of India is to make Japanese investors get interested in the infrastructure projects in a big way. The positive results of this effort are evident with nearly 475 Japanese companies having a presence in India. This indicates the interest that the Japanese Government has taken in strengthening the long-neglected economic relations with India. Previously, lured by the huge Chinese market and the cheap labour there, Japanese investors had paid little interest in India.

Despite this, the bilateral trade continues to be sluggish – an average of 4 bn. U.S. dollars which is in sharp contrast to India's bilateral trade with China which has been racing towards 30 billion dollars. Between 2002-03 and 2006-07 total bilateral trade with China has grown almost six times.

Countervailing Factors

The most important of the countervailing factors that inhibit both countries from developing an open security relationship which is directed against China is that both Japanese and Indian governments are focused on the economic development of their countries. They believe that economic development requires prolonged, peaceful and cooperative relations with their Chinese neighbour, notably one another. China depends heavily on Japan for economic assistance for technology and investment and as a market for Chinese goods. Japan is increasingly dependent on China as a source of imports and an offshore manufacturing base. At the same time, India's exports to China are dependent on large-scale Chinese imports of raw materials from India. China and India have focused on faster economic growth for compelling domestic reasons and have shaped their foreign policies to achieve this objective together.

Conclusion

In the 21st century, India seeks to establish itself as a global player in world politics. For this to happen, India has to follow its traditional policy of peaceful coexistence, i.e. Panchasheel, with enlightened and realistic assessment of its national interest and it has to develop good relations with both major powers of Asia, Japan and China. Hence, it requires a strategic and security relationship along with an economic relationship with Japan but at the same time this goal requires peace with neighbours and stability in Asia and substantial cooperation between India and China for regional peace and stability. It is also necessary if the 21st century is to turn into the Asian century.

References

1. Ashley Tellis, "China and India in Asia", in Francine R. Frankel and Harry Harding (eds), *The India-China Relationship: What the United States Needs to Know*, (The Woodrow Wilson Centre Press: Washington D.C., 2004), p.163.
2. Fazal-ur-Rehman, "Japan's New Engagement in South Asia," *Strategic Studies*, Vol. xx, No. 4, Autumn 2000, pp.70-78.
3. Feng Zhaokui, *People's Daily*, 30 April 2004.
4. http://meaindia.nic.in/joint statement/dec.2006.
5. http://coomerce.nic.in/eidb/iecnt.asp
6. Jairam Ramesh, *Making Sense of Chindia, Reflections on India and China*, (India Research Press: New Delhi, 2005), pp. 57-67.

10

India's Options in its China Policy

T. Nirmala Devi

The relationship between the two Asian giants, China and India, is of global significance today, albeit its complex nature. These two are currently the world's fastest growing economies, having immense political potential. The simultaneous rise of China and India is an outstanding phenomenon in today's world, with bilateral, regional, and international dimensions. China's relations with India originated from Buddhism from India. However, the association between the two countries was limited due to natural barrier, the Himalayan mountain range. China started maintaining relations with both independent India and Pakistan. The warm relations between India and China in the 1950s led to *panchasheel* agreement in 1954, which in Indian perception is a diplomatic negotiation for the settlement of border dispute. Later, the bilateral relations were strained markedly in 1959, followed by war in 1962, in which India paid a great penalty by losing a huge land area to China. From the late 1970s, the bilateral relations resumed, whipch were enhanced in the subsequent three decades. High level political exchanges between China and India played a crucial role in reducing the tension by resolving some of their differences. From early 1990s onwards, commerce and economic relations have become the driving force behind the Sino-Indian cooperation.

China has been showing keen interest in the South Asian Association for Regional Cooperation (SAARC), the institutional framework since its inception. It is not a geographical entity of South Asia. Its recent observer status; its substantial economic and military assistance to the members; and the recommendation of the majority of members for China's full time membership in the regional grouping denote its ongoing pro-active role in the SAARC process. Against this background, the present paper addresses the economic diplomacy of China in the SAARC region and its implications for India on one hand; and the economic inroads of China in India's trade and key investment sectors on the other. The paper is divided into four sections. The first section – introduction – presents the political and economic backdrop of China and India in a comparative framework in order to ascertain their regional and global positions. This section also provides their active role in the midst of global economic meltdown. The second explains the spread of China's influence in the form of massive economic aid to the members of the SAARC region, particularly to Pakistan. The third discusses the economic domination of China in India's trade and investment in the recent years; and finally the fourth section provides the concluding observations.

I. Introduction - India and China in a Comparative Framework:

China and India are the two big-sized Asian nations that are transforming at a rapid pace, due to which comparison is difficult. However, it is imperative to know the recent rise of both the countries on the international scene.

(i) Political Perceptions

China: Since the 1950s, China followed the communist ideology till he economy was opened in 1978 and became a socialist market economy. China today is different from what China was in 1962, owing to its isolation from the international system and keeping distance from both the super powers at bay. It differed in perception with the erstwhile U.S.S.R, another communist country. Until 1971, China maintained a visible distance from the U.S, a capitalist country and the bilateral relations improved significantly once China got its economy on track in the mid-1980s. The Sino-American trade has been increased overtime, despite the differences in political ideologies. After the disintegration of the Soviet Union, China had started.reaping the strategic opportunities from the world polity. Gradually, with the acceleration in economic performance, China has been playing a significant role in the world affairs and stood as a responsible power and stakeholder in world stability. It is seen that the political perceptions of China have been changing along with its economic might.

China has been interacting economically not only with the Western countries and most of the East and Southeast Asian countries but also with the African and Latin American countries by investing in oil and mineral industries. China has been steadily engaging these countries with a long term view on energy dependency. With its growing economic and political clout, China is forging ahead on the global platform and is showing its supremacy over the weaker neighbours in East and Southeast Asian countries.[1] Thus, its economic power is gradually transforming into political power on the global scene.

India: India followed its own distinctive political system, despite having a strong bearing of the ideology of the USSR at the initial level. It adopted a mixed path of socialism and capitalism till 1970s. The Democratic Parliamentary Republic of India gave top priority in attaining self-reliance through substitution and also public sector with a view to alleviate poverty and unequal distribution of income. From the beginning, India followed the non-alignment policy, resulting in increasing opportunities for negotiations.

The bilateral relations between India and China improved a lot from late 1970s, viz; the diplomacy of 1970s, especially noted by the exchange of Ambassadors in 1976; Rajiv Gandhi's visit to Beijing in 1988 which widened dialogue on bilateral and international issues; Premier Li Peng's and President Jiang Zemin's visits to New Delhi in 1991 and 1996 respectively; and President R.Venkataraman's and Prime Minister P.V.Narasimha Rao's visits to Beijing in 1992 and 1993 respectively in the post–cold war era; Chinese Prime Minister Zhu Rongi's visit to India in early January 2002 at a time when India's relations with Pakistan were in a state of high tension; starting of direct flights between the two countries ; Vajpayee's visit to Beijing in June 2003, resulting in China's decision to drop Sikkim as a separate country and display of published maps with Sikkim as an integral part of India; Premier Wen Jiabao's visit to New Delhi, in January 2005, which led to the first ever strategic dialogue by sidelining border dispute and improving economic ties; the visit of Pranab Mukherji, the then Defense Minister, in May 2006, signing MoU on defense cooperation; President Hu Jintao's visit to New Delhi in November 2006, another milestone in bilateral relations, paving the signing of 13 agreements and Prime Minister Manmohan Singh's visit to Beijing in January 2008, signing joint vision document.[2] All these moves have consolidated their relationship.

Since three years, there has been a war hysteria over India's relations with China, which heightened tensions. While there were reports of Chinese incursions into Arunachal Pradesh, India rejected the idea of any happening of war between the two countries, dismissing it as media hype. During the past few years, China expressed publicly and aggressively asserting that the whole of Arunachal Pradesh was a part of South Tibet. Though there was an agreement on the status of populated areas in 2005, China is now insisting on its control of Tawang, the Buddhist monastery town, in Arunachal Pradesh to secure legitimacy for its role in Tibet, if it is to accept India's claims in Ladakh. India has flatly rejected Chinese claim on this. The problem of border intrusion is continuing, because China wishes to keep its option open by not spelling out where the LoAC lies. This will make China to continue to intrude into Arunachal Pradesh and Ladakh, whenever it wishes. India and China held 13th round of talks to settle the long running border dispute in August 2009, and these talks have made a little headway. China has expressed its dissatisfaction over the visit of Indian Prime Minister Manmohan Singh to Arunachal Pradesh, parts of which China still has claims on. India has responded to this objection and asked China to stop developmental activities in areas illegally occupied by Pakistan. In return to India's concerns, China, while maintaining its own policy on Kashmir, suggested that it was a matter to be resolved between Pakistan and India.[3] Thus, the recent developments in the bilateral relations between China and India have become a matter of concern. Leaving these matters aside, both countries have decided to step up the dialogue for increased interaction and also aligned on some common global issues like WTO talks and climate change.

(ii) Economic Performance

India and China, the neighbours with a billion plus population each, viz; 1.14 and 1.32 billion in 2008 respectively and with a record of having higher GDP growth rates (7.9 and 10.4 per cent respectively in the period 2000-08) are now seeking wider access to each other's growing markets. The population growth rates of the first two populous countries in the world at 0.6 and 1.4 per cent respectively in the period 2000-08[4] demonstrate not only the individual country's strengths and weaknesses, but also the considerable impact on the global demographic scenario. Each country is having its own demographic advantage. China's lower growth rate of population reduces the social overhead costs at present, while India's favourable ratio of working age population to the old age population, i.e., the dependency ratio, determines the country's future economic prospects.

Chinese economy, currently the third largest in the world, has been registering robust growth since three decades. Hence, the per capita income of China with $ 2,940 in absolute terms and with $ 6,020 in PPP terms is more than two times to that of India with $ 1,070 and $ 2,960 respectively in 2008.[5] However, the improvement in India's per capita PPP is also significant in the recent years. For Chinese economy, manufacturing sector is the vital source of strength. The contribution of industry to the country's GDP was 49 per cent in 2008, whereas this sector continued to generate a moderate share in output of 29 per cent in India. The share of services was two-fifths (40 per cent) in China and it was well above one-half (53 per cent) of GDP in India in the same year. In both countries, agriculture continued to contribute a lower share in GDP with 11 per cent in China and 18 per cent in India in the above year. However, there was no much difference in the agricultural productivity (agricultural value added per worker in US $2000) which stood at 407 and 392 in China and India respectively in the period 2003-05, notwithstanding the considerable variation in the period 1990-92.[6]

The external sector has been playing a significant role in the growth process of the Chinese economy. The share of exports to GDP in China was 34.9 per cent in 2006, while the share of exports in India was 13.9 per cent.[7] India's exports started lagging behind those of China from 1954 onwards and the gap widened over the years, particularly from the 1990s. China's rising exports showed a surge in its share of the world exports from 3.9 per cent in 2000 to 9.1 per cent in 2008 claiming the highest global position; and India recorded a moderate growth from 0.7 per cent to 1.1 per cent after remaining unchanged from 2007 and stood at 27th place in the world.[8] The share of manufacturing exports accounted for 93 per cent in China and 64 per cent in India in their total exports in 2007.[9] India's production and export structure is different and its export dependence on manufacturing is much smaller. In the recent years, India's export dependence has been much more in knowledge-intensive services than manufacturing. The share of high tech exports in total manufacturing exports, which earns huge foreign exchange, constitutes 30 per cent and 5 per cent in China and India respectively in 2007.[10] Till the mid-1980s, the high-tech sector in China was completely dominated by the radio, television and communications and accounted for almost two-thirds of all high tech manufacturing value added. Recently, the production of office equipment and computing machinery has been rising rapidly, and accounted for two-fifths of high-tech value added, while that of earlier component had fallen from two-thirds to two-fifths.[11] Information technology hardware is thus behind the success of China's high-tech sector by contributing a greater share in its GDP. India has improved its rank from 10th position to 9th position in global commercial services exports in 2008 against China's 5th position. These two countries were among the top 10 exporters of commercial services in the world and the rest being the developed countries.[12] India's export – import ratio which revealed the share of exports in financing the imports fell from 0.8 in 2004-05 to 0.3 with China in 2008-09, while the same was positive in the case of the U.S., the U.A.E.[13] the U.K., and Singapore. The major development in the direction of India's trade is that the U.S, which was in the first position in 2007-08, has been relegated to third position in 2008-09, with the U.A.E becoming India's largest trading partner followed by China. China's first position as the largest trading partner of India in 2008 slided to the second place in the backdrop of global financial crisis. However, in the first half of the 2009-10 with oil prices moderating, China has gained a slight edge over the U.A.E. to become India's major trading partner. China remained the largest source of India's imports with a share of 12 per cent followed by the U.S. and the U.A.E with nearly 6.0 per cent shares each.[14]

The current account balance in GDP was also highly favourable to China, with an increase from 1.3 per cent in 2001 to 10.0 per cent in 2008, while it was still unfavourable in the case of India with a decline from 0.3 per cent to -2.8 per cent in the above years.[15] Unlike India, China continues to have a surplus of both the current account and the capital account even in the first half of 2009 amidst crisis. In terms of UNCTAD Survey 2008-10, China is the most preferred destination of Foreign Direct Investment followed by India, the U.S, the Russian Federation and Brazil. But with its robust economic growth, an improved investment environment and opening up of critical sectors like telecommunications, civil aviation, refineries and construction etc., India replaced China as the most promising country for business operations of Japanese TNCs. Though India was lagging behind China in FDI in general and standing at 9th place in 2008 in contrast to China's 5th place, the percentage growth rate was significantly at 85.1 against China's 10.6 in the above year.[16]

China is the largest foreign exchange reserves holder in the world with $2399.2 billion by December 2009, while India with $283.5 billion is in the fourth position after China, Japan, and Russia. The foreign exchange reserves in China increased nearly ten times from $ 216.3 billion in 2001 to $ 1950.3 billion in 2008, with an import cover (ratio of foreign exchange reserves to imports of goods and services) which nearly doubled from 79.7 to 158.2 in the above years. In the case of India, the foreign exchange reserves rose from $ 46.4 billion to $ 248 billion and its import cover from 65.0 to 73.6 in the above years respectively. Despite the decline in import cover from 95.1 in 2007 to 73.6 in 2008, a steady improvement was shown in the ratio of reserves in India.[17] The excessive investments of China's huge foreign exchange reserves are in the U.S. Treasury Bonds,[18] some of which were reportedly sold recently. This was attributed to President Obama's meeting with Dalai

Lama on February 18, 2010, by allowing Japan to retake its place as the largest foreign exchange holder of U.S. Treasury Bonds.[19]

(iii) India and China in the Midst of Global Financial Crisis

According to Kaushik Basu, an economic analyst, China remains one of the most state-owned economies of the world, notwithstanding the liberalisation of its economy since 1978. He further stated that the economic liberalisation in 1978 as well as the social and political priming set three decades before, gave a tremendous impetus for the overall growth of China. Unlike China, India does not have such social pre-condition for the policies to work, yet it has been able to grow fast because of the liberalisation of markets and also the concurrent social and political changes that have been occurring in the country.[20]

The economies of India and China are now critically associated with the global economy as never before. Though their economies are not seriously exposed to the U.S. sub prime mortgage securities, both countries could not insulate from the crisis. The global financial crisis led to shrink in the demand for goods all over the world and led to contraction of exports including that of China and India. Hence, the fall out has a negative impact on them, as external factors account a significant proportion of their economies in both countries – exports in China and knowledge-intensive services in India. The hit was more on China, an export-reliant economy, than on India. Initially, the impact was sizeable on India's out-sourcing industry and export-dependent I.T. sector, due to global slowdown in demand as well as the rise in the value of rupee against the U.S. dollar.[21] The general deceleration in import growth of commercial services in the U.S and the E.U has a negative bearing on India which recorded a decline from 12 per cent in 2006 to 7 per cent in 2008.[22] However, China and India were able to reduce the impact and overcame the crisis to a greater extent with their cautious policies.

At the beginning of the economic meltdown, the general expectation was that the two large economies, China and India, could help lift the global economy without aggravating the global imbalances. These two countries are often referred to in this context as shock absorbers and the economies of ensuring recovery. On the whole, these two countries are outperforming others with their strong domestic demand and have become powerhouses for the recovery of the world economy. As China is an export power house and the centre of world manufacturing, the world is eyeing China particularly for the global economic revival.

China is forging ahead on the global platform, both in economic and political fronts, at a fast pace. The country has increased the volume of its exports substantially and set to become the world's biggest exporter. China has displaced Canada this year[23] as the biggest supplier of imports in the U.S. In these difficult times, there is a demand for cheaper goods, in which China is specialised and therefore, the country is not impacted significantly by the fall in exports. It announced a huge stimulus package of $ 585 billion; strengthened the domestic demand through various measures; reduced the pace of deterioration in the manufacturing sector; and followed regulatory policies in other sectors. It is the world's third largest economy now with a modern military power. Thus, the Chinese economy has been doing better than the other economies in the world in the light of global economic meltdown.

India did precious little to boost its external sector till the adoption of structural adjustment programme in the early 1990s. Later, India focused on the relations with the East and Southeast Asian countries with its 'look-east policy' for augmenting its external economy. The phase-II of its 'look-east policy' included free trade pacts with these countries. Thus, India has been concentrating on the Asian markets for the past one and a half decades, while the U.S and the E.U continue to remain the preferred destinations.[24] From 2003-04 onwards, the country registered a significant growth, due mainly to the service exports. With the advent of economic recession worldwide, India's focus is on restoring growth and employment which require increased spending. A stress on savings is maintained continuously. The major task before the government is to make the industrial sector efficient and globally competitive. Despite some limitations, the country is in a better position today, as compared to many developing countries suffering from several ills including the trade reduction, contraction in exports and tourism receipts and raising unemployment levels. The impact on the Indian economy is, by and large, limited due to the country's domestic-driven growth and the adoption of a pragmatic, fundamental and cautious approach in its economic policy, while initiating deregulation in early 1990s. It followed effective supervision, prudent regulation, and careful development of financial markets and fine tuning of monetary policy etc.[25] The government announced three stimulus packages in order to revive the economy, which seemed to work well. The economy is showing the positive signals, but still it is under the grip of recession, as it has some structural weaknesses like infrastructure.

II. China in SAARC

China's immense interest in the SAARC region has been increasing overtime. The country is strategically important for the South Asian region too, due to its geographical position and its role in global affairs. Hence, some of the South Asian countries are trying to forge closer ties with China. China's observer status in SAARC grouping was supported by Pakistan, Bangladesh and Nepal. China considers South Asia as an opportunity for investment due to its attractive production base and its liberalised trading policies regarding goods and services. Alongside their rising energy requirements, China to a major extent and India to a minor extent have emerged as the largest global production hubs. In fact, a broad-based cooperation between China and South Asia would be ideal, given the endowments in natural and human resources, technological capabilities and levels of economic development.[26] However, the one-sided economic domination of China on South Asian/SAARC countries smacks of its hegemony over small states than of its assistance.

Through the extension of economic assistance to China wields tremendous influence in the SAARC region. China's economic strength in the form of its growing trade and investment activities has spread all over the region, especially to India and Pakistan. Bilateral trade between China and Pakistan has increased quite substantially due to the series of free trade agreements and the former country surpassed the E.U as the second largest trading partner of the latter, while the U.S. being the first. China's increasing volume of export trade with the SAARC members is reflected in their continuous trade deficits with the country. All SAARC countries were having huge trade deficits with China – Afghanistan with \$165 million; Bangladesh with \$2.5 billion; India with \$16.2 billion; Maldives with \$33 million; Nepal with \$406.5 million; Pakistan with \$5.7 billion; and Sri Lanka with \$1.7 billion in 2008. This is because that the exports of any SAARC country to China constituted only a smaller share in its total, viz., 3.0 per cent in Afghanistan; 7.0 per cent in Bangladesh; 9.0 per cent in India; 0.7 per cent in Maldives; 0.6 per cent in Nepal; 4.0 per cent in Pakistan; and 0.6 per cent in Sri Lanka. On the other hand, the imports from China accounted for a sizeable share in each SAARC country's total imports such as 3.0; 14.7; 11.0; 2.5; 13.0; 14.0; and 12.0 per cent respectively in the above year.[27] Evidence shows that China invests the money so generated from the trade surpluses for massive investment programmes, especially in infrastructure development and energy production in these countries. In response to the economic aid received, the majority of the SAARC countries barring India, showed positive attitude towards China's political and strategic actions and had cooperative efforts in military training exercises and accepted its 'one–China' policy.[28] Thus, it is apparent that China's huge economic assistance is compounded by its political and foreign policy motivations.

The extension of China's economic strength to the global economy from early 1980s is different from its increased interaction with the SAARC region, as is seen in the latter in the form of construction of vital ports and other key activities, particularly defense exports. China has continuously supplied sizeable economic and military assistance to the South Asian countries in general and Pakistan in particular.

After 1971, China has been supporting Pakistan by providing political and military assistance, against India's interests. At the time of cold war and also during the 1990s, China maintained a close relationship with Pakistan. China's growing defense exports of China to Pakistan over the decades include of a variety of military and nuclear equipment. The defense relationship between these two countries was strengthened from the 1960s onwards, particularly noted by the China's weapons supply to Pakistan during this decade. In return, Pakistan ceded to China a critical military route from Xingjiang through Tibet in Kashmir, which is under dispute with India, for favour of military access to China into Tibet.[29] In the 1980s and 1990s, numerous military and nuclear capabilities were supplied by China to expand Pakistan's reprocessing capability, like F-5A and F-7 fighters; several hundred tanks; anti tank missiles; and other conventional weapons; the short range nuclear capable DF-11 or M-11 missiles. In 1995, China continued to supply 5,000 ring magnets for uranium enrichment centrifuges, though denied such. In addition to this, China sold Pakistan four F-22 P naval frigates and six Z–9C helicopters designed for surface-to-surface and surface–to–air missiles together with other associated self defense systems in April 2005. The transfer of technology and training of naval personnel were also carried out in Pakistan.[30] The latest example is the sale of two nuclear reactors by China on which the U.S. seeks clarification. Thus, Pakistan's security criterion was strengthened through conventional and nuclear capabilities of China, which determined to maintain nuclear balance between India and Pakistan. Both China and Pakistan admitted that the relation between the two is all-weather friendship and both countries derived tremendous benefits from each other, which leads to all round cooperation.

China shares borders with five SAARC countries, viz., Afghanistan, Pakistan, India, Bhutan, and Nepal and also with Myanmar. China's interest in Afghanistan is mostly due to the internal security of its Muslim-dominated western province of Xingjiang from the Talibans. China helped in the process of reconstruction of Afghanistan after the defeat of the Taliban regime by pledging $ 150 million in 2002 besides wiping out Afghanistan's old debts worth $18 million in 2004. China has an agreement on its land boundaries with Afghanistan and Nepal along with a few other countries.[31] In the recent years, China's strategy with regard to the SAARC region is reflected in its :

(i) continuous assistance to Pakistan by boosting its nuclear weapons and capabilities with supplies of ballistic and cruise missiles; (ii) pledging aid for hydroelectric projects in Pakistan; (iii) supporting Pak's sponsored terrorism openly by blocking moves in the U.N security council for action against them; (iv) using areas in Kachin state of Myanmar to arm and train the northeastern insurgent group in Manipur etc. in its Yunnan province; (v) undermining India's relations with its similar actions and policies in other SAARC nations like Nepal, Bangladesh, Sri Lanka and Maldives by strengthening its presence and influence in the region;[32] (vi) creating its presence of navy in the Indian Ocean with the approval of the U.S. to compete with India; (vii) opposing India's attempts to emerge as an Asian power on par with it; and using every opportunity to weaken India by reducing the Indian influence in the rest of SAARC as well as by isolating it; and (viii) strengthening the relationship with Pakistan in order to confront India with the danger of a two-front war giving Pakistan a nuclear and missile capability for threatening India.[33]

China's recent economic inroads in SAARC are denoted by : the two contracts in Sri Lanka viz. Colombo-Kalutara road, and the second stage of Hambantota port development; the two contracts in Myanmar for improvement of port on the coast and permission for the construction of two pipelines-one for gas and one for oil; negotiations with Bangladesh for a pipeline to carry gas to Myanmar; proposals for a railway line from Gwadar of Pakistan, where China is building a port, to Xinjiang in China; and talks with Pakistan and Iran for a gas pipeline to take Iranian gas to Xinjiang.[34]

China would continue to provide assistance in upgrading the Karakoram Highway and building the Neelam-Jhelum hydroelectric project in Pakistan occupied Kashmir (PoK) including the northern areas of Jammu & Kashmir. China's presence in this region has grown in recent years with its involvement in several infrastructure projects. On October 14, 2009, China assured Pakistan of its help in development projects in PoK. China and Pakistan signed a deal for 7,000 MW hydro power project in PoK, when Pakistan President Zardari visited China and invited Chinese companies to help develop hydel and thermal projects in the region. Reacting to this, India asked China to take a long term view of relations between the two countries and to stop activity in PoK.[35]

Of late, China has agreed to give another soft loan of US $ 200 million towards the cost of construction of the second phase of Hambantota port during the visit of Chinese Vice Premier Zhang Dejiang to Colombo from June 10 to 12, 2010, in addition to the loan of $ 360 million in the first phase.[36] Bangladesh and China signed a defense cooperation agreement in 2002, which emphasized more on military training and maintenance of the Bangladesh armed forces. Along with the assurance of other sops provided by Chinese Vice Premier during his visit to Dhaka from June 13 to14, 2010, China is likely to consider Bangladesh's request for financial and construction assistance for the expansion and modernisation of the Chittagong port in the coming years. The 'string of pearls', connecting Bangladesh, Sri Lanka and Maldives is another example of China's strategic intentions in the region, which may have long term implications for India. China's competition for the domination of the Indian Ocean is another concern for India, along with the U.S.

China has been playing its own pro-active role in SAARC through its policies, in order to advance its influence in the region and enhance the autonomy of the member states and thereby undermining the strength of India, in lieu of a direct military confrontation with India. All these moves are showing the growing strategic and economic influence of China in India's neighborhood and surmounted tension for India. Its extensive port development activity in Myanmar, Bangladesh, Sri Lanka and Pakistan and actively supplying weapons to these countries and tightening borders with Nepal are enough to create disturbance in SAARC and destabilise India's supremacy in the region. These actions are aimed at preventing India's strength and influence in the region, while simultaneously enhancing its own superiority over the other members of SAARC through its long term strategy for the monopoly. In the Indian perception, China's dual capable transport links, coupled with its eastern and western flanks, display its encircling strategy rather than its geo-economic interest. In all, China has encircled India with its base in India's neighborhood and diminishes India's advantage of unique centrality in the SAARC region and its comprehensive strategy.

China's relations with the SAARC countries, particularly with India, cannot be judged easily. On one side, it is shifting away from its former policies of siding with Pakistan on Kashmir dispute, indicating the emphasis on positive relations with India than with Pakistan, perhaps due to the alignment between the U.S. and India to contain its own country.[37] On the other, it is making incursions into Indian territory and creating a war-type situation.

In the true sense, it appears that there is no dilution of China's overall strategies in South Asia/SAARC and in the entire Indian Ocean to contain India, as is evident from its enhanced military and nuclear ties with Pakistan and few other SAARC countries. Thus, 'containment' of India has been sought by China through transfer of conventional and nuclear weapon capabilities to Pakistan and active use of Chinese diplomatic, economic and military muscle across India's neighbourhood.[38] To counter the Chinese influence in Pakistan, India will need to enhance its economic interaction with China itself, and at the same time building confidence in the rest of SAARC countries with its economic and political milieu.

III. China in India

The policies for developing energy, trade and investment linkages, common for both China and India, are gaining increasing momentum now-a-days. More recently, both countries have proved that if good macro economic policy is combined with appropriate social and institutional policies, it would result in a reasonably sound economy. In the light of this, competition between the countries is inevitable in the current global economic environment.

(i) China's Trade with India : After the resumption of bilateral trade in 1978, India and China signed the 'Most Favoured Nations' Agreement in 1984 and since 1988, it was resolved to widen and deepen the bilateral relations in the form of trade and other economic relations.

The total two-way trade in 1991 was $265 million, which by 1998 had reached $11.9 billion. Since 2001, bilateral trade grew at an average rate of around 36 per cent. India-China trade touched $25.05 billion in 2006, exceeding the $20 billion goal set for 2008 by the two countries in 2005. At the Singh-Hu summit in 2006, a new bilateral trade target of $40 billion by 2010 was declared. This target was again revised in January 2008 to raise the annual volume of trade to $ 60 billion by 2010.[39] By end 2007, India had become China's 10th largest trading partner, while China had become India's largest trade partner in 2008 with bilateral trade reaching 52 billion, however fell to $43 billion to stand at the second place in the event of economic meltdown.[40] Of late, the situation is again changing. The rising trade deficit of India with China, a cause for concern, relates to the challenge before India to diversify its export basket to China. This refers to the long pending market access to pharmaceutical, I.T, and engineering companies and high tariff imports.

A decade ago, India's focus was westward and China's concentration was on the Pacific. Asia including Association of South East Asian Nations (ASEAN) became the major destination of exports and imports for India from the 1990s, which rose to over 50.0 per cent and 61.7 per cent respectively in 2008-09.[41] In spite of this increasing trade pattern, India is lagging behind China's trade and commerce strategy which has its deep roots in the ASEAN's market also.

The continuously increasing Sino-Indian trade was significant in the wake of economic meltdown from 2008. The impact of the global meltdown has not yet affected this bilateral trade. There is a huge demand for Chinese machinery in India for developing its manufacturing sector. China's demand for Indian products includes raw materials, mainly metals and ores. In other words, India's exports led by minerals and raw materials or low-value added items, in contrast to the imports of electronic goods, organic coke and briquettes, medicinal and pharmaceutical products, telecommunication equipment, electric equipment, organic chemicals and light industrial goods. India's exports to China in 2008-09 amounted to $ 9.3 billion against $10.8 billion in 2007-08 marking a decline of 14.39 per cent, whereas India's imports from China were $31.3 billion against $27.1 in the respective years showing a robust growth of 16 per cent.[42] This shows the direction in which the bilateral trade balance is flowing.

Antidumping probes is another area of conflict between India and China. Out of the 42 cases of antidumping probes India launched, China accounted for 17 cases. This was followed by safeguard duties on aluminum products from China, a five year duty on Vitamin-C and extension of a ban on dairy products. This is common under WTO framework and China faced similar action from the U.S on car tyres.[43]

(ii) China's Companies in India: Alongside the import and export trade of commodities, the multi-dimensional cooperation on engineering contracting, technology trade and two-way investment and others supported by various agreements are also significant and contributing to intensified bilateral relations. But there is an imbalance between the two countries in these sectors, owing to the Chinese domination and hence the inroads of China into the key sectors of Indian economy are a matter of concern. Chinese companies started in a big way in India during 2004-08, when the ruling coalition party took the support of Marxist party. These companies are continued even after the Marxists stopped supporting the ruling party. The reason for this is the preference of the Indian corporate houses for the Chinese companies which bring together their workforce on three-month tourist visas for cheaper emoluments. China's construction companies in India have been bringing a large number of Chinese workers without employing Indian workers. This is a practice which China has been following in African countries where there is a severe shortage of labour.[44] But the Indian experience is that foreign companies from countries like Japan, South Korea and the Southeast Asian region did not bring labour from their countries. In view of the growing unemployment of the educated and semiskilled labour force, especially at a time when global financial crisis impacts the employment scenario, India raised objection to this.

The Chinese companies are surging from infrastructure projects to power and telecommunications. Thus, India has become the largest overseas market for Chinese companies undertaking projects worth $12.9 billion.[45] The power companies of China are giving tough competition to the domestic units such as BHEL. Indian industrial chambers like Assocham asked the government to levy import duty on Chinese power equipment, which is giving direct competition to the domestic industry. Together with the problems of unemployment and competition, there is a security threat also for the country. India has reconsidered its decision to allow Chinese telecommunications in sensitive areas[46] for its security concern and put restrictions on its import. It is known that the government is allowing the Chinese in telecom companies in south India, away from the borders.[47] All these have added to the list of strains between the two countries. When India objected to a dam China is constructing on Brahmaputra river, China has responded by dismissing the plan recently. India is also establishing its companies in China, mostly in the I.T sector. Its service exports have stepped up their activities with some of the leading companies, viz. Infosys, TCS and Wipro and also I.T institutes like NIIT. Most of these are not working on a big scale, as China is in India. The State Bank of India in Shanghai is providing services by fostering the expanding trade between the two. Indian manufacturing units are setting up shop in China, ready to take on the Chinese market. Its companies like Sundaram Fasteners of TVS have been sourcing parts for China, particularly in the auto sector.[48] NIIT is the only shining example of the success of Indian enterprise in China.

China is well aware of its political pressure points which can be used at appropriate time on different countries in order to use its political clout. This is evident from the comparative silence of the U.S on human rights issues relating to Tibet and Xinjiang. The reason is attributed to the U.S need for continued purchase of the Treasury Bonds by China, the largest foreign investor in the U.S Treasury Bonds at a time of economic meltdown. Now, China is using this type of pressure points on India by making intrusion in Arunachal Pradesh and declaring it as disputed area in order to resist India's influence on Tibet.[49]

China is still pestering some kind of disputes not only with India, but also with other neighbouring countries which are militarily weak. China's quest for supremacy and hegemony is evident from the occupation of Tibet; teaching lesson to Vietnam; taking Hong Kong in its fold and more or less similar move towards Taiwan. Responding to China's latest incursions and objections towards its internal matters, India asked the country to stop taking development projects in disputed areas. The intention was to pay China back in its own coin for objecting to development work in disputed areas under India's control while following a similar practice in disputed territory elsewhere. India is in a position to play the role of a balancer in the ongoing rivalry between China and the U.S. However, China's policy towards India is to prevent closer relationship between the two.[50]

In the past two decades, high level political visits and exchanges have now become the norm in both India and China and people to people ties have grown and common interests and positions have been identified on key international issues. In fact, the historic accord of 1988 firmed up the subsequent bilateral agreements and vision documents in 1993, 1996, 2003, 2005, and 2008. It is suggested that the best way to forge a high level bilateral political agreement would be on the model of Deng-Rajiv accord of December, 1988, because it ensures the maintenance of balance and tranquility on boundary claims.[51]

IV. Conclusion

With common strengths and export destinations, both India and China are bound to compete in international markets. India-China relations have seen a maturity in the recent years. The interactions between the two countries can be broadly categorised into three major phases: The first phase (1976-87) was characterised by expanding mutual good will and trust; the second (1988-95) witnessed five formal summits towards consolidating CBMs; and the commencement of the third phase with President Jiang's visit to New Delhi in November 1996 when concrete decisions on more contentious issues including the border dispute were taken.[52]

The relationship between India and China is a complex one. On the one hand, the increasing trade relations, high level political exchanges, and a common understanding on certain global issues contributed to greater trust and confidence. But the ongoing border dispute, anti-dumping measures of India from the cheap Chinese goods, competition for oil and gas, and the naval competition in the Indian Ocean are the major areas of concern for both. These problems are acting as speed bumps.[53] Importantly, China's enhanced economic and military assistance to Pakistan is a matter of serious concern for India. China's close interaction with Pakistan in defense and nuclear matters on the one hand and India's strategic relationship with the U.S. and Japan on the other, strengthened this trust-deficit between the two countries. In addition to this, they would increasingly compete for leverage in the international arena.

On some selected global issues, India and China have shared common interest. These two countries have cooperated in forums such as the G-20, WTO talks and the BRIC group, besides climate change and shared the common goal of restructuring the IMF and World Bank. The role of these two economies is particularly crucial in the wake of global economic meltdown in reducing the intensity of the crisis and ensuring recovery in the world economy. This underscores the political as well as economic understanding between the two countries for restricting the West from global protectionism and importantly for a peaceful co-existence in Asia. In the context of global economic architecture, both countries must strengthen their economic clout by jointly standing up on core issues.

India has arrived at a stage in international politics, when it has to demonstrate maturity in its relations with powerful countries. The differences with China would not be allowed to obstruct the mutual relations. The development strategies of India and China should take the centre stage in the backdrop of the economic meltdown rather than wasting time on rigid and long running issues.

Currently, China is a rising power and is most likely to overtake the U.S as the country with the highest GDP in a couple of decades as per some projections. It wants to be the dominant power in Asia in the immediate future, showing an unequal relationship with other major Asian powers. According to K. Subrahmanyam,[54] a strategic analyst, the two main reasons for China disturbing India are: (i) its increasing relationship with the U.S which has entered into a new phase and may act against China's growing political power; and (ii) the competition from India as a major global player in future. He further explained that India is the only nation that has the potential to challenge China in the long run with a comparable population, particularly with the advantage of younger age population and with its significant economic clout.

The above reasons, along with its dissatisfaction on India's Tibet policy, make China to pressurise India in the recent times. Though the bilateral relations went through a rough patch for some time, the differences were not multiplied by the two countries, in view of the all-round development in bilateral relations. India, while trying to strengthen its bilateral relations, should convey its core interests to China.[55] India has the responsibility to protect its national as well as regional interests. It should step up its regional policy in SAARC through appropriate measures to win over the confidence of the member nations. India's commitment to open regionalism in the subcontinent from the second half of the new millennium is evident from its support to the entry of China and Japan into SAARC framework as observers. This is reiterated by the then Foreign Minister, Pranab Mukherji that India does not seek an exclusive sphere of influence, but a shared sphere of mutual development and cooperation in South Asia.[56]

It is time for India to enhance its naval capacity and also to reach out East and Southeast Asian countries, some of the Indian Ocean Rim countries and other global players, like the U.S. and Japan to strengthen the strategic relationship and to build a stable balance of power in Asia. Some strategic analysts like K.Subrahmanyam.[57] Have suggested that increase in India's economic growth to 10 per cent by exploiting all available favourable factors in the international economic and political system is also providing solution. While others like Subramanian Swamy.[58] Cautioned India to change the bottom-line that China has a veto over the U.S. actions in South Asia. Otherwise, the U.S. partnership is not going to mitigate India's problems with China. In all, majority of scholars advocates that augmenting the country's military capability immediately, while working for peace and making all major powers taking part in India's growth and security, is the immediate alternative to follow the cooperative mechanism with China.

References

1. *Business Line* (2009), September 15.
2. Mohan Guruswamy and Zorawar Daulet Singh (2009), *India-China Relations–The Border Issue and Beyond,* (New Delhi: Viva Books), pp. 92-111.
3. *The Hindu* (2009), October 15.
4. World Bank (2010), *World Development Report*, Table. 1, New York: Oxford University Press, p. 378.
5. *Ibid.*
6. *Ibid,* Table.4, p. 386.
7. UN ESCAP (2008), *Statistical Yearbook of Asia and Pacific,* New York, Table. 21.2, p.154.
8. Govt. of India, Ministry of Finance (2009-10), *Economic Survey*, Table.7.5, p.155.
9. World Bank (2009), N. 4, Table. 5, p. 386.

10. *Ibid.*
11. Jayati Ghosh and C.P. Chandrasekhar (2009),"Global trade in a time of crisis", *Business Line,* July 28.
12. Govt. of India, Ministry of Finance, N. 8, (2008-09), p.144.
13. *Ibid*, (2009-10), Table 7.11, p.163.
14. *Ibid*, pp.160-2.
15. *Ibid,* (2008-09), table. 6.3, p.128.
16. *Ibid,* Box.6.3, p.134.
17. *Ibid,* (2009-10), Table 6.6 & 6.7, pp.134-5.
18. B.Raman (2009) "Chinese Economic Monitor- Note No.5", January 22, South Asia Analysis Group, Paper No. 3020.
19. *Ibid,* (2010), "Chinese Sale of U.S. Bonds: Linked to Dalailama's Meeting with Obama?", February 19.
20. Kaushik Basu (2009), "China and India: Idiosyncratic Paths to High Growth", *Economic and Political Weekly,* September 29, pp. 43-44.
21. Shalendra D.Sharma (2009), *China and India in the Age of Globalisation*, New Delhi: Cambridge University Press, p. 272.
22. Jayati Ghosh and C.P. Chandrasekhar (2009), N.11.
23. G. Srinivasan (2009), "India-China: Complex Engagement", *Business Line,* October 1.
24. P.S. Suryanarayana (2009), "India's new burst of Economic Diplomacy in East Asia", *The Hindu,* August 21.
25. Deepak Mohanty (2010), "Lessons from the financial crisis", *Business Line*, February 15.
26. Mavara Inayat (2007), "The Broadening Horizon of SAARC", *Regional Studies* (Islamabad). Vol. XXV, No. 3, Summer.
27. IMF (2009), *Direction of Trade Statistics*, Washington, D.C.
28. B. Raman (2009), N.18.

29. Rollie Lal (2007), "China's Relations with South Asia" in Joshuva Eisenman, Eric Heginbotham, and Derek Mitchell (eds.), *China and the Developing World*, New Delhi: KW Publishers Pvt. Ltd., pp.143-44.

30. *Ibid.*

31. *Ibid,* pp.145-46.

32. G. Parthasarathy (2009), "Chinese designs on the border", *Business Line*, September 17.

33. B. Raman (2009) "India-China : Dangerous Hysteria", September 8, South Asia Analysis Group, Paper No. 3397.

34. *Ibid,* "China's Strategic Intrusions in India's Neighbourhood", September 14.

35. *The Hindu* (2009), October 16.

36. B.Raman , "Chinese interest in Hambantota, Chittagong Ports- An Update", June 16, 2010, South Asia Analysis Group, Paper No. 3862.

37. Rollie Lal (2007), N.29, pp.146-47.

38. G.Parthasarathy (2009), N. 32.

39. Mohan Guruswamy and Zorawar Daulet Singh (2009), N. 2, p. 108.

40. *The Hindu* (2010), May 31.

41. P.S. Suryanarayana (2009), N. 24.

42. G. Srinivasan (2009), N. 23.

43. *Ibid.*

44. B. Raman (2009) "Chindia: China all over India", September 29, South Asia Analysis Group, Paper No. 3437.

45. *Ibid.*

46. *The Hindu* (2010), May 31.

47. B. Raman (2009), "Chindia: China all over India", n. 44.

48. An International Business Initiative (2009), "India-China Growing Partnership", *The Hindu*, October 1.

49. B. Raman (2009), "Chinese Economic Monitor- Note No. 5", N.18.

50. G. Parthasarathy (2009), N. 32.

51. *The Hindu* (2009), October 19.

52. Mohan Guruswamy and Zorawar Daulet Singh (2009), N. 2, p.110.

53. B. Raman (2009), "Strange Bed-fellows", August 31. (Institute for Topical Studies, Chennai.

54. K. Subrahmanyam (2009), "Coping with rising China", *The Hindu*, October 10.

55. Rasheeda Bhagat (2009), "The Dragon Frowns", *Business Line,* October 20.

56. Mohan Guruswamy and Zorawar Daulet Singh (2009), N. 2, p.127.

57. K. Subrahmanyam (2009), N.54.

58. Subramanian Swamy (2009), "Myth and Reality in India-China Relations", *The Hindu*, September 18.

11

Recent Trends in Vietnam's Relations with China and India

M. Prayaga

India and China are Asia's two emerging powers. Being the two fastest growing economies, these two Asian giants are playing significant role in the international affairs. Vietnam is seeking to develop friendly ties with China, its immediate neighbour and source of security threat, and India, which is perceived as a traditional friend, ready to help Vietnam, whenever the latter was in need of it. Therefore, the study of Vietnam's relations with China and India about which Hanoi has contrasting perceptions becomes interesting and gains contemporary relevance.

Vietnam is the only country in Southeast Asia that was brought under the Chinese cultural orbit, though the cultural affinities between the two contiguous countries did not ensure an atmosphere of peace and security between them. Hence, the recent spurt in ties between Vietnam and China, which stands in sharp contrast to those during the Cold War that had resulted in fierce war, puzzled many international political analysts. Yet, it was the cumulative effect of the domestic and global changes that pushed these two borders-sharing, culturally close, politically identical, centrally planned and reform-driven economies to forge closer ties. In spite of the deep-seated distrust, it had harboured towards Beijing, Vietnam edged close to China, evidently because of global changes.

Following the *Doi Moi* or Renovation, which was unveiled at the Sixth Party Congress in 1986, Vietnam intensified its economic integration with world economies, and also consciously gave up its isolationist policy in order to cultivate relations with all the countries, particularly China. The decade-long estrangement ended when both the countries succeeded in getting their bilateral relations normalised in 1991. Since then, the rapid growth of the relations had begun documenting significant achievements.

The major ice-breaking development between the two was the unravelling of the border issue. Both sides wanted to turn the border into an area of peace, friendship and cooperation. Accordingly, they have signed two landmark agreements on Land Border and on Tonkin Gulf Demarcation and established diversified relations with each other. Still, the fear of Chinese security threat in South China Sea and economic domination continues to lurk in the bosom of the Vietnamese.

India and Vietnam apart from sharing historical connections have established steady growth in their relations significantly in the post-Cold War era. India's 'Look East' policy-unveiled to re-engage Southeast Asian countries, has become leverage to further shore up multilateral ties with Vietnam. On the other hand, changing geopolitical equations in Asia compelled Vietnam to forge closer strategic relations with India. Mutual understanding made them active partners in regional and trans-regional mechanisms for promoting peace and security in the region.

This paper is an attempt to present an account of Vietnam's relations with China and India in the political, economic and strategic spheres in the contemporary period.

Evolution of the Sino-Vietnam Relations

Vietnam which was annexed to the Chinese empire, wrenched itself free in the first century A.D. after a bitter struggle that lasted over one thousand years. The bitter past continued to impact the attitude and policy of the posterity. It was only after the advent of the French colonialism that the threat from the north effectively dissipated and the border between China and Vietnam was defined and demarcated. The communist movement forged bonds of friendship between China and Vietnam since 1930. The Democratic Republic of Vietnam (DRV) set up in 1945, under the leadership of Ho Chi Minh, received crucial help from China during its struggle with the French.[1] However, Beijing's acceptance of the division of Vietnam at the 17th parallel in 1954 Geneva Conference, remained unpalatable for Hanoi until the reunification in 1975.[2]

On the other hand, for strategic reasons, China continued to offer critical help during the Vietnam War in 1960s. Beijing's assistance to Hanoi tapered off, following the China's détente with the United States in 1972, when Vietnam was getting ready for a large scale military assault against the American-backed forces in South Vietnam. Vietnam aligned itself with the Soviet Union which generously offered the military aid needed for its final assault on the South. After 1975, hostilities between Vietnam and China were fuelled by the perceived threat to the economic and cultural interests of the ethnic Chinese in Vietnam from the ongoing process of Vietnamisation and the exodus of the ethnic Chinese.[3]

The period of over three decades relations from 1945 that lasted well, yielded to a period of estrangement which climaxed with their spar on Cambodia. Giving an incisive insight into the historical hostility that characterised Sino-Vietnam relations, the historian Willam J. Duiker noted: "On the Asian political landscape, the dispute over Cambodia has been the most visible manifestation of a deep and jagged fault running between China and Vietnam.... The root of the problem, a legacy of mutual suspicion and periodic conflict, goes back 2000 years to the first emergence of direct ties between the organised governments in the two countries".[4]

On the question of the ethnic Chinese, the outraged China suspended the economic and technical assistance to Vietnam and directly assailed Vietnam's policies toward Kampuchea.[5] The Sino-Vietnamese relations, which were under severe strain, were on the wane following Vietnam's military intervention in Cambodia on 25 December 1978, which resulted in the replacement of China-backed government of the Democratic Kampuchea (DK) by a pro-Vietnamese government. The overthrow of the friendly DK government dealt a tremendous blow to the power and prestige of China. Having harped on the "the need to teach Vietnam a lesson", China now felt that the time had come to translate its words into action and launched a "self-defensive counterattack" along the land border with Vietnam on 17 February 1979 and withdrew behind the borders on 5 March 1979. By these deeds, China surely earned no merit but betrayed, rather exhibited its hegemonistic behaviour to its neighbours.

In order to bring Hanoi around, China sought to subject Vietnam to increasing pressure through international isolation besides its military threats. Vietnam, which managed to stick to its own agenda without yielding to China for most of 1980s, finally climbed down to "do a bit of kowtowing to the Chinese".[6] Thanks to the continuous and consistent pressure from its "patron" and major ally, the Soviet Union. Moscow too was willing to normalise relations with China. The Soviet delegation, having attended the Sixth National Congress of Vietnam Communist Party (VCP) in December 1986, felt the need for an early settlement of the Cambodian issue and the normalisation of Vietnam's relations with China.[7]

Vietnam's Sixth Party Congress

In its historic Sixth Party Congress held in 1986, VCP along with launching the economic reforms, initiated changes in its China policy. Vo Dong Giang, the Special Envoy of Vietnam Foreign Ministry, at a Press Conference in December 1986, noted: "The political report, made at the Congress, once again reaffirmed that Vietnam is ready to negotiate with China at any time, at any level and in any place, in order to normalise relations between the two countries".[8]

However, Vietnam, compelled by the challenging domestic economic crisis, heightened by decades of economic stagnation, foreign embargos and the drying up of external financial support, from the Soviet Union and the East European allies, made a determined bid for developing relations with China. Hence, Vietnam made certain positive gestures to propitiate China. In June 1988, the Vietnam National Assembly deleted a hostile reference to China, namely the phrase "Chinese hegemonists", from the preamble of the 1980 Constitution of the country.[9] Satisfied with Vietnam's addressing its major demand, namely, the withdrawal of its troops from Cambodia in September 1989, China, which was also subjected to international isolation imposed, following the Tiananmen incident in June 1989, welcomed détente. The end of Cold war also proved to be catalytic in fortifying the relations between the two. It is felt that the "sense of insecurity, in a new and different world, nudged the two neighbouring states towards cooperation."[10]

The inward looking foreign policies played a significant role in bringing the two closer. Vietnam felt, "China was not just a neighbour, but a big power with which Vietnam should have good ties. China meanwhile, also saw Vietnam as an important bridge to engage Southeast Asia and prevent other great power's influence in its southern border".[11] In addition, China felt that, Vietnam's long coastline over 3,300 km on the South China Sea, was important for its oil imports and critical for security in the sea-lanes.[12]

The changing trend in Sino-Vietnam relations was characterised by a series of exchanges of official and unofficial visits and enhanced trade and economic relations. A significant step in the direction of normalisation of the relations between the two was taken in September 1990, when a secret summit meeting was held in Chengdu in Southern China, where President Jiang Zemin met VCP Chief Nguyen Van Linh, Premier Do Muoi and former Premier Pham Van Dong. Thoroughly pleased with the growing positive trend in Sino-Vietnamese ties, the two communist neighbours got their relations normalised on 5 November 1991 when the VCP General Secretary Do Muoi, Premier Vo Van Kiet, Chinese Communist Party General Secretary Jiang Zemin and Prime Minister Li Peng issued a joint statement to that effect after their closed-door meeting in the Great Hall of the People. In a written statement, Do Muoi said normalization was "of great historic significance" and would pave the way for positive exchanges in cultural, scientific, economic and other spheres.[13] After the normalisation of relations was announced, 'Friendship Pass' was re-opened in April 1992, and air travels between Guangzhou and Ho Chi Minh City, and between Beijing and Hanoi were resumed in May and June 1992 respectively.[14]

Relations after Normalisation

By taking forward the process of normalisation of relations on the political front, China and Vietnam took further steps. In November –December 1992, Premier Li Peng paid an official visit to Vietnam. In the course of his visit, Li Peng said: "China stands for the settlement of disputes between countries through peaceful negotiations without resort to force." Sharing Li's sentiments, Premier Vo Van Kiet said: "All these problems left by history will be solved through negotiations".[15] The significance of the visit was that it marked the first by a Chinese Prime Minister in 21 years. Yet another important step taken by China and Vietnam, was the conclusion of an 'Agreement of Fundamental Principles on Territorial Conflicts' in 1993, in order to find an amicable solution to border disputes in the Gulf of Tonkin.[16]

The growing relations between the two were highlighted by the Four-day "official goodwill visit" of President Jiang Zemin to Vietnam in November 1994. During the visit of Jiang who led a 150-member Chinese delegation, three economic and trade accords and agreements were signed. Leaders of both sides agreed to improve bilateral ties. They took a decision to negotiate rival claims to the Spratly Islands in the South China Sea, which straddle major supply lines and fishing grounds.[17]

The growing relations increased the exchange of high level visits further. To start with every year, more than 100 delegations from state to local levels of both sides were exchanged and this number rose to 267 delegations in 2009. In 1999, when the Secretary of the Communist Party of Vietnam, Le Kha Phiew, visited Beijing along with him, the Chinese President Jiang Zemin, announced a "16 Word Guideline" of "friendly neighbourhood, comprehensive cooperation, long-term stability, and future orientation" and the four-good-point-spirit of "good friends, good neighbours, good partners, and good comrades" for improving strong bilateral relations and to take them to new heights. This spirit has been successfully utilised by Vietnam and China to resolve the outstanding disputes relating to the land border and maritime rights in the Gulf of Tonkin between 1995 and 2000.[18]

Since normalisation, Vietnam and China began to have exchange of visits of heads of state, particularly after the dawn of the present century. Some of the Chinese leaders visited Vietnam more than once. Former President Jiang Zemin, visited Vietnam in February 2002. Premier Zhu Rongji visited Vietnam in Dec.1999. Hu Jintao visited Vietnam twice in December 1998 and in April 2000 as its Vice President and paid his state visit, as President in November 2005. During his 2005 visit, he even addressed the Vietnam's National Assembly and announced a deadline for the demarcation of land border by 2008. By way of complementing the Chinese gesture of visits, almost all Vietnamese elite leaders visited China : Prime Minister Phan Van Khai in October 1998; in February 2000, in May 2004 and in June 2005, Le Kha Phieu, former General Secretary of the CPV, in February 1999, Tran Duc Luong, the then President, in December 2000 and in July 2005, Nong Duc Manh, General Secretary of the CPV, visited China in August 2006 and the incumbent President Nguyen Minh Triet, in May 2007.

Vietnam and China established 'Steering Committee for Vietnam-China Bilateral Cooperation' (SCBC) in November 2006 to build consensus on the bilateral ties, political exchanges, economic and trade cooperation, people-to-people contacts and cultural exchanges, and to sort out mutually the issues relating to boundary. In this series four meetings were held alternately, in Vietnam and China : First in Vietnam in November 2006; Second in China in January 2008; Third in March 2009 in Vietnam and the fourth and the latest in the series in China in July 2010. In the third meeting, President Minh Triet said to the Chinese State Councilor Dai Bingguo, that 2008 is the "harvest year" for Sino-Vietnamese relations, as the land border between the countries was successfully demarcated.[19] On the importance of relations between the two, Vietnam's Prime Minister Nguyen Tan Dung said to the visiting Chinese Foreign Minister Yang Jiechi in April 2008: "The mountains and rivers of Vietnam and China are adjacent, cultures similar, ideologies shared, and destinies interrelated." For their durable relations both sides emphasized the need to set up a hotline between senior leaders of the two nations to "handle issues of major concern".[20]

However, based on these outward expressions of friendship and cordiality, one cannot say that favourable relations are prevailing between two countries. Vietnamese leadership, an admixture of pro-Chinese and moderates who had opposed the Vietnam's alignment with China, followed a policy of comforting different factions in the polity and in the public. While promoting the strengthening of close political relations with China, Vietnam was mindful of its own security and national interests. Towards developing a counter weight to China's strategic interests in the South China Sea, Vietnam adopted a policy of getting its own security partnerships with the US, India and Japan fortified. Vietnam also signed "reliable partnership" with Japan and "strategic and comprehensive cooperative relationship with India", two potential powers of Asia in 2003.[21]

Economic Relations

Economic relations between Vietnam and China developed significantly during 2000-09. Mutual accommodation and consensus being the acknowledged guiding principle in shaping the relations among nations, both Vietnam and China got engaged together in many bilateral and multilateral driven mechanisms.

Driven by international economic trade liberalisation and mounting cooperation among the nations, the relations of Vietnam and China evolved into a model in the changing trajectories in the region. Vietnam has been carrying out an economic renovation for more than two decades. This process was the result of transformation of the centrally planned economy to the market-based economy and from an agricultural base to an industrialised one. Buoyed up by '*doi moi*' economic reforms, Vietnam wanted to become an economically vibrant country in the Southeast Asian region. A turning point in this direction, was achieved by the normalising relations with its Southeast Asian neighbours. In this context, Vietnam has taken leverage of its economic renovation programme to develop its trade and economic relations with its neighbours. Vietnam became a member of Association of Southeast Asian Nations (ASEAN) in 1995. Thus, an integration with the region provides a springboard to become a member in ASEAN Regional Forum (ARF) and Greater Mekong Sub-Region (GMSR) which embraces Cambodia, China, Lao People's Democratic Republic, Myanmar, Thailand and Vietnam. This sub-region is shaped to promote free flow of goods as well as people in the sub-region. Interaction between Vietnam and China at regional and sub-regional level helped to sort out differences mainly in trade, land border and territorial issues in South China Sea.

Further, under the economic cooperative framework, Vietnam and China gave due attention to the "Two Corridors and One Economic Belt" project for the development of two impoverished regions of their countries. The first corridor covers from China's Kunming to Vietnam's Lao Cai, Hanoi, and Haiphong; the other one connects China's Nanning with Vietnam's Lang Son, Hanoi, Haiphong and Quang Ninh provinces. Besides, the economic ring covers China's Guangxi, Guangdong, Hainan, Hong Kong and Macao and 10 coastal localities of Vietnam. When the project comes to full operation, the local peoples' standard of living would get better with promising employment opportunities, growth of social services and infrastructural development. The Asian Development Bank (ADB) in December 2007 approved US$ 1.1 billion, the biggest single loan in its history, for the construction of a modern 244-kilometer highway project linking Kunming city in China with Hanoi, and Hai Phong and Cai Lan ports in Vietnam. Since Vietnam is the only country in ASEAN having both land and maritime boundaries with China, it is conjectured that, this project would play a key role in ASEAN-China FTA in connecting both regions for sustainable development in the region.[22]

Though there are huge differences between Vietnam and China, the similarities such as political systems, opening of economies, geographical proximity and historical connectivity gave chance to get their relations advanced. The frequent exchange of visits between leaders of the two countries laid a solid foundation for "long-term stability, future orientation, good neighbourly friendship and all-round cooperation". On the basis of mutual respect, good trade relations grew between these countries.

One of the awe-inspiring developments of the recent period has been the emergence of China as an economic giant. Vietnam did benefit a lot through growing trade relations with China like the neighbouring ASEAN region which benefited by the rapid growing China market.

Trade Relations between Vietnam and China, 1998-2009

Vietnam and China have expanded and deepened their economic cooperation. Indeed, an accordance of China's Most Favoured Nation status to Vietnam helped in realizing many milestones in bilateral trade. The bilateral trade grew to unexpected levels and even surpassed the set targets by both the countries. For the bilateral trade, which was only $ 32 million in 1991, the two countries set a target of US $ 5 billion to be achieved by 2005. But, the target was achieved by 2003 itself. The target set for 2010 with a total value of US $ 10 billion was obtained in 2006. (Vietnam's export accounted for US $ 3.03 billion and import amounted to US $ 7.39 billion). In 2009, the bilateral trade reached US

$ 20.8 billion. The bilateral trade volume accounts for 0.6 per cent of China's total foreign trade and 12 per cent of Vietnam's total trade.[23] With the enormous growth of Vietnam's exports and imports to China, the atter became the largest trading partner replacing Japan.[24]

From 2000 to 2003, Japan was the top trading partner of Vietnam, with total bilateral trade value of US $ 5.9 billion. However, since 2004, China has surpassed Japan and thus started becoming the largest trading partner of Vietnam. But a such trading relationship was marred by Vietnam's trade deficit with China.[25]

Vietnam's imports increased rapidly from US $ 1.6 billion in 2001 to US $ 13.8 billion in 2008. Vietnam's export value to China was estimated at US $ 4.7 billion in 2008. Vietnam's import value from China developed slightly, particularly in 2007 and 2008 with import values of US $ 12.6 billion and US $ 15 billion respectively.[26] The table shows that in 2009, the imports worth US $ 16,441 million were four times greater than its exports worth US $ 4,909 million to China. Obviously, the imports were more than doubled in two years (2005 -2007). Thus, Vietnam became a net importer of goods from China. [27]

In the composition of the export of goods from Vietnam, there are more than 100 goods where as Vietnam imports more than double the number of goods from China. Vietnamese exports mainly include, raw materials such as coal, oil, rubber, iron ore; Agricultural products like food, tea, vegetables and cashew; frozen sea food, handicrafts, fine arts and shoes. China imports large quantities of raw materials from all over the world to sustain the high growth rates of its economy and also for its simmering demand for energy needs. Increasing raw material imports have been a major factor driving Vietnam's trade with China.

The variegated imports from China include, machinery equipment for cement and sugar factories; machines, transport vehicles; oil and raw materials (cement, pesticides and fertiliser; food products and consumer products such as medicines, electronic products and textile fabrics). China is the chief source of Vietnam's machinery, computers, chemicals and textiles. Vietnam is a net exporter of oil and coal; China is also a net exporter of coal. Importing coal from Vietnam, China is time-saving inexpensive as well as the transport costs. Since many of the Chinese coal mines are in the northern part, it is convenient to import coal from Vietnam for its southern-located plants. Chinese goods fill Vietnamese markets. These differences in economic capacity and structure, as well as in global weight, create a general asymmetric framework for the economic

Table 1: Trade relations between Vietnam and China, 1998- 2009 (millions of US$)

Year	*Vietnam's Exports to China*	*Vietnam's Import from China*
1998 #	440.1	515
1999	746.4	683.4
2000	1,536.4	1,401.1
2001	1,417.4	1,606.2
2002	1,518.3	2,158.8
2003	1,883.1	3,138.6
2004	2,735.5	4,456.5
2005*	3,228.1	5,899.7
2006	3,242.8	7,391.3
2007	3,646.1	12,710.0
2008	4,850.1	15,973.6
2009	4,909.0	16,441.0

Source: Trade statistics for the years 1998 to 2004, Vietnam General Statistics Office 2004 in Ha Thi Hong Van and Do Tien Sam. "Vietnam – China Trade, FDI and ODA Relations (1998-2008) and the Impacts upon Vietnam."
*Trade statistics for the years 2005 to 2009. *Statistical Year Book of Vietnam 2009*. Statistical Publishing House. 2010.

relationship. Vietnam is a "perfect external market for Chinese goods because of similar economic conditions and consumer cultures and low transportation costs."[28]

China has become a leading trade partner of Vietnam. In 2006, the bilateral trade volume was US $ 10.32 billion (Vietnam's export was $ 3.03 million and import was $ 7.39). The bilateral trade volume accounts for 0.6 per cent of China's total foreign trade volume and 12 per cent of Vietnam's total foreign trade volume. On the list of trade commodities, some critics viewed that Vietnam exports low-value raw materials to China and imports high-value goods and technology from China, required for the growing Vietnamese economy.[29]

During this period, the glaring development was the trade deficit against Vietnam. Since 2001, the trade deficit has been constantly increasing. In 2001, the deficit was US $ 211 million, US $ 1.7 billion in 2004, and US $ 3.5 billion in 2006 and US $ 9 billion in 2007.[30] Vietnam's normalisation of relations with its former rival, the US, has improved the bilateral trade. The trade deficit with China has been balanced by Vietnam through its trade surplus with the United States[31] as well as by increasing substantial the exports to the two neighbouring countries.

The two chief reasons for the disparity in trade are lack of enforcement laws and illegal importation of goods from China to Vietnam at the border. As the two countries share an unwieldy long border, the unofficial border trade has grown considerably alongside the official bilateral trade. The other reasons have been the total lack of marketing strategies, consumption and legal system. The Chinese products are relatively cheaper, more diverse and plentiful meeting the needs of socio-economic groups, particularly the low-income groups.[32] Border trade assumes importance for the local people in improving their job opportunities, income, people to people contacts and even revenue generator for the local governments on both sides. The trade including diverse goods such as crude oil, gas, vegetables and fruits and services, has become an informal way to develop quality of lives of the border communities, who naturally attract low attention from the governments. In the 1990s, the border trade value between Vietnam and China stood at 90 per cent of the total trade turnover.[33] But by 2005, the border trade declined to reach 10 to 15 per cent of the import-export turnover because of various tax and other required measures taken by the two sides. The effective implementation of FTA between China and ASEAN countries would ensure freer flow of goods sans tax.

One positive outcome of the bilateral trade, is the sustainability of trade turnover. When the major world powers have been the victims of global financial crisis, the bilateral trade volume between Vietnam and China in 2009 reached a high record of more than $ 20 billion (See Table). China has become the second consecutive 5-year Vietnam's largest trading partner.[34] The fostering trade relations made them to agree to jointly celebrate 2010 as the 'Vietnam-China Friendship Year'.

Investment

As part of its economic rejuvenation, Vietnam opened its economy for investments. Initially, some East Asian countries like Singapore, Taiwan, Japan and Korea were the biggest investors who dominated the investment list with nearly 50 per cent of the total committed capital. The inflow of investments has been a welcome opportunity for Vietnam. In recent times, Chinese investments too grew tremendously. China's foreign direct investment stood at $ 146 million in 61 projects in 2003 ranking fifth among foreign investors in Vietnam.[35] By 2007, China had invested US $ 1.182 billion in 437 projects in Vietnam. Chinese investors focused the investment on industry and mining, with more than 70 per cent of their total investments. China provides US $18 million as non-refundable aid to help build a Vietnam-

China Friendship palace. But, Vietnam's investment in China is tiny, mostly concentrated on Yunnan and Guangxi, with a total amount of US$ 240,000. According to the China Ministry of Commerce (MOFCOM), the engineering contracts completed by Chinese companies in Vietnam had reached US$ 1.92 billion in 2006 and China's total non-financial foreign direct investment (FDI) had reached US$ 48.79 million in 2006.[36]

Aid and ODA

Aid programmes are generally carried out by a country to understand the national interests of other country at the international level. China recognised the importance of the aid as a catalyst to improve friendly relations with other countries. China, under its ASEAN Agricultural Technical Training Programme, is providing agricultural techniques in regard to production, research and dissemination for 3 to 4 people each from Thailand, Vietnam, Cambodia, the Philippines, Indonesia, Myanmar and Laos besides meeting their accommodation and training expenses. Chinese aids were used to build satellite television stations, power plants, cultural facilities, cement and steel factories, and in the construction of infrastructure facilities in many Southeast Asian countries, including Vietnam.[37]

China is also one of the official donors of the Official Development Assistance (ODA) to Vietnam. It provided US $ 18.42 million as non-refundable aid to health care units. It also pledged around US $ 40.5 million in soft loans to upgrade a number of Chinese cooperative and built projects in Vietnam.[38] During 1992-2004, China pledged $ 312 million of ODA for the upgrade of a number of projects built with the Chinese cooperation in Vietnam, including expansion of the Thai Nguyen Steel production complex, a railway route connecting Hanoi with Ha Dong town.

Tourism

Since tourism is one of the prime foreign receipts generators, both the countries focused attention on widening and strengthening this sector. Normalisation of relations and multilateral meetings of both sides emphasized the need to improve tourism for the development of economies, particularly in border areas for improving social harmony. Encouraged by the governments of both sides, the number of Chinese visitors to Vietnam increased year by year. Chinese tourists accounted for 26.5 per cent of total international tourists visiting Vietnam and their share is more, when compared to other East Asian countries. The number of Chinese visitors rose to 717.4 thousands in 2005, but as a result of economic meltdown, only 518.9

thousands visited Vietnam in 2009. Still in the visitors list, Chinese top the list.[39] Similarly, 167,700 Vietnamese tourists visited China in 2004. Both Vietnam and China have a huge potential for cooperation in tourism industry.

Issue of Land Border

The swift development in their bilateral relationship in the wake of normalisation, has created conducive conditions for the two countries to resolve their differences over the land border and the Gulf of Tonkin with political sagacity. Their strategic thinking is that a good overall bilateral relationship is the significant foundation for the two countries to settle the lingering differences and to resolve border issues within the purview of international laws. Vietnam and China had a legal border-line under the 1887 French-Qing agreement, with about 300 landmarks planted on site. A century later, it became volatile because of China's punitive war in 1979 and was further complicated by regular border skirmishes.[40] In the background of historical animosity between the two, demarcation and planting of the landmarks do not make a simple and easy task. It needs a constant political will besides mutual consensus, to solve the issue.[41] The Vietnam-China land border runs about 1,400 km, connecting the seven northern provinces of Vietnam (Lao Chau, Dien Bien, Lao Cai, Ha Giang, Cao Bang, Lang Son and Quang Ninh) with two southern provinces of China (Yunnan and Guangxi). China positively worked out with Vietnam in solving the border problem and thereby completed the process of demarcation of land border. Accordingly, the two powers signed "Convention on the Vietnam-China Land Border" on 3 December 1999. Joint Working Groups were formed to enhance mutual cooperation and to build the consensus between the two. Though the process started after the normalisation of relations, it took another decade for the final approval of demarcation on both the sides in 2009.[42] Another area which equally attracted both the nations is the Gulf of Tonkin. Since the normalisation in 1991, the frequent exchange of visits at different levels made possible the delimiting of the Tonkin Gulf. The two sides signed a historic **Tonkin Gulf Agreement** on 25 December 2000 demarking maritime boundary and accommodating fishing rights. As part of the security agreement, both conducted naval exercises. Beijing's naval ships made periodical visits to Vietnamese ports. Naval forces of both countries' got their cooperation enhanced in order to conduct joint patrol on the Beibu Gulf. In December 2009, two navy fleets conducted their joint patrol at Beibu Gulf.[43] Vietnam and China oil and gas companies agreed to conduct joint surveys in the area.

The South China Sea Dispute : Paracels and Spratlys

The Paracel islands in the north and the Spratly islands in the southern sector of the South China Sea, are economically viable (under sea fossil oil and gas resources) and strategically significant in the region. Therefore, China and Vietnam have rival claims on both the archipelagos. On the whole, the Spratly islands have been claimed by six countries including Vietnam, China, Brunei, Malaysia, the Philippines and Taiwan. The claims of Vietnam and China are based on historical grounds whilst the claims of other four rested on Exclusive Economic Zones (EEZ) and continental shelf. Consequently, Paracels and Spratlys have become political hotspots and form the bone of contention in the region.

Even before the formation of the SRV, Chinese forces violently seized the Paracels from Vietnam in 1974. Both the nations made continuous claims on their sovereignty over Paracels by releasing historical proofs in support of their argument. Since Paracels is under the effective control of China, Ang Cheng Guan, a Scholar on Vietnam China studies, felt "it is unlikely that Vietnam will be able to regain"[44] the islands group.

Another dispute concerns the Spratly islands. Soon after the Cold war ended, it became a new flashpoint in the Southeast Asian region. It has been seen by many countries as a crucial test for peace and security in the region. The dispute has provided periodic points of tension and anxiety in Southeast Asia about the menace of the Chinese military prowess demonstrating its aggressive diplomatic policies. Following the normalisation of relations between Vietnam and China, the negotiations over the Spratly evolved steadily. A Joint Working Group was established in August 1994 for peaceful settlement of the dispute. The issue also assumed importance when ASEAN urged all claimants to resort to peaceful consensus to solve the problem. Accordingly, in 2002, China and ASEAN signed a "Declaration on the Conduct of Parties in the South China Sea" (DOC) to solve the issue amicably. Approaches to solve the conflict were undertaken through different mechanisms for conflict management. China adopted a policy to mitigate the fears of its neighbours. This was manifested in China signing the DOC wherein it committed itself to the task of using peaceful means for the resolution of territorial disputes. In 2003, it signed the Treaty of Amity and Cooperation (TAC) with ASEAN and the Code of Conduct (COC) in March 2005, to settle the dispute.

Challenges to Vietnam

In the name of solving the problem among the members at the South China Sea, China has been adopting ambivalent relationships with Vietnam and ASEAN members which pose a threat to regional order. The Chinese record on security and sovereignty issues has been betraying a latitude between its promises and fulfillment as China periodically demonstrated and indulged in aggressive actions against Vietnam and other Southeast Asian countries over Spratlys. In 1988, a Naval skirmish occurred over Spratlys between these two powers at Johnson Reef, resulting in the sinking of Vietnamese ships and the consequent missing of sailors in the incident. This incident became a concern about the expansionist designs of China and pushed Southeast Asian countries to revise and redraw their security relations in the ASEAN region.

In another incident in 1990s, the overlapping claims have led both the states to award concessions to oil companies in the areas of dispute – the Chinese to Crestone Energy Corporation in 1992 and Vietnam to the Mobil corporation in 1994. Both sides have denounced these actions as illegal. China deployed two warships in July 1994 to prevent Vietnam's activities which led to tension in the region. A further incident in March 1997 was the Kantan affair. China sent oil platform Kantan-III and two pilot ships to conduct exploratory oil drilling in an area, claimed by Vietnam as its exclusive economic zone in the Tonkin Gulf in March 1997. Vietnam protested vehemently and explained Vietnam's position to the ASEAN ambassadors. During the row with China, the Commander of the US Forces in the Pacific went to Hanoi, to be reckoned the highest US military official to visit Vietnam since normalisation.[45] By doing so, the US told China obliquely, that Washington was interested in the peaceful settlement of the problem without any use of force or show of force.

Problems and Tensions

Hanoi continues to draw protests from Beijing for inviting foreign contracts for exploring possible oil and gas resources in the disputed areas and for planning a tourist cruise service to the Spratly islands. Violence flares up on the occasion of the kind. In January 2005, the Chinese border guards opened fire on Vietnamese fishermen and killed nine for having allegedly entered into Chinese waters. Vietnam, therefore, made quiet efforts to balance China by entering into security cooperation with the United States, Japan, India and Russia. Some Vietnamese elites openly supported an American military presence in the region to counterbalance China. In 2004, Admiral Thomas Fargo, the Commander of US Forces in the Pacific, and General James L. Campbell, the Commander of US Army Forces in the Pacific, paid a visit to Hanoi. A US naval vessel made a port call in Vietnam for the first time since 1975, at Da Nang in 2004. In 2007, Admiral Gary Roughead, Commander of the U.S. Pacific Fleet, visited Vietnam. Military ties were strengthened between the U.S. and Vietnam when Naval ships, USS Blue Ridge and USS Lassen, paid a good will visit to Da Nang port in November 2009.[46] The recent Chinese military assertiveness in the Western Pacific and the South China Sea provides a stimulus for stepped up U.S.-Vietnam military cooperation. Carlyle Thayer, an authority on Vietnam, opined that in preventing China, "Vietnam sees the U.S. presence as a hedge against China's rising military power".[47]

India - Vietnam Relations

The time-tested traditional ties of India and Vietnam are characterised by mutual trust and support. Their relations were deep rooted during the struggle for their national independence. The two great leaders Pandit Jawaharlal Nehru and Ho Chi Minh shared views against imperialism. India benignly supported the reunification of Vietnam, which was divided during the Cold War years. India was against ostracising Vietnam and consequently opposed the US intervention in Vietnam. After Vietnam's successful reunification in 1975, India was one of the few countries who extended whole hearted support for its reconstruction and also granted 'Most Favoured Nation' status to Vietnam.

Even though India and Vietnam have two different political systems, they forged close bilateral relations. Both were dependents of the erstwhile Soviet Union for economic and strategic benefits. Soon after the implosion of the Soviet Union, both ascribed to market-oriented economic reforms and pursued pragmatic foreign policies. India and Vietnam felt the need for ushering in a new era of friendship and cooperation in the context of changing global milieu. India unveiled its covetous 'Look East Policy'(LEP), wherein Vietnam assumed a pivotal role in strengthening India's relations with the other countries of the Southeast Asian region. After pulling itself out of the Cambodian quagmire, Vietnam under *doi moi* chose the path of normalisation of its relations with its neighbours as well as integrated itself with the much successful ASEAN. While Vietnam became a member of ASEAN in 1995, India obtained ASEAN Full Dialogue Partnership and became a member of ASEAN Regional Forum (ARF). As India's relations with ASEAN deepened, New Delhi's relations with Hanoi which include wide gamut of areas – political, economic, social, cultural and strategic – have witnessed steady growth.

Economic Cooperation

Exchange of high-level visits by both sides offered great opportunities and facilitated wider scope for cooperation between the two countries in different areas. The visits pushed forward the process of mutual support and cooperation in political as well as economic spheres. Building on the confidence and mutually beneficial cooperation, the India-Vietnam Joint Business Council has promoted trade and investment since 1993. The cordial relations were further strengthened following the promulgation of "Joint Declaration on the Framework of Comprehensive Cooperation Between the Republic of India and the Socialist Republic of Vietnam As They Enter the 21st Century" in 2003. The effective implementation of several bilateral agreements and MoUs signed between them became a catalyst in the consistent growth of trade relations. After the liberalisation of their economies, the trade between India and Vietnam has galloped from US $ 72 million in 1995 to over US $ 1 billion in 2006; US $ 1.53 in 2007 and US $ 2.055 billion in 2008.[48] However, the trade balance is heavily in favour of India. The trade commodities include agricultural products, handicrafts, textiles, electronics, crude oil and metals. The pro-investment atmosphere facilitated the Government of India-owned company, Oil and Natural Gas Corporation (Videsh) Ltd., and private enterprises like Essar and Tata Steel, to bolster their investments in Vietnam. India became the 6th largest investor in Vietnam with US $ 4.6 billion in 2007, its biggest in any ASEAN country.[49]

Strategic Partnerships

In the post-Cold War period, India and Vietnam tried to reinforce their security relations in order to promote peace and prosperity in the region. After their increased involvement in the ASEAN framework, the two nations displayed cooperation and understanding in regional and multilateral organisations for mutual benefit. In that process, the two became the most trustworthy partners. Vietnam supports India's bid for membership of the United Nations Security Council and the Asia Pacific Economic Cooperation (APEC). India helped Vietnam to get access to WTO. Closer association of India and Vietnam in regional mechanisms like ARF, EAS and trans-regional cooperative mechanisms such as MGC which was founded to promote transportation, tourism, human resources and culture among the member states, paved the way for India's increased involvement in the spheres of economic development and investments in Vietnam.

Emerging China's strategic presence in Asia, following the power vacuum created after the disintegration of the Soviet Union, alerted India and Vietnam, the former allies of the Soviet Union, for pursuing a new era of cooperation. P.V. Rao, an Area Studies specialist, felt, "both were equally concerned over the prospect of China filling the strategic space vacated by their common friend".[50] Amid new security realignment in the region, both looked to develop a strong strategic cooperation in the region. Defence cooperation assumed importance in bilateral relations. Their relations were cemented after Indian Defence Minister Fernandes' visit to Vietnam in 2000 when both signed a 15-point Defence Assistance Agreement which created an institutionalised framework for regular meetings between the Defence Ministers of both the nations. The navies and Coast Guards of both countries have been conducting regular joint exercises. Besides, India offered considerable expertise to the Vietnamese Navy in safeguarding its marine properties in the Gulf of Tonkin and the South China Sea.[51] On the strategic front, the long bonhomie and political solidarity between the two reached new heights when a Joint Declaration on Strategic Partnership was signed by the Prime Ministers of two countries, Manmohan Singh and Nguyen Tan Dung in July 2007. Towards strengthening security relations, Indian Defence Minister A.K. Antony, visited Vietnam in December 2007 and announced that, "New Delhi will transfer 5,000 items of naval spares belonging to Petya class of ships to Vietnam to make many of the ageing vessels operational.[52] He also said after the conclusion of the First ASEAN Plus Eight Defence Ministers Meeting in Hanoi in October 2010, that, "New Delhi will provide support to Vietnam to enhance and upgrade the capabilities of Services in general and the Navy in particular and India will help Vietnam in its capacity building for repair and maintenance of its platforms".[53] Further, an MoU on defence cooperation facilitated the supply of military hardware, ammunition, propellants, MIG spares and aircraft batteries besides providing training facilities. As both possessed military hardware supplied by the former Soviet Union, these two nations have tremendous scope for cooperation in defence industries besides expanding training facilities for military personnel.

India's sustained security cooperation enabled naval goodwill visits to Vietnam and offer of technology in defence and e-technology and technical support to the Vietnamese Navy. As part of the training programme, 49 Vietnamese officers had participated in army and navy courses in India and 64 officers had attended English language courses. Gen. Phung, while expressing his gratitude for providing training facilities to Vietnamese officers, said the Indian-trained Vietnamese military officers "are bringing back valuable knowledge and skills to their work areas".[54] New Delhi has been offering nuclear technical training and assistance to the Vietnam scientists working in nuclear research reactor at Da Lat in Vietnam.

An interesting feature of India-Vietnam bilateral relations is their growing concern about China's assertive posture in the South China Sea maritime region after its emergence as a global power in recent years. This has heightened the tension in the South China Sea, particularly among six claimants of the Paracel and Spratly islands. In the past, Vietnam and India bore the brunt of their northner's aggression. In the context of shifting geopolitical scenario in the region, India and Vietnam have improved their strategic cooperation in safeguarding the sea lanes in the South China Sea. The most significant development in the maritime cooperation was Vietnam's Vice-Admiral Hien's offer of the port of Nha Trang in the South China Sea for use by the Indian Navy. The Indian naval flotilla has been voyaging frequently between the Andamans and Nha Trang.[55] However, India and Vietnam made it explicit that their joint naval exercises were not aimed at any country, but to strengthen India-Vietnam traditional ties. The engagement in security cooperation is mutually beneficial as both can benefit especially in training and the sharing of information on anti-terrorism, sea piracy and transnational crimes. India can draw Vietnamese army expertise in jungle warfare and guerrilla tactics in dealing with insurgency movements effectively.

Meira Kumar, Lok Sabha Speaker, during her visit to Vietnam in May 2011, while admiring Vietnam's achievements in socio-economic development and poverty reduction, noted, "since the two countries lifted their relations to strategic partnership level, bilateral cooperation has been boosted in science and technology, culture, society, diplomacy, security and defence as well as in international forums".[56]

Conclusion

It is an irrefutable fact that Vietnam-China bilateral ties have undergone remarkable change and both have displayed keen desire to work towards a new era of economic accommodation. Yet, the disputes in the South China Sea are figuring much in their relations. On the contrary, Vietnam's relations with India are affable. India-Vietnam relations aim at promoting their interests for mutual benefit as well as for establishing peace and security in Asia. As the Southeast Asian region is becoming an arena of interest for the great powers again, Vietnam seeks to develop further friendly cooperation not only with India but also with China.

References

1. China claimed that in the past it provided the DRV with economic assistance of more than US $ 20 billion and sent more than 20,000 advisers and 300,000 soldiers. Tatsume Okabe, "Coping with China," in Jacques Morley and Masashi Nishihara (eds.), *Vietnam Joins the World*, ME. Sharpe, New York, 1997, p. 117.

2. Nayan Chanda, *Brother Enemy*, New York, 1986, pp.126-127.
3. Pao-min Chang, *The Sino-Vietnamese Territorial Dispute*, New York, 1986, p. 5.
4. William J. Duiker, "Looking Beyond Cambodia: China and Vietnam," *Indochina Issues*, No. 88, June 1989.
5. *Ibid.*
6. *Ibid.*
7. *Summary of World Broadcasts (SWB)*, FE/4446/C1/6, 19 December 1986.
8. *Ibid.* FE/8445/C/5, 18 December 1986.
9. *Asia 1989 Yearbook*, p. 251.
10. Do Thi Thuy, "The Implementation of Vietnam-China Land Border Treaty: Bilateral and Regional Implications," S. Rajaratnam School of International Studies, Singapore, 5 March 2009, p. 3.
11. *Ibid.*
12. Subhash Kapila, "Vietnam in China's Strategic Calculus: An Analysis." www.southasiaanalysis.org/%5Cpapers17%5Cpaper1609.html.
13. Chen Jiabao, "A New Era Begins in Sino-Vietnamese Relations," *Beijing Review*, 18-24 November 1991, p. 4.
14. Ang Chung Guan, "Vietnam-China Relations Since the End of the Cold War", *Working Paper*, Institute of Defence and Strategic Studies, Singapore, November 1998, p. 3. www.ntu.edu.sg/idss/WorkingPapers/Wp01.pdf.
15. *The Daily Yomiuri*, 1 December 1992.
16. *International Herald Tribute*, 4 December 1992 and *Asia 1994 Yearbook* Hong Kong, p. 222.
17. *Indochina Digest*, 25 November1994; *International Herald Tribune*, 23 November 1994; *The Daily Yomiuri*, 23 November 1994.
18. Brantly Womack, *China and Vietnam : Politics of Asymmetry*, New York, 2006, pp. 26-28.
19. "Vietnam Stance: to 'comrades and brothers' to properly deal with the spirit of maritime disputes", http://wuxinghongqi.blogspot.com/2009/03/vietnam-stance-to-comrades-and-brothers.html.

20. http://www.chinapost.com.tw/china/national-news/2010/07/05/263316/ Vietnam-China.htm.
21. Alexander L. Vuving, "Changing Synthesis of Strategies: Vietnam's China Policy Since 1990," paper presented at Conference on "Regenerations: New Leaders, New Visions in Southeast Asia", Yale University, New Haven, November 11-12, 2005, p.15.
22. "ADB Approves Largest-Ever Project Loan for Billion-Dollar Highway Linking Ha Noi, Kunming", http://www.adb.org/media/Articles/2007/12330-vietnamese-highways- developments; Do Tien Sam and Ha Thi Hong Van, "Vietnam-China Relations and Building the "Two Corridors, One Economic Circle," at the International conference on China's Future: Pitfalls, Prospects and the Implications for ASEAN and the World, Kuala Lumpur, 5-6 March 2009.
23. www.vnemba.org.cn/en/nr050706234129/
24. Hai Thi Hong Van and Do Tien Sam, "Vietnam-China Trade, FDI and ODA Relations (1998-2008) and the Impacts upon Vietnam," www.ide.go.jp/English/ Publish/.../01_vietnamandchina.pdf
25. Ha Thi Hong Van, "Comparison of Vietnam and East Asia (China, Korea and Japan) Economic Relations." in Mitsuhiro Kagami (ed.), *Japan and Korea with the Mekong River Basin Countries*, BRC Research Report, No. 3, Bangkok, 2010, p. 263.
26. *Ibid.* p. 243.
27. Hai Thi Hong Van and Do Tien Sam, N.24, p. 370.
28. Brantly Womack, N. 18.
29. Hai Thi Hong Van and Do Tien Sam, N.24, p.376.
30. Do Thi Thuy, N. 10.
31. Brantly Womack, N. 18.
32. Ha Ti Hong and Do Tien Sam, N.24, p. 372.
33. Ha Thi Hong Van, N.25, p. 232.
34. Vietnam Stance: to "comrades and brothers" to properly deal with the spirit of maritime disputes", http://wuxinghangqi.blogsport.com/2009/ 03/vietnam-stone
35. www.mofa.gov.vn/cn/cn-vakv/ca-tbd/nr040818094447/ ns050117143913.
36. http://gpj.mofcom.gov.cn/accessory/200704/1177554168731.pdf.

37. Zhang Haibing, "China's Aid to Southeast Asia," in Saw Swee-Hock (ed.), *ASEAN-China Economic Relations*, Singapore 2007, pp. 250 and 260.

38. www.mofa.gov.vn/cn/cn-vakv/ca-tbd/nr040818094447/_ns050117143913

39. *Statistical Year Book 2010*, Statistical Publishing House, Hanoi, 2010, p. 490.

40. Do Thi Thuy, N.10.

41. *Ibid.*

42. "China, Vietnam settle land border issue," http://news.xinhuanet.com/ english/ 2009-02/23/content_10878785.htm

43. http//.news.xinhuanet.com/English/

44. Ang Cheng Guan, N. 14.

45. Alexander L. Vuving, "Strategy and Evolution of Vietnam's China Policy : A Changing Mixture of Pathways," *Asian Survey*, Vol. XLVI, No. 6, November December 2006, p. 815.

46. Denny Roy, "Southeast Asia and China: Balancing or Bandwagoning?" *Contemporary Southeast Asia*, Vol. 27, No.2, 2005, p. 316. And http:// vietnam.usembassy.gov/chronology.html

47. Crlyle A. Thayer, "Vietnam's Defensive Diplomacy : Hanoi Signals that it Views an American Military Presence in the Region as Legitimate," *The Wall Street Journal*, 19 August 2010.

48. Nguyen Huy Hoang, "Exploring Areas for Cooperation in Vietnam-India Economic Relations in the Context of ASEAN-India Free Trade Agreement," in Vijay Sakhuja (ed.), *India-Vietnam Strategic Partnership: Exploring Vistas for Expanded Cooperation*, New Delhi, 2011, p.19.

49. Pankaj K. Jha, "India-Vietnam Relations: Need for Enhanced Cooperation," *Strategic Analysis*, Vol. 32, No. 6, November 2008, pp. 1094-1095, Vibhanshu Shekhar, "Indian Investment in the Indochina: Emerging Trends," http:// www.ipcs.org/article/southeast-asia/indian-investment-in-the-indochina-emerging-trends-2741.html

50. P.V. Rao, "India and Vietnam: Forging a Durable Strategic Partnership," in Vijay Sakhuja (ed.), n. 48, p. 151.

51. John Cherian, "Friend in Need," *Frontline*, Vol. 24, Issue, 14, July 14-27, 2007.

52. India, Vietnam to Boost Defence, Strategic Cooperation http://www.india-defence.com/reports/3652; also see, Subhash Kapila, "Vietnam-India: Time to Make Partnership Truly Strategic," http://www.southasiaanalysis.org/%5Cpapers22%5Cpaper2169.html

53. India and Vietnam to Expand Defence Cooperation Covering all Three Services, http://www.indian-military.org/news-archives/indian-army-news/1072-india-and-vietnam-to-expand-defence-cooperation-covering-all-three-services.html

54. "India, Vietnam to Boost Defence, Strategic Cooperation," N. 52.

55. Bharat Karnad, "Good morning, Nam," *Deccan Chronicle*, 7 July 2011.

56. "Vietnam, India agree to deepen relations," http://www.intellasia.net/news/articles/ governance/111324882.shtml

12

The Sino – Indian Border Problem: Need for Pragmatic Approach

L. Premashekhara

I

It is an irony of history that the frontier separating Asia's two giants– China and India– was transformed from the one guarded by a few hundred club-wielding policemen into world's highly militarised one in a surprisingly short period in the latter half of 1950s. The frontier erupted almost suddenly, led to acrimonious charges and counter-charges eventually culminating into the border war of October – November 1962 that wounded India's pride. Although several attempts were initiated by both governments in the form of bilateral talks and confidence building measures in the 1980s that led to several agreements initiating an era of mutual economic and scientific cooperation, the border issue remains unresolved and raises its ugly head like a hydra time and again. This paper attempts to analyse the actual nature of the problem and raises certain questions about the very genuineness of the problem itself. In other words, the aim of the paper is to probe with the help of the "Three Frontiers Theory" (see next page for details) whether there is really a border problem between the two countries *now*. It also attempts to make a hypothetical analysis on the possibilities of this *unresolved* border dispute leading to one more round of bloody conflict between today's two fastest growing economies in the world.

What all happened, in the realm of Sino-Indian relations during 1949-62, has become an inseparable and unforgettable chapter in the history of modern India. The plethora of material, painstakingly researched and compiled by numerous scholars,[1] conclusively establishes that there were two broad sets of reasons for the war of 1962. The Indian insistence on the legitimacy of one of the several lines that put the whole of Aksai Chin under its control and New Delhi's undue haste in getting it accepted by Beijing either through negotiations or through low-key military operations during 1959-62 described as "Forward Policy" belong to the first set of reasons. On the other hand, frequent changes and shifts in China's claims and stances form the second set of reasons.

Before proceeding further' it is relevant at this point to introduce the basic principles of the "Three Frontiers Theory" in order to properly equip the reader to understand and appreciate the contents and conclusions this paper tries to present.

> The Three Frontiers Theory classifies the frontiers between the states of the world into three categories– (i) Single-edged frontiers, (ii) Double-edged frontiers, and (iii) Dull frontiers. Single-edged frontier is the one that gives strategic advantage to one of the two states say State A. Double-edged frontier provides strategic advantage to both State A and State B. The Dull frontier does not give any strategic advantage to either.
>
> The frontier, that existed between and the boundary line that separated Germany and France during 1871 to 1919, was a very good example of single-edged frontiers. It provided considerable amount of strategic advantage to the newly unified Germany vis-à-vis France, thereby acting as a single-edged frontier in Germany's favour. There are innumerable examples for double-edged frontiers and perhaps the most striking one is the Radcliffe Line that separates India and Pakistan. This Line provides strategic advantage to both countries, thereby forcing the two to maintain constant vigil on each other's motives and moves. The present line of control or the de-facto frontier between India and China is the best example of dull frontiers. It doesn't provide any kind of strategic advantage to either and has eliminated the usefulness of an armed conflict between the two neighbours ever since it was created as a result of the border war of 1962.

> For the sake of convenience the state that enjoys strategic advantage in the case of a single-edged frontier is referred to as **Ridge State**, and the one that is deprived of that advantage as **Valley State.** This nomenclature has been coined on the basis of the general assumption that one who positions himself on a ridge tends to possess advantage vis a vis the one in the valley below. In the case of a double-edged frontier, the two states on its either side can be called **Plain States;** since both of them are on equal footing just like two contenders standing on an even surface enjoy relatively equal amount of advantage among themselves. Similarly, in the case of dull frontiers, the states that lie on either side of that can be called as **Canyon States** since a canyon hardly allows the two adversaries on its either side to gain any advantage against one another (Premashekhara, 2008: 13-14).

The Sino – Indian frontier saw military activities in a major scale on its eastern flank during the beginning of the second decade of the previous century. It was India that initiated those military activities and China did the same in the western flank forty years later. These military moves, first by India and followed by China later, together are, according to the "Three Frontiers Theory", attempts on the part of New Delhi and Beijing to convert "Single-edged Frontiers" against themselves into "Dull Frontiers".

II

There existed no linear boundary[2] between India and China before an attempt for creating one for the first time in history was initiated by India during 1911-14. In fact, no linear boundary existed between empires/kingdoms of Asia in the historical past. What separated one from the other was a broad stretch of land of varying width usually being a geographical landmark like a mountain, or a desert and the like. Interestingly, rivers which are closer to linear boundaries in nature hardly acted as lines that separated one empire from the other. Usually these frontiers (between two empires) were uninhabitable areas or areas with sparse tribal or nomadic population which was numerically a minority and militarily insignificant and consequently played no role in the regional politics of the time thus posed no threat to or undermined the interests of the empires which they separated. The reason for Asiatic states not attempting to establish linear boundaries was probably the frequent changes in the location of frontiers. The constant warfare between the states never allowed a particular stretch of land to remain as a frontier for a time span adequately enough for it to secure acceptance and legitimacy. Thus, absence of permanent frontiers was the reason for absence of linear frontiers or at least attempts at establishing them.[3] It was so in the case of India and China too. Of course, the mighty Himalayas were regarded as the traditional frontiers between the two civilisations. But the fact is that it was not quiet most of the time. Military activities involving the armies of Tibet, Nepal, Punjab (the Sikhs), Kangra, Jammu, Kashmir, Ladakh, Hunza, Baltistan and, occasionally, imperial China were common during the historical period causing constant shifts in frontiers. As a result, when "the Republic of India and the People's Republic of China, after they came into existence, had faced an unfinished task: How to convert their frontiers into legal boundaries" (Swamy, 2001: 39).

Before 1911 Tibetan suzerainty extended to areas south of the Himalayas in the eastern sector.[4] In other words, the present north-eastern state of Arunachal Pradesh was not under the political and military control of British India. The traditional frontier between Tibetan territories and British India ran roughly along the northern edges of the Brahmaputra plains far below the mighty Himalayas which were traditionally believed to be an impassable wall providing absolute protection to India from any invading army from the north.[5] The British Indian troops in Assam would have been put under tremendous stress, if Tibet became expansionist or it came under stricter Chinese control once again, as was the case before the decline of the Beijing-based imperial authority.[6] In this way this line acted as a Single-edged Frontier in favour of Tibet of which China was the suzerain and thus India found itself in the unenviable position of a Valley State.

In order to eliminate any future threat from either Tibet or China or Russia, a section of the British Indian authorities conceived a plan of pushing the Indo-Tibetan frontier to the higher reaches of the Himalayas and also delineate it. Colonel Francis Younghusband led an expedition in 1911 into the Tibetan territories, south of the Himalayas, and successfully established Indian authority there. These territories, which British India established *de-facto* control, were christened "North Eastern Frontier Agency (NEFA)".[7] An unsuccessful attempt to formalise Indian sovereignty over these newly acquired territories was made by the British Indian authorities during 1913-14. When the tripartite negotiations involving India, China and Tibet held in Shimla in 1913 failed to produce the desired result, Sir Henry McMahon, the then Foreign Secretary of the Indian government arranged bilateral talks with Tibet in New

Delhi in March 1914. The boundary line he proposed and got accepted by the Tibetan representative in this meeting bore his name and ran almost right along the crest of the Himalayan Mountains, thus establishing a natural boundary between India and Tibet. The Tibetan authorities in Lhaasa, however, soon repudiated their representative's action of accepting the McMahon Line. As a bigger blow to the Indian official's plan, the Chinese government too declared that any agreement between Tibet and India would be "illegitimate and null" (Swamy, 2001: 42).

Sir Henry McMahon had a vision about the necessity of linear boundary for the security of India which, unfortunately, was not understood and shared by his superiors in New Delhi and London at that time. His efforts which were aimed at converting the Single-edged Frontier against India in the eastern sector into a Dull Frontier were met with opposition not only from Chinese side but by the very government he represented. The then Viceroy, in his report to London, disowned McMahon's dealings with the Tibetan representative. The British government too expressed it's disapproval of McMahon's moves by transferring him from India to Egypt (*Ibid.*). Even the Survey of India did not include NEFA in India in its maps. Thus Sir Henry McMahon became a tragic hero in the saga of India's quest for converting Single-edged Frontier into Dull Frontier in the eastern sector.

The British authorities finally accepted the relevance of McMahon Line in the 1930s and maintained that it was India's legal boundary with Tibet and the Survey of India too followed suit by publishing maps that showed NEFA as Indian territory for the first time in 1938. After some initial hesitation, the government of independent India too echoed this view when Prime Minister Jawaharlal Nehru asserted in the Parliament: "Our maps show McMahon Line is our boundary and that is our boundary-map or no map. The fact remains that we stand by that boundary, and we will not allow anybody to come across that boundary." (Maxwell, 1997: 75). This assertion by Nehru is a clear indication that the government of independent India accepted the perception of the erstwhile British colonial regimes regarding the necessity of McMahon Line for India's security. It demonstrated its resolve to continue the policy of converting Single-edged Frontiers against India into Dull Frontiers when it annexed in February 1952 Tawang which the British had left with the Tibetans despite it being located south of the Himalayas as well as the McMahon Line. China which had established politico-military control over Tibet an year ago did not react to the Indian move at all. "This puzzling silence can be construed as China's acquiescence in India's filling out in the McMahon Line" (Maxwell, 1997: 73). In the Sino-Indian war of October-November 1962, the Chinese People's Liberation Army (PLA) violated the McMahon Line, crossed the Himalayan Mountains occupied Tawang and made significant gains further south.[8] The Chinese government, however, declared unilateral cease-fire after a month long campaign, vacated all the occupied areas including Tawang and withdrew its army to its own territory, north of the McMahon Line. Though this action of Beijing has all elements of a typical Chinese riddle, it is not difficult to decipher it. Had the PLA remained in the areas south of the Himalayan Mountains for some more time, it would have been cut off from China once the mountain passes got closed due to heavy snowing during winter which was about to set in. In such an eventuality, the Chinese soldiers would have become sitting ducks for Indian army and the impressive victory achieved by the PLA would have turned into a great fiasco for Beijing (Premashekhara, 2008: 17). The Chinese realised the fact that it would be difficult or even impossible for them to keep NEFA (present Arunachal Pradesh) under their control during winter, since the Indians enjoyed easy access to that territory throughout the year including winter months. The peculiarity or uniqueness of this region is that a Chinese controlled Arunachal Pradesh would act as Single-edged Frontier in India's favour during winter and in China's favour during the rest of the year! It would, in a way, act as a Double-edged Frontier. It means this frontier would never be quiet. In order to avoid such a situation, Chinese authorities realised the fact that it would be wise to regard the McMahon Line as boundary line since it was a Dull Frontier and did not provide strategic advantage to either of the powers, did nothing to disturb it except issuing statements staking their claim on the territories south of the McMahon Line. Thus the Sino-Indian frontier in the eastern sector was first converted by the British into a Dull Frontier during 1911-14 and was accepted by the Chinese as such later in 1962.[9]

III

The Sino-Indian frontier in the western sector is more complex in nature than its eastern counterpart. Here, it was China that converted a Single-edged Frontier in India's favour into a Dull Frontier. There existed no clearly delineated boundary between Ladakh region of Jammu & Kashmir and Uyghur Xinjiang (formerly Sinkiang) and the British exhibited least interest in having one ever since they came to possess Kashmir following their victory over Maharaja Ranjit Singh in the Fourth Sikh War in 1839. The governments in both London and Kolkata,[10] however, were alarmed when an Imperial Russian army led by Capt. Grombechevsky reached Hunza in northern Kashmir in 1888 after his successful campaigns in Central Asia. The Russians, if allowed, were capable of threatening the densely populated Punjab which also had the distinction of being the bread basket of British India.

A careful study of British India's frontier policy in the north shows that London and Kolkata always wanted "friendly buffers" lying between densely populated regions of northern India on the one hand and imperial Russia and China on the other. Their attitudes towards and dealings with Afghanistan, Swat and Tibet were all demonstrative of this policy. Capt. Grombechevsky's entry into northern Kashmir evidently disturbed British India's "friendly buffers" policy, exposed densely populated northern India to potential dangers unless London did something drastic against the Russians. The British apprehension and their threat perception *vis a vis* the Russians were demonstrated by Capt. Algermon Durand, the well-known frontier expert when he said "the game had begun" (Woodman, 1969: 72). Northern Kashmir suddenly assumed strategic importance and led to the British efforts at defining Kashmir's boundaries with Afghanistan in the north-west and China in the north-east. They did conclude an agreement with Kabul formally delineating Afghanistan's border with India in 1893. The Russian threat in the north-west was considerably reduced when the British signed a treaty with Moscow on 11 March 1895 according to which a narrow corridor called "Wakhan" was created between the Russian controlled Tazhik territories on the one hand and Swat Valley of the newly created North West Frontier Province (NWFP) and Gilgit region of the princely state of Jammu & Kashmir of the British Indian Empire on the other, and the same was placed under the control of Kabul (Premashekhara, 2008: 22).

With regard to the issue of delineating Kashmir's boundary with China in the Aksai Chin region,[11] the British contemplated three lines – Ardagh-Johnson Line, Macartney-MacDonald Line, and Trelawney Saunders Line.[12] While the Ardagh-Johnson Line,[13] running along the Kuen Lun Range in the north and northeast, placed the whole of Aksai Chin within the territory of Kashmir, the Macartney-MacDonald Line,[14] on the other hand, put much of Aksai Chin in Sinkiang. The earlier Trelawney Saunders Line[15] ran along the Karakoram Range and thus placed the whole of Aksai Chin in Sinkiang (Lamb, 1964: 86).

The British, however, did nothing serious to get any one of these lines accepted by Beijing as there appeared to be no consensus among the various officials and bodies dealing with Indian affairs in London and Kolkata. Initially John Ardagh's views of placing the entire Aksai Chin in India gained acceptance in London when he argued that China's weakness made it useless as a buffer between northern frontiers of British Indian Empire and the Russian Empire. Highlighting the eagerness with which Russia annexed the whole of Central Asia in less than forty years and advanced its borders towards India, Ardagh predicted that Moscow would eventually annex western part of Sinkiang and pose serious threat to India's security in the Kashmir region and argued for extending Indian sovereignty right up to the Kuen Lun Range with the whole of Aksai Chin within Indian territory (Maxwell, 1997: 32). Although he conceded that in general sense the Karakoram mountains formed a natural boundary, "easy to define, difficult to pass and fairly dividing the people on either side", he rejected this mountain range as proper border as it's very "physical condition" would deny Indian army of proper information regarding the movement of the enemy on the other side (*Ibid.*). The officials in India, however, rejected Ardagh's views as "impractical theorising of an armchair general" (*Ibid.*). The Viceroy Lord Elgin "warned" London that any attempt to implement the Ardagh-Johnson Line and bring Aksai Chin under Indian control would "entail a real risk of strained relations with China and furthermore might precipitate the very Russian advance which Ardagh wished to forestall".[16] London accepted the Indian officials' point of view and approved the Macartney-MacDonald Line and the same was proposed to the Chinese on 14 March 1899 (*Ibid.*: 33). Thus, this Macartney-MacDonald Line was the only border line British India officially ever proposed to China. The Chinese, however, never replied to this proposal.

The British lost their interest in the issue, once the Russian threat disappeared, following the Anglo-Russian Convention of 1907 and China ceased to be a source of threat as it plunged into political instability following the revolution of 1911. These developments, and several other similar ones which the history of the British Empire, in Asia in particular and the world in general, is replete with, amply demonstrate that London's attitude towards India's borders with its neighbours was determined not by India's interests and it was the empire's interests *vis a vis* other empires that guided the British in this regard. It was the two variables of Russia and China that shaped London's policy towards India's borders. In the words of Stephen

A. Hoffmann:

> They [the British] had to be concerned with the political and strategic implications for the empire of any boundary agreement concluded with other powers bordering India. Such powers included Russia and China, and relations with them were seen from London as set by such matters as Anglo-Russian dealings in Europe and the Middle East and British interests on the mainland of China. Thus, London tended toward the avoidance of forward claims and lines.
>
> (Hoffmann, 1990: 14).

Thus, the "British approach towards the border was that of an imperial power and not one of defending Indian nation state". (Swamy, 2001: 42). Despite these historical ambiguities and absence of any formal treaties, the government of independent India unilaterally accepted a slightly modified Ardagh-Johnson Line as the international boundary between India and China insisting on New Delhi's sovereignty over the whole of Aksai Chin. This stand was not effectively challenged as long as civil war raged on in China and Chinese frontier remained receded far away from India as Tibet enjoyed independence and Sinkiang experienced Russian influence. Once China achieved political stability under the communists following their victory in the civil war in 1949 Tibet lost its independence to the new central government in Beijing, Sinkiang was once again reverted to Chinese rule and consequently, China's frontier once again came closer to that of India. History repeated itself then and Aksai Chin once again became a *disputed* territory.

The British maps had shown no marked boundary at all in the Sino-Indian frontiers from Nepal to Afghanistan. The Survey of India continued to reproduce the same maps for several years after independence. It, however, published maps in 1954 marking a definitive boundary between India and China in the western sector which placed the whole of Aksai Chin in India. India did insist time and again that Aksai Chin belonged to it but did nothing to establish its authority there. New Delhi became aware of Chinese presence in that region only when the Chinese media announced in 1957 that their frontier guards and about three thousand civilian builders had completed the construction of a road there. Although the Indian ambassador in Peking reported this matter to New Delhi in September 1957, the latter took ten full months to send a patrol team in Aksai Chin to find out whether the Chinese claim on road construction was true.[17]

Then onwards, began a series of allegations, accusations, counter-accusations and failed negotiations with China firmly holding on to its claim. Beijing on its part changed its claims over border lines frequently pushing the same westward every time thus arousing Indian anxiety greatly (Woodman, 1969: 245-78). All these finally led to the border war of October-November 1962 which resulted in the Chinese occupation of all the areas right up to the Karakoram Mountains. Beijing's attitude here was markedly different from its policy in the eastern sector. Here, the PLA didn't withdraw from the region as it did in the east; instead, maintained that the Karakoram Mountains were the traditional frontier between Kashmir and Sinkiang and the same must be accepted as international boundary between the two countries. Beijing was reasonable in thinking that the extension of Indian sway over areas beyond the Karakoram Mountains would make Aksai Chin a Single-edged Frontier in India's favour throughout the year except the winter months and seriously undermine Chinese security in and control over Tibet. Hence, they wanted to limit Indian control up to the Karakoram Mountains only thus creating a natural and Dull Frontier between the two countries.[18]

Neither any government in London nor any British Administrator in India had ever attempted to extend India's control beyond the Karakoram Mountains although such an idea was contemplated whenever Russian, and Chinese to a lesser extent, threat came closer to India's northern frontiers. At the same time, they never accepted any hostile element being present on this side of the Mountains. In other words, they wanted mighty mountain ranges to form India's northern frontiers in both eastern and western sectors. They extended Indian authority up to the Himalayas in the east during 1911-14 and maintained that Macartney-MacDonald Line which ran almost along the eastern slopes of the Karakoram Range was India's limit in the western sector. They were well aware of the danger the empire was to face, should it cross the Karakoram as the areas beyond that mountain range were indefensible from Indian side. The government of independent India, however, lacked such wisdom and followed an ill-conceived and audacious policy and challenged Beijing's authority over Aksai Chin when China emerged, with a fiercely nationalist government under the communists, stronger after decades of chaos and re-uniting all the regions under strong central authority. The British had avoided such a daring policy during their heydays as global power and China offered little resistance. The policy India followed towards China with regard to the border issue was geographically unscientific, strategically illogical, politically irresponsible and militarily suicidal. It was doomed to end in disaster and humiliation, and that is what happened finally.

IV

The above analysis shows that the Sino-Indian frontier which was Single-edged in India's favour in the western sector and in China's favour in the east was converted into a Dull Frontier during the period between 1911 and 1962. Although Beijing and New Delhi have not officially accepted the change, they have not done anything significant to disturb the *status quo* and alter the so-called "Line of Actual Control" (LAC) since the end of the war of 1962 giving the indications they feel that there exists no border dispute between India and China. Of course, there have been minor incursions into each other's territories, the Somdorong Chu incident of June 1986 and the Kongka Pass incident of July-August 2009 being the major ones. Such incidents are bound to occur when borders are not defined in written agreements and delineated on land. Both countries handled these incidents in positive manner and never allowed the situation on the ground to deteriorate. The Indian government's handling of the situation in the present case is particularly remarkable. It has not given in to media outrage and remained calm maintaining that there were inbuilt mechanisms to handle these kinds of situations effectively. This is markedly different from New Delhi's attitudes during similar situations before the war of 1962. Reality being so, it is unlikely that India and China will go to war over the boundary issue again. Such a war will alter the Dull Frontier created over a period of half a century of military moves and push India and China to situations similar to the one existed before 1962 which is not going to serve the interest of either country.

In fact, New Delhi and Beijing have concluded, apart from the significant "Agreement on the Maintenance of Peace and Tranquillity Along the Line of Actual Control in the India - China Border" signed during the official visit of Prime Minister P. V. Narasimha Rao to the Chinese capital in September 1993,[19] several agreements to maintain peace along this LAC. Therefore, it can be safely assumed that both New Delhi and Beijing have realised the fact that the present LAC is the scientific boundary between the two countries. Their hesitation to officially convert the LAC into official international border is understandable. Such a move will, especially in India, create strong public resentment. Such resentment is actually the result of lack of understanding of history on the part of the Indian people. A careful analysis of the historical documents and proper understanding of events in the past 120 years, demonstrate clearly enough that India has been the gainer in its border row with China. India now possesses Arunachal Pradesh, which was in fact not a part of its territory before 1911. On the other hand, Aksai Chin, which is under Chinese control now was part of Indian territory only in maps as a result of

British India's ambiguous policies and independent India's cartographic expansion in 1954. In reality, India never controlled that region.[20] If the Indian public is properly educated on historical facts, they may not oppose any move by their government to convert the LAC into international boundary.

In fact, the Chinese offered to convert the LAC with minor modifications into international border between the two countries in the fifth round of border talks held during 1983-84. This meant China was ready to recognise Indian sovereignty over Arunachal Pradesh, provided India accepted Chinese sovereignty over Aksai Chin. The Indian government, however, rejected it (Sali, 1998: 113, Ganguly, 2009: 14). The Chinese offer was wise in more than one respect and Indian acceptance of the same would have solved the vexed border row, freed Indian armed forces from the tremendous burden they have been shouldering and radically overhauled Sino-Indian relations. It is difficult to gauge whether China still favours such a solution to the border problem. However, it is in the interest of the Indian people and government to probe the matter and work for legitimising the LAC as international border and formally establish "Dull Frontiers" which will remove the threat of any armed conflict between the two Asian giants. A Dull Frontier with China is very much in India's interest. It will free India from the tremendous tension along its northern borders and help New Delhi to deal with challenges and threats emanating from other sources and directions more effectively and decisively.

References

1. Some of them are: Hoffmann, Steven (1990), *India and the China Crisis*, Oxford University Press, Delhi; Lamb, Alastair (1964), *The China – India Border: The Origin of the Disputed Boundaries*, Oxford University Press, London; .... (1966), *The McMahon Line*, 2 Vols., Routledge and Kegan Paul, London; .... (1975), *The Sino Indian Border in Ladakh*, University of South Carolina Press, Columbia; Maxwell, Neville (1970), *India' China War*, London; Swamy, Subramanian (2001), *India's China Perspective*, Konark Publishers Pvt. Ltd., New Delhi; Woodman, Dorothy (1969), *Himalayan Frontier*, Barrie and Rockliff; London.

2. A Boundary is a geographic line agreed to in diplomatic negotiations (delineation), jointly marked out on the ground (demarcation), thereafter visualised on a map (cartography), and accurately formalised between two sovereign governments (treaty), in which each thus recognised the limits of its own and that of its neighbour's territory. See: Swamy, Subramanian, (2001), *India's China Perspective*, Konark Publishers Pvt. Ltd., New Delhi, p. 39.

3. Perhaps the first ever linear boundaries in continental Asia were established by the Russians to separate their newly conquered Central and Northeast Asian territories from Sinkiang and Manchuria of imperial China in the second half of the 19th century. British and French colonisers followed suit in Southeast Asia at the end of that century

4. The areas, lying south of the Himalayas and north of the Assam plains, were not parts of Tibet in the strict sense. Arunachal Pradesh, as that region is known today was fragmented and was under the control of several tribal chieftains. These chieftains in turn owed their allegiance to the Tibetan rulers in Lhasa.

5. In other words, the boundary line that now separates India's two northeastern states of Assam and Arunacal Pradesh was roughly the boundary between British India and Tibetan territories.

6. The threat the British rulers were apprehensive of at that time was in fact not coming from either the Chinese or the Tibetans. The Imperial Russian advance into Central Asia had begun in the middle of the 19th Century. The Russian campaign was swift and decisive and by late 1880s, the Russians annexed what are now called Central Asian Republics and their armies were knocking at the doors of Kashmir and Chinese Turkestan. A Russian army led by Captain Grombechevsky actually landed in Hunza in Northern Kashmir in 1888. At the same time Peking's authority over the remote western province of Sinkiang was gradually weakening because of various politico-social, ethnic and religious reasons. There was a danger of Russians extending their sway over that region and then entering into the adjoining Tibet. Had they succeeded in that adventure then they would have posed serious threat to both Northern and Northeastern regions of India.

7. NEFA was a part of the state of Assam for some times. In 1972, it was accorded the status of a Union Territory with a new name of Arunachal Pradesh. Full statehood followed suit fifteen years later in 1987.

8. The Chinese army came right up to Bomdila, just 80 kilometer north of Tezpur and 40 kilometers away from oil fields at Dig Boi and thus threatening to enter the Assam plains.

9. Though the Chinese have not given up their official claim over Arunachal Pradesh yet, the fact remains that they have not done anything significant to disturb the McMahon Line since 1962, despite their overwhelming superiority against the Indians as far as military strength is concerned. Though the Somdorong Chu incident of 1986 created some resentment in New Delhi, it was amicably settled by the end of the year and was soon forgotten.

10. Kolkata, or Calcutta as it was known till recently, was the capital of the British Indian empire during the 19th Century and it enjoyed that position until the capital was shifted to the newly built city of New Delhi in 1911.

11. Aksai Chin is a triangular elevated tableland lying between the Karakoram Mountains in the west, Tibetan Plateau in the east, and Kuen Lun mountain range and low lying Uyghur Xinjiang (Sinkiang) beyond in the north. Geographically, it is an extension of the great Tibetan plateau. It is easily accessible from the Chinese side, whereas the high-rise Karakoram Mountains deny India similar easy access.

12. These names were coined by Alastair Lamb (1964) in his book: *The China – India Border: The Origin of the Disputed Boundaries*, Oxford University Press, London.

13. This line is called "Ardagh-Johnson Line" as it was prepared way back in 1863 by Survey of India explorer W. H. Johnson and later proposed to the government of India in 1897 by the chief of British military intelligence in London, Major General Sir John Ardagh. See: Woodman, Dorothy (1969), *Himalayan Frontier*, Barrie and Rockliff; London, pp. 360-65.

14. This line was suggested to the Viceroy Lord Elgin by George Macartney, the British representative in Kashgar and proposed to the Chinese, on behalf of the viceroy, by Claude MacDonald, the British minister in Peking.

15. This line was drawn by the India Office cartographer Trelawney Saunders for the Foreign Office in 1973.

16. The full text of Viceroy Elgin's official communication to London can be found in Dorothy Woodman, (1969), *Himalayan Frontier*, Barrie and Rockliff; London, pp. 364-65.

17. One of the two patrols, that went towards the southern section of Aksai Chin, reported in October that the Chinese had indeed built a road there. The other patrol that went to the north disappeared. It was later learnt that they had been detained and later 'deported back' to Indian territory by the Chinese. The unfortunate patrol team was lucky to be discovered and rescued after being dumped by the Chinese at the Karakoram Pass far away from any nearby Indian post.

18. Karakoram Mountains are the second highest mountain ranges in the world next only to the Himalayas.

19. For the full text of this Agreement, see: Sali, M. L., (1998). *India-China Border Dispute- A Case Study of the Eastern Sector*, (A.P.H. Publishing Corporation, New Delhi, pp. 288-92.

20. It's interesting to note that Indians learned of Chinese presence in Aksai Chin only when Beijing officially announced in mid-50s that it had completed the construction of a road in that region.

REFERENCES

Ganguly, Swagato, "Grouchy Tiger, Misread Dragon" in *Times of India*, (Chennai), 8 October 2009.

Hoffmann, Steven (1990), *India and the China Crisis*, Oxford University Press, Delhi.

Lamb, Alastair (1964), *The China – India Border: The Origin of the Disputed Boundaries*, Oxford University Press, London.

.... (1966), *The McMahon Line*, 2 Vols., Routledge and Kegan Paul, London.

.... (1975), *The Sino Indian Border in Ladakh*, University of South Carolina Press, Columbia.

Maxwell, Neville, (1997), *India' China War*, Natraj Publishers, Dehra Dun.

Premashekhara, L., (2008), "Three Frontiers Theory: An Explanation to India – Pakistan Animosity" in *International Journal of South Asian Studies* (Pondicherry), Vol. I, No. 1, January – June 2008, pp. 13-32.

Sali, M. L., (1998). *India-China Border Dispute- A Case Study of the Eastern Sector*, A.P.H. Publishing Corporation, New Delhi.

Swamy, Subramanian (2001), *India's China Perspective*, Konark Publishers Pvt. Ltd., New Delhi.

Woodman, Dorothy (1969), *Himalayan Frontier*, Barrie and Rockliff; London.

13

Energy Security of India and China: Some Reflections

A. Subramanyam Raju

Energy security has become an important concern to most of the countries, particularly, the developing countries in the world. Energy availability is one of the requirements to eradicate poverty and improving standards. Safeguarding energy security has thus become an important element in foreign policy. India and China have low levels of energy production and per capita consumption. They depend heavily on indigenous coal to meet energy requirements. China and India are possessing first and fourth largest coal reserves respectively, in the world. They are the largest emitter of green house gases and they rank second and fourth respectively in the world. Their development is linked up with the environment and they need to play a constructive role in reducing the green house emissions.

China and India are the second and seventh largest consumers of oil in the world. Their demand for energy consumption is likely to increase. Both the countries are largely dependent on energy imports and are emerging as major players in the oil and gas market in the world. To meet the future demand, both the countries had incorporated their policies in their foreign policy. Both have realised the need for coherent and enduring foreign energy security policy to secure energy imports without any disturbance. Energy policies of both countries are linked to both politics and the security domain. They depend on sea for their energy imports and hence they need to protect the maritime routes (sea lanes of communication).

Economic reforms, population growth, urbanisation, demographic transition and growing transport sector are resulting in a rapid demand for more and more energy. Many people in India and China still lack access to electricity for their basic needs. The demand for energy consumption is likely to increase in future. Both countries are largely dependent on energy imports. Energy security is linked up with both growth and poverty. On one hand, they have to provide enough commercial energy for growth and on the other hand they have to minimise the inequality between urban and rural people's consumption levels of energy.[1] China and India have been projected as the second and third largest economies by 2020. They have been exploring various options to meet their demands through investment abroad and through bilateral/ multilateral cooperation in the energy sector.

In most of the rural areas of China and India, people use non-commercial energy for their consumption that causes air pollution leading to respiratory, heart and lung problems.[2] There are about 600 million Indians who do not have access to electricity and over 700 million people are using traditional biomass as the primary fuel for the most of their basic needs.[3] There are about 80,000 villages, which are yet to be electrified. Out of these 18,000 villages can be electrified by using renewable resources. Over 800 million inhabitants out of China's total population of 1.3 billion live in rural areas. Among them, 300 million people do not have access to electricity.[4] The consumption level of energy of both the countries has been increased since 1980: 4.3 per cent per year by China and 5.4 per cent by India. The International Energy Agency forecasted that energy demand in both the countries would be doubled by 2030. There is unevenness of development between the different areas and between rural and urban areas in both countries. Both have to address to minimize the disparity.

The paper analyses the existing energy situation in both India and China and their investment abroad. This paper examines both countries' initiatives for cooperation with the neighbouring countries in the energy sector. This paper further analyses competition as well as cooperation between them in addressing their energy requirements.

Energy Security Scenario

India: The Indian government had set up a group on *India's Hydrocarbon Vision 2025* in February 1999. The recommendations put forth by the group are: 100% exploration coverage of Indian sedimentary basins by 2025; exploration in the frontier and deep water areas; offering of attractive fiscal terms; abroad investment in exploration of oil and gas resources; self-sufficiency in Petroleum refining and Storage of oil in various locations.

Table 1: India's Position in Global Energy Production and Trade-2004

	Crude Oil (Mt)	*Coal (Mt)*	*Natural Gas (BCM)*	*Petroleum Products (Mt)*
Global Production	3923	5878	28721	3719
Indian Production*	34 (0.87)	430 (7.32)	32 (0.11)	108 (2.9)
Indian Consumption*	130 (3.31)	454 (7.72)	32 (0.11)	107 (2.9)
Global Trade*	2235 (56.97)	778 (13.24)	838 (29.18)	825 (22.18)
Indian Imports**	96 (4.30)	37 (4.76)	6.9	9.75 (1.18)
Indian Imports Dependence	73.85	8.15	—	—

*Figures in parentheses are percentage of global production;
**Figures in parentheses are percentage of global trade.

Source: EIA, *International Energy Outlook* 2006, Washington DC: US Energy Information Administration, 2006, cited in Nitya Nanda, "Trading in the World Energy", in Logia Noronha and Anant Sudarshan (eds), *India's Energy Security*. London. Routledge. 2009. p. 52.

The data about India's energy production and its trade given in the Table-1 reveals that India is depending more on importing oil than on others. It is the sixth largest importer with a share of 4.3 per cent. Though India produces a large amount of coal but it has become the sixth largest importer of coal. India's trade in natural gas is not significant because of infrastructure constraints and liquefied natural gas imports started only in 2004. In 2002, India spent Rs. 84,000 crore to obtain oil to meet sixty-nine per cent of its oil fuel needs.[5] Its crude oil requirement is seen as growing to 364 mtpa by 2025 from 100 mtpa of now. India's economy is growing since the economic reforms were undertaken. If it has to grow at the rate of eight per cent as per projection, there should be uninterruptible supply of oil. Most of its oil comes from the Middle East. This may make India vulnerable to any event that may cause instability in that region. Any disruption in the oil supplies from the region or any price hike by the oil producers of the region could affect India's economy.

The future energy requirements by India are given in the Table-2. The energy demands from 1997-2020 are going to increase rapidly. For instance, the demand for oil and gas by 2020 would be required more than what it consumed in 1997.

China:

The main objectives of China's energy policy are: Increasing China's control over its energy supplies and maximising the domestic output of oil and gas; increasing investment in overseas oil fields and diversifying the sources of oil and gas supply; the construction of a strategic petroleum reserve system and other infrastructure to bring oil and gas more easily to the Chinese market; closing off oil fields in western China for emergency use; the continued development of Chinese naval forces to protect China's energy supplies.[6] If there is any blockade of sea lanes in the Malacca Straits or in the South and East China seas, then China would become vulnerable, because most of its energy resources ship through these routes. It has been direct economic interest in securing its demands in other regions (Middle East, Russia, Central Asia, Africa and Southeast Asia). The China National Petroleum Company (CNPC)

Table-2: Projected Requirement of Fossil Fuels

Fuel / Unit	*1997*	*2010*	*2020*
Coal (MMT)	233	378	516
Oil (MMT)	111	203	304
Gas (BCM)	33	78	147

Source: *World Economic Outlook, 2000*

realised the importance of securing China's energy demands and it spent $8 billion in 1997 for oil concessions in Kazakhstan, Venezuela, Iraq and Sudan. The government had invested billions of dollars in hydro-electric power schemes like Three Gorges and Ertan which contribute a larger portion of the electrical power supply of central and eastern regions of China.[7]

On the basis of projection given by the International Energy Agency, China's energy demand for coal, oil, gas, nuclear and hydro will increase annually till 2030. However, the demand for biomass and other renewable are going to be negligible (see Table-3). It shows that China's dependency over the fossil fuels will be continued.

Investment abroad

India: One of the recommendations put forth by the group in its vision 2025, was to explore the resources abroad through investment to secure its imports. The Oil & Natural Corporation (ONGC), ONGC Videsh Lmtd (OVL), Gas Authority of India Limited (GAIL) and private companies like Reliance Company have entered into a production-sharing contract. Negotiations are going on for oil explorations in other countries. Table-3 shows India's investment in oil and gas reserves in different parts of the world:

China: Chinese national companies have been involved in exploring oil and gas in countries in Asia, Africa and Latin America. Twenty-eight per cent of Chinese oil imports come from Sudan, Angola, Congo, Nigeria and other African countries. China's companies are very active and aggressive in expanding their presence in other countries.

Having discussed the energy scenario and their investments abroad by India and China, in the following section, an attempt is made to focus on their energy cooperation with others.

Table-3: Energy Demand in China (million tons of oil equivalent)

Year/Fuel	*1971*	*2002*	*2010*	*2030*	*2001-30*
Coal	192	713	904	1,354	2.3%
Oil	43	247	375	636	3.4%
Gas	3	36	375	636	5.4%
Nuclear	0	7	21	73	9.0%
Hydro	3	25	33	63	3.4%
Biomass and Waste	164	216	227	236	0.3%
Other Renewables	0	0	5	20	0%
Total	405	1,244	1,940	3,018	2.60%

Source: *World Energy Outlook 2004*, (Paris: International Energy Agency, 2005), p. 264.

India's and China's Energy Cooperation with their Neighbour Countries:

India and China have realised the fact that it is essential for them to have bilateral/multilateral cooperation to meet its energy needs.

India and Pakistan[8]: India's relationship with Pakistan is very important because any gas pipeline to India from the Middle East/Central Asia would require Pakistan's involvement and partnership. Pakistan has a 500 Kv primary transmission system extending from Jumshoro in the south to Tarbela and Peshawar in the north. All the lines are close to India's borders and may not require very complex transmission extensions. Pakistan's Power Minister stated: "There is a complete network on our side of course, on their (India) side as well. What we need are the connections, which would take a couple of weeks."[9] If Pakistan exports its surplus of power, it not only gets revenue[10] but also it

Table-4: Indian Companies' Investment on Abroad

Country	*Companies*	*Estimated oil resources*
Libya (Ghadames Basin)	OVL: 49% IPR (US): 51%	Estimated oil reserves of 645 million barrels
Sudan (Greater Nile)	OVL:25% China National Petroleum:40% Petronas:30% Sudan National Oil Company: 5%	Estimated oil reserves of 1 billion barrels
Syria	OVL:60% IPR (US): 40%	Reserves yet to be estimated
Iraq (Block 8 Western Desert)	OVL: 100%	Reserves yet to be estimated
Iran (Farsi Offshore)	OVL: 40% Indian Oil: 40% Oil India:20%	Estimated oil reserves of 540 million barrels
Yemen	Reliance: 30% ONGC:40% BP:30%	Reserves yet to be estimated
Myanmar (A 1 block off Rakline Coast)	OVL:20% GAIL:10% Daewoo:60% Kogas:10%	Estimated reserves 14-16 tcf of gas
Vietnam (Nam Conson Basin)	OVL:45% PetroVietnam:5% BP:50%	Estimated reserves of 2.04 tcf of gas
Indonesia (Coal fields)	Tata Power Corporation: 30%	———
South Sumatra	Reliance Company	
Russia (Sakhalin-I)	OVL:20% Exxon-N:30% Sodeco:30% SMNG-S:11.5% RN Astra:8.5%	Estimated reserves of 1.15 billion tones of oil and 20 tcf of gas.
Venezuela (San Cristobal oil field)	OVL: 40% PdVSA (Petroleos de Venezuela S.A.): 60%	40,000 barrels barrels a day

can help the power plants to use their power at 80% capacity than the present 60%. If the plants run at 80% capacity utilisation, the tariff would decrease to 3.5 - 4 cents. However, there is no mutual acceptance in fixing the price per unit. There has been an asymmetry in the power tariff between these two countries. They have to sort out their differences and as a result both will benefit from power deal.

India and Bangladesh[11]: Bangladesh contains natural gas reserves of around 16.3 trillion cubic feet (tcf). Further, it is estimated an additional 32.1 tcf

Table-5: Investments by Chinese Petroleum Companies in Overseas oil and gas exploration and development:

Country	Project name or Location	Project nature	Approx. date	Value US $m
Kazakhstan	Aktyubinsk	Oil development and production	1997	4,000
Kazakhstan	Uzen	Oil development and production	1997	1,300
Kazakhstan	JV with ONGC of India	Oil exploration	1998	
Turkmenistan		Oil fields services	1997 & 2002	14 & 52
Azerbaijan	Kyursangi, Karabagly	Oil field development	2002	52
Russia	East Siberia	Oil exploration and production	2001	
Iran	Balal	Gas/oil development and production	1999	
Iraq	Al Ahdab	Oil development and production	1996/7	1,300
Kuwait	Various	Oil development and production, and refineries		3,000
Sudan	Various fields	Oil development and production, and pipeline	1998	700
Venzuela	Two fields	Exploration	1998	385
Peru	Talara	Oil field rehabilitastion	1993	25
Mongolia		Oil production and refining	1998	30
Indonesia	Repsol's assets	Exploration and production	2002	585
Papua New Guinea		Block 160 and Kamusi Exploration	1994	
Egypt		Oil and gas development	1999	
Thailand	Banya	Oil development and production	1993	
Canada	Calgary	Oil production	1992/3	11
Nigeria	Niger delta	Exploration	1998	
Nigeria	Chad Basin	Oil exploration	1997	

Source: Philip Andres-Speed, Xuanli Liao and Roland Dannreuther, *The Strategic Implications of China's Energy Needs* (New York: Oxford University Press Inc, 2002), p. 34.

in undiscovered reserves. It has apprehension in exporting gas to India. Bangladesh will certainly benefit if it exports gas to India. An analyst rightly pointed out: "Dhaka's inclusive, and perhaps increasingly irrelevant debate on gas exports reflects the tragic sub continental tradition of wallowing in isolation and poverty rather than creating shared wealth."[12] However, recently, both have agreed to set up a joint venture 1,320 mw power plant. This plant (two units: 660 mw each) has to be constructed in southern Khulna in Bangladesh and will be operational within two years. India has agreed to offer 250 mw at the rate of Rs. 2-2.5. India's National Thermal Power Plant (NTPP) and the Bangladesh power Development Board (BPDB) signed the MoU on 19 February 2010. The project required 130 km grid connectivity: 85 km in India and 45 km in Bangladesh). The cost of the grid shared by both: Tk. 200 crore by India and Tk. 1100 by Bangladesh. Dhaka has to invest more to set up a Hi-Voltage Direct Current (HVDC) substation because the capacity of the transmission will be increased.[13]

India and Bhutan[14]: India and Bhutan had an agreement related to hydroelectric power supply. Under this agreement, Bhutan is supplying power to India from Chukha Hydro Electric Project (336 MW). There is another project –Tala Hydro Electric Project (1020 MW), which is under construction and the surplus power from this project will be supplied to India. Bunakha (180 MW) and Wang Chu (900 MW) projects are planned and Sankosh project (4060 MW) is under process. Bhutan is exporting eighty per cent of its energy generation to India, which accounts for thirty per cent of its GDP. According to Indian sources, about sixty per cent of Bhutan's GDP accrues from exporting of surplus power from three hydro power station (Kurichu, Chukha and Tala) and the generation will increase once work on four more stations (Punatsangchu, Wangchu, Bunakha and Sankosh) is completed.[15] Through Chukha Project, Bhutan earned Nu 1,454 million as profit in 1998-1999 from its power export to India. As a result, it is in a position to increase revenues through the supply of power to India and to its own industries in the country. India provided technical and financial support to this project. Its share was Rs. 2.45 billion with sixty per cent grant and forty per cent loan. Bhutan was able to redeem the entire cost of the project in five years. India is able to supply power to West Bengal, Orissa and Northeastern parts of India. However, India has to upgrade its transmission lines to increase its access to Bhutanese power.

India and Nepal[16]: Nepal is possessing the largest hydropower potential (83,290 MW) in South Asia. However, due to various reasons, Nepal is not able to tap its hydro resources. It is able to install only 283 MW capacities. There are proposals between India and Nepal for hydroelectric cooperation. Projects like Pancheswar Project, which has the capacity of about 6000 MW, needs special institutional and financial assistance. The other project - West Sati (750

MW) is also proposed to develop to export power to India. Factors such as technical, production and supply constraints and political differences hit cooperation hard between the two countries.

India and Other Countries in Southeast Asia[17]: Presently, India imports crude oil from Malaysia and Brunei and it is about 5.4 per cent of its total imports from the world. It also imports 3.5 per cent LPG from Malaysia. Since the ASEAN countries- Indonesia, Malaysia and Vietnam have about one per cent of world's proven oil reserves and three per cent of the world's proven gas reserves,[18] India can work towards enhancing its energy trade with them.[19]

India-Pakistan-Iran Gas Pipeline

India and Pakistan had signed a memorandum of Understanding in July 1993 regarding exploring the prospects of a natural gas pipeline from Iran to India via Pakistan. In 1995, Pakistan and Iran had signed an agreement to construct a pipeline from South Pars gas field in Iran to Karachi in Pakistan and with an extension to India. However, due to various factors it has not been materialised. It was estimated that a 2700 km overland gas pipeline through Pakistan would cost about $3.1 billion. Out of this amount, India has to bear about $1 billion and the rest by Pakistan and Iran. Later the BHP Billiton revised the cost to about $7 billion. If it is materialised then Pakistan will get $700 million as transit charges from India every year.[20] India has reservations about the onshore pipeline project on the following grounds: (a) India is keen on full-fledged economic relations with Pakistan. It would be possible only if Pakistan gives MFN to India. India has already granted MFN to Pakistan in 1995;(b) India has doubts about the safety and security of the gas line in the light of the ongoing tensions between the two countries; (c) India has to live at the mercy of Pakistan; and (d) there may be threats from the fundamentalists and terrorists of Pakistan to the pipeline. In spite of these reservations on the part of India, the proposed project can still be pursued on the ground, as it is mutually beneficial for both.

Turkmenistan-Afghanistan-Pakistan-India (TAPI): India and Pakistan can import gas from Turkmenistan via Afghanistan. The Turkmenistan-Afghanistan-Pakistan-India (TAPI) line will run from the Dauletabad gas field to Afghanistan. From there, it will be laid from Herat to Kandahar and then through Quetta and Multan in Pakistan. The final destination of the pipeline will be the Indian town of Fazilka, near the border with Pakistan. The 1,680 km pipeline from Turkmenistan will transport 100 million standard cubic meters per day (mscmd) of gas from the Dauletabad gas field and India will have share of 60 mscmd.[21] The pipeline will be 1420 mm in diameter with a capacity of 3.3 billion cubic meters (bcm) of natural gas annually. The cost of the project is estimated at $3.5 billion in 2005. However, the cost was now estimated about $7 billion. This proposal is yet to be discussed by all the parties. This would be another channel to import gas to fulfill some of India's energy demands.

Myanmar-Bangladesh–India Pipeline:

Myanmar possesses significant energy reserves: gas in Yadana field and another deposit in the Bay of Bengal. GAIL conducted feasibility studies for a 550 to 600 kms. long offshore pipeline to connect India through Bangladesh. However, in the case of supplying gas to India, Bangladesh wants pipe line to be laid along its existing roads and highways and the project to be managed jointly by both, remove the existing trade barriers between the two countries. Bangladesh wants India to allow a free trade corridor to Nepal. It is very unfortunate that Dhaka refuses to allow supply of gas through its soil despite knowing that it would benefit $100 million per annum as transit fee. In case of Bangladesh's continued refusal to permit gas to be supplied to India, an alternative route of the pipeline will have to go under the sea in the Bay of Bengal, where pipes may have to be laid as deep as 6,560 ft. under water, which would be highly expensive. The pipeline cost may be more than $2 bn even if an economical route is followed.

China-Southeast Asia: China has identified Southeast Asia as an important source of energy resource. Its major energy imports pass through the Malacca Straits. Sixty per cent of its crude oil comes from Middle East through Malacca Straits. Energy security concern is one of the factors that led to territorial dispute in the South China Sea, where China and some of the ASEAN countries (Philippines, Vietnam, Malaysia and Brunei) are claiming their jurisdiction. However, China has jointly ventured along with some of the above Southeast Asian countries in exploring oil and gas in the South China Sea. The South China Sea is an area comprising over 200 islands, rocks and reefs and Paracels and Spratly groups. The need for energy has made the Southeast Asian countries and China to involve jointly in exploring energy resources. Energy cooperation between China and the Southeast Asia initiated in 2002. Chinese Offshore Oil Corporation purchased seventeen per cent stake in the Tangguh natural gas field. In 2005, China, the Philippines and Vietnam signed an agreement for joint surveys in the South China Sea, which led to cooperation and minimise rivalry over the disputed region. For China, Malacca Straits which is the shortest route to China from the Middle East and Africa reduces 2,000 km than by sailing by the Sunda Strait. Thailand exports half of its total LNG exploration (350,000 tons) gas to China, which is about five per cent of China's imports. China and Myanmar had joint exploration in 2001 and in 2005. Myanmar allowed China to explore deep water areas off its coast in the Indian Ocean. Before signing an agreement with India, Myanmar signed a MoU with the Chinese company PetroChina in early 2006 to supply gas to China from the A-1 field over a thirty year period. China gave soft loan of $84-million to Myanmar for laying a 2380-km pipeline connecting the gas site at Kyaukphyu (Myanmar) to Ruili (Yunnan province of China). China also agreed to pay $150 million annually for thirty years as a transit fee for the 990 km stretch through Myanmar.

China-Central Asia: The Central Asia has abundant oil and gas resources. For instance, Central Asia has petroleum reserves about fifty billion barrels and natural gas over eight trillion cubic metres.[22] China is seeking to reduce its dependence on SLOC by developing overland pipelines to import oil and gas from Central Asia. A 200,000 bpd pipeline was planned between Kazakhstan and China's northwest in early 2006.[23] At present, China is importing crude oil from Kazakhstan and Russia. China has, for the first time, explored the gas reserves of Central Asia i.e. gas pipe line (double line: A and B and has a length of 1,833 km.) from Turkmenistan to China via Uzbekistan and Kazakhstan. It is expected that initially capacity will be 10 bcm and will increase to 40 bcm later. It will be the second biggest buyer of Central Asian gas after Russia, which is importing 50 bcm from the region.[24] China has given $3 billion loan to Turkmenistan to develop the huge South Iolotan gas field and promised $10 billion in loans to Kazakhstan, which already supplies oil to China through pipeline. It is reported that China controls one-third of Kazkhstan's oil reserves. China Guandong Nuclear Power Co (CGNPC) plans to develop uranium deposits in Kazakhstan with reserves of 40,000 tonnes. It is carrying out more than fifty investment projects in Turkmenistan and has set up over 100 joint ventures in Uzbekistan.[25] China and Russia had signed seven agreements on cooperation for energy resources on 17 February 2009: to construct a pipeline, a long term crude oil trading and a financing scheme between the China Development Bank and the Russia Oil Pipeline Transport Company. The Chinese Vice Premier Wang Qishan said: "We hope the two sides will give a full play to the bilateral energy negotiation mechanism to promote the bilateral energy cooperation to score substantial outcomes."[26]

China- Middle East: The Middle East holds two-thirds of the world's oil. China imports fifty per cent of its oil from the Middle East. The IEA forecasts that China will import about seventy per cent of its oil from the Middle East. China's imports of oil from Iran increased from 738,000 tons in December 2006 to 2.214 million tons in January 2007.[27] Iran is the third largest supplier of crude oil and it supplied 287,000 bpd to China in 2005. Iran and China had numerous agreements in energy sector.[28]

China- Africa: Africa has become an important player in the world energy security strategy. The main suppliers of oil to China are: Angola, the Republic of Congo, Equatorial Guinea and Sudan. Twenty-three per cent of China's oil imports come from Africa (730,000 barrels a day). It was predicted that oil imports by China will be increased in future and thus Africa will be of great strategic importance to China's oil supply. The African countries have less infrastructure facilities to explore the resources. China is able to help these countries in exploring the energy resources. For instance, forty per cent of Sudan's oil market is controlled by China. There are other countries in Africa, where China is collaborating to develop better technology for alternative energy resources and economisation of petroleum resources.[29] There are about seven hundred Chinese companies established in different parts of Africa.

Competition/Cooperation:

When energy availability is one of the requirements for development, India and China would invariably compete each other in fulfilling their energy demands. For instance, India has lost in bidding oil fields in Iraq. In June 2009 OVL along with OAO Gazprom of Russia and TPAO lost their bidding of Zubair oilfield. ONGC has failed in its bid to win a major oil field in Iraq. The consortium of ONGC Videsh, Oil India Ltd., and Turkish Petroleum Corp (TPAO) lost to consortium led by China National Petroleum Corporation (CNPC) to develop the Halfaya oilfield. CNPC along with its partners: Petroleum Nasional Bhd (Petronas) and Total SA bid lower than OVL-led consortium. CNPC had offered 5.35 lakh barrels a day from the current 3,000 bpd at a cost of $1.40 a barrel, whereas the OVL group had a bid at $1.76 a barrel to output to 5.5 lakh bpd.[30]

India and China have interest in efficiency-enhancing coal technologies and thus development of coal technologies could be a potential area of cooperation between them. They are exploring possibilities to liquefy coal so that they can avoid dependence on imported oil. Hence sharing of experience in technology could be mutually beneficial. Both can cooperate in the construction and joint management of crude oil stockpiles to bring down the costs. Tajikstan and Kyrgyzstan have substantial hydel potential and if hydel projects are built, electricity can be transported through the Xinjiang district of China to Himachal Pradesh or Ladakh (bypass Pakistan). Chinese have pioneered oil recovery technology that helps sustain production at ageing oil fields for longer periods of time.

Joint Ventures: In 2004, China and India had signed an agreement to prevent their companies getting in each other's way when exploiting natural resources in other countries. For instance, on 5 December 2005, ONGC and CNPC made a joint $537 million bid to buy the al-Farat oilfields in Syria. In January 2006, ONGC Videsh Ltd and the CNPC agreed to place joint bids for promising energy projects in other countries. They are also working on an acquisition on Russia. Recently, OVL and GAIL have taken 12.5 per cent stake in China pipeline project in Myanmar. They were allowed to invest $1 billion in gas fields (A1 and A3 blocks), which will supply gas to China through pipeline. OVL and GAIL hold 17 per cent and 8.5 per cent stakes respectively in bringing to production the gas fields in the two blocks.[31] They realised that more can be gained from cooperation than competition in the field of energy. For instance, China CNPC agreed to pay $4.18 billion for PetroKazakhstan, to outbid ONGC. They realised that they can gain more from cooperation than competition in energy sector.[32] Their expertise can be used in basin evaluation and drilling. Indian companies could offer state-of-the art IT-enabled exploration and production services. Both can collaborate in the construction of hydel projects and transmission networks, pooling capital and technology. Both can collaborate in R&D to bring the down the cost of wind turbines. China can bid for construction of pipe lines in India, whereas India can set up refineries in China.

Conclusion

India and China can create a better future for their people through mutual understanding and cooperation. They can address the quest for energy by sharing their experiences, collaborative analysis of the current situation and assessing future scenarios and prospects for energy needs. Both are trying to foster cooperation with each other on energy matters while keeping options open for more intensified competition. Energy security cannot be attained on a purely national basis but through cooperation with other countries. India and China are emerging as powerful economies and major players in Asia. Their growth rates are around eight to nine per cent. Their energy imports pass though maritime routes and hence protection of SLOCs cannot be achieved without cooperation of each other.

References

1. For details see Anant Sudarshan and Logia Noronha, "Contextualising India's Energy Security", in Logia Noronha and Anant Sudarshan (ed), *India's Energy Security*, London: Routledge, 2009, p. 3.

2. For instance, according to Indian government report an estimated 0.59 million Indians die each year due to polluting traditional fuel.

3. Surya Sethi, "India's Energy Challenges and Choices", in Noronha and Sudarshan (ed), n.1, p.19.

4. Valentine V. Craig, "China's Opening to the World: What does it mean for U.S. Banks?" see http://www.gov/bank/analytical/banking/2005nov/article1.html

5. Anup Jayaram & Rajeev Dubey, "India's Oil Hunt", *Business World*, Vol.23, No.7, 8-14 July 2003, p. 31.

6. Cited in Amardeep Athwal, "China's and India's Energy Policies", in Amardeep Athwal, *China-India Relations: Contemporary Dynamics,* London: Routledge, 2008, p.103.

7. Philip Andrews-speed, Xuanli Liao and Roland Dannreuther, *The Strategic Implications of China's Energy Needs*, Adelphi Paper 346, New York: Oxford University Press, Inc., 2002, p. 30.

8. For more details, see A. Subramanyam Raju, "India's Energy Security: Challenges and Opportunities", in B. Mohanan Pillai (ed), *India's Foreign Policies: Continuity and Change.* New Delhi: New Century Publications, 2010, pp. 35-46.

9. *The Hindustan Times*, 16 January 1999.

10. Mahendra P. Lama, "Economic Reforms and the Energy Sector in South Asia: Scope for Cross-Border Power Trade", *South Asian Survey,* Vol.7, No.1, January-June 2000, p.18.

11. Raju, N. 8.

12. *The Hindu*, 12 November 2002.

13. *Ibid*, 21 February 2010, p.12.

14. Raju, N. 8.

15. *The Hindu*, 22 December 2009, p. 10.

16. Raju, N. 8.

17. A. Subramanyam Raju, "India and Southeast Asia: Energy Cooperation". Paper presented at the International Seminar, *India-Southeast Asia: Strategic Convergence in the 21st century, organaised by the centre for SAARC Studies, Andhra University Vishakapatnam, March 2008.*

18. Partha Pratim Pal & Mitali Dasgupta, "Does A Free Trade Agreement with ASEAN Make Sense?", *Economic and Political Weekly*, Vo.43, No.46, 15 November 2008, p. 11.

19. For more details see, Raju, N.17.

20. G. Pathasarathy, "The Quest for Energy Security", see http://www.rediff.com/news/_2001/jul/106gp.htm.

21. *The Hindu*, 23 April 2008.

22 http:/www.chinaenergy.gov.cn/news.php?id=13022. Vitaly Kozyrev, "China's Continental Energy Strategy: Russia and Central Asia". Gabriel B. Collins, Andrew S. Erickson, Lyle J. Goldstein and William S. Murray (eds), *China's Energy Strategy: The Impact on Beijing's Maritime Policies*, Maryland. Naval Institute Press, 2008, p. 209.

23. David Pietz, "The Past, Present, and Future of China's Energy Sector". Collins, Andrew, Lyle and William (eds.), N.22, p. 55.

24. *The Hindu*, 12 December 2009, p.14.

25. *Ibid.*

26. www.chinaview.cn

27. Ahmed Hashim, "China's Evolving Relationship with Iran". Collins, Andrew, Lyle and William (eds.), N.22, p.172.

28. For details see Dan Blumenthal, "Concerns with Respect to China's Energy Policy", in Collins, Andrew, Lyle and William (eds.), N.22,, p. 424.

29. Clifford Shelton, "The Energy Component of China's Africa Strategy". Collins, Andrew, Lyle and William (eds.), N. 22,, p.190.

30. *The Hindu*, 12 December 2009, p.15.

31. *Ibid*, 19 February 2010, p.15.

14

India and China in the Post-Cold War Years: Dexterous Quest for Competitive Edge in Southeast Asia

Tridib Chakraborti

The civilisational linkages and cultural contacts between India and China, imprinted in the annals of world history, failed to maintain their continuity in the cold war years. The contacts, a record of friendly exchanges dating back to centuries and interaction, did not last long with the advent of Muslim rule in India. Since the end of the Second World War, India's relations with China were cordial in nature. Following the establishment of new governments in India and China, both established diplomatic relations and their ties were quite normal. However, this state of relations underwent sea change following the 1962 border war. Since then, Sino-Indian relations have experienced profound upheavals, starting from the total loss of benign warmth to hyper-tension in the 1960s and 1970s, and from rapprochement in the 1980s to readjustment and pragmatic understanding in the 1990s and onwards. Presently, New Delhi and Beijing are attempting to put the past behind and forge new understandings based on the emerging global realities. Thus, it might sound quite paradoxical that despite several commonalties in terms of historical experiences, societal structures, cultural values and domestic economic conditions, the bilateral relations between India and China have waded through a mixed taste of sweet and sour. This nature of relations naturally had a spill over effect and coloured the ties with the countries of the Southeast Asian region. Today, in the context of the New Global Order, both India and China have emerged as competitive economic powerhouses and have gained buoyancy among the members of ASEAN. Their rise is a delicate and intricate combination of a discernment of sweet and sour opportunities and threats for the ASEAN members. During the cold war years, India and China's relations with Southeast Asia were determined by cold war politics. India's relations with Southeast Asia were principally confined due to the former's close alignment with the Soviet Union, considering its own national interests and its legitimisation of the Vietnamese-backed Kampuchean government in 1980, which resulted in drifting apart of India and the members of ASEAN.

Like India, China's relations with the countries of Southeast Asia in the cold war years, were more bitter than sour. During this period, relations were transformed from suspicion and fear, at first driven by ideology and later on largely based on territorial disputes. China's interactions with the ASEAN countries were concluded solely on a bilateral basis and no institutional linkages were formally forged between them. During most of this period, the countries of ASEAN followed the 'two China' policy, which irritated the state of mind of the ruling Chinese elites. Moreover, ASEAN members' suspicion of China originated during the cold war years owing to the latter's ideological support to the local Communist parties, ranging from fomenting Communist insurgencies to "teaching lessons" through military action in various countries of Southeast Asia, with the exception of Singapore and Brunei. China ended such support over time and the last support was given to Burma, which also ended in the 1980s. However, the situation changed with the death of Mao Zedong and the emergence of Deng Xiaoping as the Chairman of the Communist Party of China. Through his 'Four Modernisation' programme, Deng's first priority was to augment China's geopolitical importance in the global arena and pursue stable relations with neighbours. This state of relations further brought them close to each other following Vietnam's invasion of Cambodia in January 1979 and China's support to the ASEAN cause against Vietnam for the rest of the cold war years. This was strengthened with the announcement of the then Chinese Premier, Li Peng's four principles in November 1988, during his visit to Thailand, in developing its relations with the ASEAN countries. The purpose of the article is to identify and analyse the realms in which India and China are competing as well as cooperating with each other for gaining an advantageous edge in the Southeast Asian/Asia Pacific region.

Descent of Soviet Union and the Effects of Changing Global Order on India and China

The years between 1989 and 1991 were a landmark phase in the history of the 20th century. With the fall of Soviet Union and the emergence of a new global order, the period was characterised by positional shifts among all the international actors. The ideological tussle between capitalism and communism had faded in no time, making it the boulevard for globalisation. The sudden demise of the former Soviet Union impelled New Delhi to embark upon a frantic search for new trade doorways and links throughout the world, leading to a drastic paradigm shift in its overall foreign policy outlook. India, under the leadership of Prime Minister, P.V. Narasimha Rao, announced its New Economic Policy in July 1991. This resulted in that New Delhi, for the first time in its foreign policy domain, turned its face and expressed its willingness to develop economic links with the ASEAN countries because of its success "as a regional grouping of countries". The ASEAN countries, having vividly realised the growing importance of the role of economic diplomacy in the relations between nations, were convinced about the seriousness of India regarding its liberalisation policy. It was also felt by them that with the rise of India, they could reduce their dependence on Japan, the Western countries, and China in trade and economic relations. Subsequently, ASEAN's response was vindicated by India's exaltation of the status from 'Sectoral Dialogue Partner' to 'Full Dialogue Partner', from 'Full Dialogue' to 'Summit Partner' (2002) of ASEAN and finally from 'Summit Partner' to 'East Asian Summit Partner' in 2005. This sweeping promotion of India in the ASEAN orbit accelerated by Narasimha Rao's official announcement of 'Look East' policy through his 'Singapore Lecture' in September 1994, and was further spearheaded when on 4 September, 2003, the then Indian External Affairs Minister, Yashwant Sinha, at the Plenary Session of the Second India-ASEAN Business Summit, held in New Delhi, officially declared Phase II, also known as India's Move East Policy. Thus, India's 'Look East' policy has been the reformation of its foreign policy strategy, a clear response to the end of cold war, aimed to upgrade diplomatic and economic relations with the region and put them on a greater, expanded and regular foothold. This close interaction also gave India an opportunity to develop an 'Asianist' discourse. Within two decades of implementing New Economic Policy, India has emerged as an important Power House, along with China in global politics. New Delhi's post-Cold War ASEAN policy and ASEAN's Look West policy have also grown nearly for two decades. During these years, total merchandise trade in 2008-09, stood at over US$ 45 billion, making the exports target to the region look realistic by 2010. India's trade with the Southeast Asian countries, during 2007-08 was US$ 390, 88.33 million – 10 times more than the year 1992-93, though the Balance of Trade has always tilted in favour of ASEAN. Besides this, ASEAN is India's fourth-largest trading partner and Indo-ASEAN trade has been growing at a compounded annual growth rate

(CAGR) of 27% since 2000. Among these countries, Malaysia and Singapore are India's most prominent trading partners and its trade with Laos has been the least in value terms (as per 2008-09 trade statistics). However, the trade turnover declined quite sharply in 1997-98, because of the 'East Asian Financial Crisis'. Since 1999, trade flow has recovered. In fact, growth in India's exports to Southeast Asian countries in the recent years has been much higher vis-à-vis other important destinations. In 2007-08, when India's trade with the world stood at US$ 413 billion, ASEAN accounted for more than 10% of India's global trade.

With the growing economic liberalisation, ASEAN entrepreneurs have also undertaken FDI in India in crucial infrastructure sectors, such as telecommunications, heavy industry, fuels, hotel and tourism, chemicals, fertilizers, textiles, paper, pulp and food processing. Malaysia, Thailand and Singapore have become the major sources of FDI into India. From a negligible amount in 1991, cumulative approved FDI from ASEAN has reached more than US$ 5 billion. Compared to other regional groupings, ASEAN is the fifth most important market in the world in terms of Indian exports and fourth in terms of imports. Moreover, FDI from ASEAN during April 2000 – July 2008 totaled US$ 6.0 billion, and ASEAN accounted for 8% of India's total FDI inflows (US$ 74.8 billion). New Delhi has also set up joint working groups with Malaysia, Indonesia etc. for working towards Comprehensive Economic Cooperation Agreement (CECA). The Framework Agreement has laid a strong base for the eventual establishment of an ASEAN-India Regional Trade and Investment Area (RITA), including FTA in goods, services and investment. On 13 August 2009, the India-ASEAN FTA for goods was finally signed in Bangkok. This is an unprecedented event in the history of Indian foreign policy and a good beginning for New Delhi's ultimate integration with the Southeast and the further East Asian regions.

Unlike India, the geographical advantage and overseas ethnic Chinese configuration has given China a lead to develop ties with the countries of Southeast Asia. Subsequently, China has adhered to a peaceful foreign policy, on the basis of the Panchasheel, and the ASEAN members have welcomed China's participation in regional economic cooperation, in spite of their past bitter experiences. On 19 July 1991, Chinese Foreign Minister, Qian Qichen participated in the 24th ASEAN Foreign Ministers' Meeting in Kuala Lumpur, where he expressed willingness to develop better ties with these countries. This willingness on the part of China bore fruit within a short span of time and it joined multilateral dialogue processes since the 1990s, including ASEAN+3,

ARF, EAS and Full Dialogue Partnership of ASEAN. Besides, in December 1997, Chinese President, Jiang Zemin and the ASEAN leaders organised their first informal summit (ASEAN+1) and issued a joint statement of establishing partnership of good neighbourliness and mutual trust, thus putting into place the framework for all round growth of relations. Since then, China-ASEAN linkages have been highlighted by frequent exchange of high-level visits. An important event in the development of China-ASEAN relations was Beijing's accession to the Treaty of Amity and Cooperation, signed in November 2003. This growing cordiality between China and ASEAN was further deepened when the Framework Agreement on ASEAN-China Comprehensive Economic Cooperation was signed in October 2003 at Bali, to establish China-ASEAN Free Trade Area (CAFTA). Thus, within a short span of time, trade between ASEAN and China increased rapidly, expanding to US$ 231.1 billion in 2008, from US$ 19.5 billion in 1995. In 2007, trade registered US$ 202.6 billion. Last year, it grew to US$ 231.12 billion, maintaining 14% growth. China is the third largest trading partner of ASEAN, while ASEAN has become the fourth largest of China. At the end of February 2010, Chinese enterprises invested US$ 8.6 billion in ASEAN countries.

Presently, both India and China are enjoying the elevated status from Full Dialogue and Summit Level Partners of ASEAN and thereby both are competing for increasing their spheres of influence in the region. China has performed more effectively in trade with ASEAN than India. As New Delhi has signed FTA in goods and not in services in 2009 with the region, India would compete with the Chinese economic advantage in the days to come. India's economic performance with ASEAN members is good enough, unlike the past years, but it is no match with China. Therefore, the rise of China and India as powerhouses is regarded as a delicate and intricate combination of a perception of sweet and sour opportunities for ASEAN members.

Preservation and Procurement of Energy as a Colluding Point

Secondly, procurement and preservation of energy security has emerged as a major locus of conflicting interest between India and China. The increasing use of energy remains the point of intense competition between them for tapping global energy resources. Since 2001, China has developed a national energy strategy ('going-out') initiated by Premier, Zhu Rongji. As a result, Chinese oil companies accelerated their hunt for overseas oil assets as part of this strategy. The largest deal ever made by China's National Offshore Oil Corporation (CNOOC) was its US$ 585 million purchase of the equity of Repsol-YPE's five oil fields in Indonesia. In total, it brought China about 40 million barrels of oil a year. In the same year, CNOOC acquired a 12.5% interest in BP's Tangguh LNG project in Indonesia for US$ 275 million.

Like China, in order to sustain economic growth, India has made energy security its current area of focus. In an effort to ensure access to energy resources, India is focusing its attention in the Middle East, Africa and Latin America. Although India has lost in many joint biddings with China, both have decided to cooperate as well. India generates only 3% of its electricity from nuclear power and this low level of production stimulated the US-India Civilian-Nuclear Agreement of July 2005. In this, India has come up against China's similar desire for regional leadership and seniority. Thus, energy has become a source of both cooperation and competition between China and India in recent years. To this end, they signed a 'Memorandum for Enhancing Cooperation in the Field of Oil and Natural Gas' on 12 January 2006. As India reaches into the Malacca Straits, Beijing has improved its port facilities in Sittwe (Myanmar), Chittagong (Bangladesh), and Gwadar (Pakistan), in order to protect sea-lanes and ensure uninterrupted energy supplies. India is also wary of China's efforts to engage its South Asian neighbours in military and economic matters, which implies that China is pursuing a two-pronged strategy of lulling India into complacency with greater economic interaction, while taking steps to encircle India and undermine its security.

A typical example cited in this connection is Myanmar's gas-field project. Chinese presence in Myanmar's oil and gas fields has been observed quite seriously by India. CNOOC signed six contracts on production sharing with the Myanmar Oil and Gas Enterprise (MOGE) from October 2004 to January 2005. China National Petroleum Corporation (CNPC) and its subsidiary Chinnery Assets have been awarded contracts to upgrade the four old oilfields in central Myanmar. India has clearly lost an important diplomatic initiative in the attempt to counter Chinese influence in Myanmar. New Delhi eventually reached an agreement with Myanmar to purchase the gas with conditions based on 'take or pay'. It emerges that Myanmar has come out as the winner in the Sino-India competition for energy, while tensions mounted between New Delhi and Beijing.

Competition of Power Strength between India and China

Thirdly, the emergence of India and China as economic powerhouses has thrown up new power competition in regional geopolitical balance. Both countries, in the post-Cold War years have outwardly begun to rub shoulders in different parts of the world. China has gushed ahead in acquiring economic and military capabilities to achieve broader strategic objectives than India.

Resource procurement in the new millennium has added to maritime rivalry between India and China and both are seeking to forge closer defence and security ties with resource-supplier nations. Nearly 90% of Chinese arms sales reach countries located in the Indian Ocean region. For its part, India has countered by promoting defence cooperation with Oman, Israel, Maldives, Madagascar, Seychelles, Myanmar, Singapore, Indonesia, Thailand, Vietnam, Taiwan, the Philippines, Australia, Japan, and US. Maritime competition is set to intensify as Indian and Chinese navies show off their flags in the Pacific and Indian oceans with greater frequency. Therefore, the Sino-Indian rivalry in South and Southeast Asia, and the northern Indian Ocean (especially the Malacca Straits) may well be a dominant feature of future Asian geopolitics.

Based on the possibility of growing power competition, both countries have strengthened their military modernisation and development programmes. The growing military budget between India and China remains another area of conflict. China's military spending in 2008 was about US$ 84.9 billion, while that of India was US$ 30.0 billion.

As I have already discussed, earlier that energy is a source of cooperation and competition between China and India in the Asian region. This energy competition is also reflected in their assertion of naval power antagonism. Chinese advancement in the domain of its Navy has remained a matter of concern for India, whose submarine technology has assumed greater significance in recent times. The People's Liberation Army Navy (PLAN) has decided to extend its influence into the Indian Ocean region, which naturally challenges India's regional position. By entering the Indian Ocean (possibly with the help of Myanmar), the Chinese Navy would be seeking to exert its influence in the Straits of Malacca. Moreover, in recent years, China has noticed the shift in India's nuclear doctrine from "regional limited deterrence" to that of "regional overall deterrence" and for that India has committed to expanding and modernising its Air Force, in addition to maintaining the stature and strength of its Army. India's military has a strong peace-building role as well. As of March 2007, India was the third largest provider of peacekeeping forces to the UN.

Furthermore, as India reaches into the Malacca Straits, Beijing is creating a "string of pearls" surrounding India by developing strategic port facilities in Sittwe, Myanmar; Chittagong, Bangladesh and Gwadar to the port of Hambantota, drilling for oil off the Coast of Northeast Sri Lanka. The "string of pearls" strategy, however, offers a forward presence for China along the sea lines of communication that now anchor China directly to the

Middle East. India is wary of China's efforts to engage its South Asian neighbours in military and economic matters. To counter this posture, India has entered into bilateral defence cooperation agreements with Malaysia, Vietnam, Singapore, Laos and Indonesia and has assisted the armed forces of Myanmar and Thailand. New Delhi holds periodic joint naval exercises with these countries and participates in a biannual gathering of regional navies, MILAN, to make its presence felt in the region. It is concerned about growing links between China and Myanmar, with which it shares land and maritime borders, and has in recent years, de-emphasised its support for democracy, based on the policy of 'constructive engagement'.

Multilateral Diplomacy of India and China: From Passive to Active Play

Fourthly, since the fall of Soviet Union, there has been a drastic change of foreign policy agenda of the various Third World countries. Both India and China are skillfully using Asia-Pacific regional organisations to develop better linkages with the individual members, since they feel that multilateralism is a safer and better way to expand international influence. Beijing has been busy carving out a large sphere of influence to subdue Japan and Taiwan, and weaken US-South Korean alliance in Northeast Asia, Southeast and South Asia. In fact, China is presently dependent on multilateral organisations to curtail the US influence in the region, attempts to marginalise Japan and show occasional strength to Taiwan and has an ambition of encircling India. In other words, China is using 'soft power' remedies to nurture 'alliances with many developing countries to solidify its position in the WTO, flex its muscles on the world stage and act as a counterbalance to US power'. China targets Southeast Asia as a region with a very assertive ASEAN policy, particularly since July 1994, when China became a Full Dialogue Partner of ASEAN and a member of the ARF. In 2001, China joined the WTO, and in November 2002, it signed two documents: a framework trade agreement designed to establish an ASEAN-China FTA by 2010, and with ASEAN members, a Declaration on the Conduct of Parties in the South China Sea, relinquishing violent means of dealing with disputed sovereignty claims in these waters. In October 2003, it became the first major Asian state outside ASEAN to sign ASEAN's Treaty of Amity and Cooperation. More importantly, its willingness to negotiate multilaterally with rival Southeast Asian claimants in the territorial disputes over the Spratly Islands reassured them that Beijing is serious about its "peaceful rise". It also expressed willingness to work towards peace by signing the Southeast Asia Nuclear Weapons-free Zone Treaty. China's diplomatic overtures to ASEAN can be interpreted as attempts to preempt member-states from increasing their bilateral security cooperation with the US. Besides this, China is also an active partner of EAS. Thus, Beijing has engaged the region at all levels, bilaterally and multilaterally, and has been at the forefront in the establishment of new regional institutions. Presently, many ASEAN countries are less vocal of China being a threat; rather they profess China as an opportunity.

Like China, India's pragmatic foreign policy has every reason to deepen its independent relationships with the major nations of Southeast and East Asia and engage all regional institutions. This process started with the opening up of its economy and announcement of 'Look East' policy and its willingness to develop better economic ties both with the ASEAN as a regional organization. India has stepped up its bilateral security and military cooperation across the region by signing multiple defence agreements with the majority countries of Southeast Asia. Although India's arms exports are well below the level of the Chinese volumes, these are set to grow. India is already committed to servicing some of the Southeast Asian fighter aircraft purchases from Russia and training the military personnel to operate them. From being a lone ranger, India has begun to emphasize the virtues of security multilateralism.

Besides this, both the Asian giants are vying with each other for increasing their sphere of influence in the South and Southeast Asian regions. In the South Asian region, India's position has not been favourable among the SAARC members. Moreover, India is an active member of the Mekong-Ganga Cooperation (MGC) and the Bay of Bengal Initiative for Multi-Sectoral Technical and Economic Cooperation (BIMSTEC). China, on the other hand, has recently received 'observer status' in SAARC, but is neither a member of BIMSTEC nor MGC. Both countries are engaged in competitive regionalism and they face each other on many platforms, like EAS and SCO. Interestingly enough, India's MGC excludes China, while China's Greater Mekong Project does the same to India. Although, both are stressing on regionalism, China has a better edge than India. China is a member of almost all regional fora along its periphery, some of which are China's initiatives, where its trade figure remains higher than India. An example can be cited in this connection: the Indo-ASEAN trade is just one- fifth of the Sino-ASEAN trade, which is over US$ 200 billion.

However, in the present global order, the story of India-China relations is not completely bitter in nature and there is space for both neighbours to cooperate. For example, in India's northeast and China's Yunnan province, the Bangladesh-India-Myanmar-China (BIMC) or the Kunming Initiative has the potential to churn the region into a zone of prosperity. Similarly, enduring partnership between the two via SCO, ARF, or the EAS has the potential to curb transnational crime, terrorism, drug menace and sea piracy.

Soft Power Diplomacy as a Competitive Tool between India and China

Fifthly, since the end of the cold war, both India and China have shelved their bitter past isolation and aim to develop their economic and political clout in the pursuit of building alliances and partnerships through soft power as an instrument. According to Joseph Nye, soft power is the ability to attract and persuade rather than coerce. It stems from the attractiveness of a nation's culture, ideals and policies and it refers to the power to attract or to induce emulation. However, not all attractive power is soft power and not all soft power evokes emulation. Therefore, soft power generally means not power that induces emulation, but power that induces respect. It is a wide range of non-material power – ideas, norms, values, and cultural products. The modalities, which China has used to enhance its soft power diplomacy, include the use of Official Development Assistance (ODA), successful public and formal diplomacy, and the use of economic and political tools such as investment and regional trade agreements. It has also used various other means of its soft power diplomacy - its conventional concept of Panchasheel; accommodating security; unconditional foreign aid; limited sanctions; mutual adjustment; international democracy; cultural diplomacy; a consultative, but non-pluralistic political organisation, global media (including CCTV-9, China's English-language satellite news channel, and the English-language editions of China Daily); educational exchanges, both in China and overseas (e.g., the establishment of Confucius Institutes to offer Chinese language courses abroad, the creation of English and Hindi language graduate programmes in Chinese Universities, and the development of financial aid programmes for foreign students who wish to study in China); etc. By engaging this strategy, the popularity of the Chinese language and cultural studies has grown immensely. In Southeast Asia, there are 21 Confucius Institutes providing language courses and these are sites for cultural transmission, intercultural exchange, and Chinese learning, conveying China's soft power resources to its ASEAN neighbours.

Besides this, the involvement of overseas Chinese for China's economic development and improvement of the economic indices of the respective countries in Southeast Asia has generated an image of better understanding. China's willingness to mediate disputes in the region and to accept the role of a regional leader against drug, human trafficking and other non-traditional security threats has proven to be a benefit for its new policies as well. China is actually using traditional tradecraft in a very soft manner, flavoured with charm. Its role in the Asian financial crisis has increased the allure of China's model of economic development to most Southeast Asian countries. China mainly through Official Development Assistance (ODA) has already penetrated more into the ASEAN region, the Indochina States and Myanmar. Moreover, in April 2009, China has announced a new investment fund and loan package to help assuage the shock of the global financial crisis for ASEAN, besides providing US$ 39.7 million for "special aid" to Cambodia, Laos and Myanmar, to meet the "urgent needs". Furthermore, Beijing has increased its cooperative aid package, including an offer of 2,000 government scholarships and 200 Master's scholarships for public administration students over the next five years. Beijing has donated 300,000 tons of rice to an emergency East Asia reserve intended to boost food security and proposed a China-ASEAN scheme to create high quality, high-yield crop demonstration farms in ASEAN countries. China's surging foreign assistance and government-supported economic projects have been appreciated by ASEAN members. However, this Chinese posture failed to satisfy all the countries of Southeast Asia, because of the former's plans to build a series of hydroelectric dams on the upper reaches of the Mekong River, which flows through and sustains the livelihoods of large populations in many mainland ASEAN states. While some of ASEAN countries may still be skeptical of China's rising regional clout, its recent aid proposals will no doubt be warmly welcomed across the region.

India is probably China's closest soft power 'competitor' in the Southeast Asian region. Until recently, India generally received negative media attention and was often portrayed in the Western media as a poor country. In spite of this dismal projection by the biased Western media, India, to a large extent, has been successful in deploying its soft power resources in the form of human capital, commerce, banking; a massive movie industry; a huge shift of IT operations from the UK and US to Indian cities such as Bangalore, Calcutta and Hyderabad; a vibrant scientific community, and world class higher education and research in many sectors. India also reaps the benefits of an excellent knowledge of the English language and Western culture. Unfortunately, in this competitive global order, the sustenance of India's historical benign image towards the countries of Southeast Asia has lost its rhythm if one compares it with China's use of soft power. New Delhi should draw lessons from its northern neighbour regarding the latter's constructive engagement with the Southeast Asian countries. Following the footsteps of Beijing's active usage of Chinese diaspora, India should employ modalities about the way of promoting and utilising the Indian diaspora settled in different parts of Southeast Asia, to re-build the genetic ties it has with these countries. There are three important avenues – education, culture, and multimedia – through which India can make use of its soft power. With reference to ASEAN's call to minimise the Development Gap within it, in November 2002, ASEAN leaders approved the Initiative for ASEAN Integration (IAI) work plan. India, being a responsible 'Dialogue Partner' of ASEAN has actively played a constructive role in the programme and has successfully completed the "Railway Training Programmes for 48 trainers from Cambodia, Laos, Myanmar and Vietnam (CLMV countries) in India". In addition, India is successfully implementing a project called "India-Singapore Joint Training Programme for CLMV in English language Training". This active focus of New Delhi on the IAI has been looked upon by ASEAN countries as a sign of India's commitment to ASEAN and its forward-looking processes. However, this initiative of India has not been too momentous like China and for that, trade initiatives such as the India-ASEAN FTA could help further. In some countries in Southeast Asia, India must provide more aid, and thereby engage in "lobbying-like" behaviour to win Southeast Asian mindset for their projects. New Delhi must upgrade its official image and improve its public diplomacy mechanism through the Indian Council for Cultural Relations, which is a nodal agency to project Indian soft power. The ICCR has to be more active in reaching out to wider sections of the population in Southeast Asia. It should establish more Indian language and cultural institutes and increase the scholarships for students to continue higher education in India. India must also promote tourism as a vehicle to develop better linkages with Southeast Asian countries. More Indian books, television shows, and joint university collaborations should be encouraged to this end. Indian policy-makers should explore the value of focusing on economic cooperation, restoring physical connectivity, and shedding the ancient notion of cultural superiority.

Conclusion

Having analysed the competitive and complementary fervour between India and China in Southeast Asia, the fact remains that there are lesser chances of any physical war between them in the coming years. However, an economic power struggle as well as the craving for becoming an important strategic player on the world stage might emerge in a clash of interest between them. After decades of frosty relations, India and China are in the midst of a rapprochement based on their desire to have peaceful borders and avoid hostile relations, in spite of the recent hot language exchanged between them with reference to the legitimacy of Arunachal Pradesh, the show of strength through naval maneuvers from the South China Sea to Bay of Bengal and quest for preservation of energy resources in Myanmar and other parts of the globe. Although China and India have been strategic adversaries since the Sino–Indian border war of 1962, which cemented India's alignment with the Soviet Union and China's strategic partnership with Pakistan, that situation has rapidly moved in the opposite direction, in the context of the New World Order. This resulted in India's growing interest in establishing cordial ties with its powerful neighbour, though it remains wary of China's intentions in South and Southeast Asia and its slow pace in resolving the border dispute. It is a fact that the impact of the India factor on the future of Sino-ASEAN relations will depend on the extent to which India's economic potential is translated into political and strategic influence. India is still relatively weak in terms of economic and political power, while its broader geopolitical ambitions have, to some extent, been held in check by its rivalry with China. India has a long way to go in competing with China in Southeast Asia, where economic and political relations are tilted largely in Beijing's favour. Today, both countries intend to be interdependent, harmonious, complementary, as well as competitive and mutually restricted to each other in the Southeast Asian region, for overall sustainable development, owing to their individual quest for survival.

References

1. Hao Yufan and Huan Guofang (eds.), *The Chinese View of the World*, Pantheon Books, New York, 1989, p. 221.

2. Tridib Chakraborti, "India's Southeast Asia Policy in the 21st Century: Perambulating the Horizon", in Y. Yagama Reddy (ed.), *Emerging India in Asia Pacific*, New Century Publications, New Delhi, 2007, pp. 157-158.

3. Tridib Chakraborti, "India's Southeast Asia Policy in the 1980s and 1990s : Contrasting Shades in Foreign Policy Priorities," *Jadavpur Journal of International Relations*, Department of International Relations, Jadavpur University, Calcutta, Vol. 1, 1995, p.150.

4. Tridib Chakraborti, N. 2, p.158.

5. Tridib Chakraborti, "India's Look East Policy: Time for Stock-Taking", *World Focus*, New Delhi, Vol. 30, November-December, 2009, p. 464.

6. *Ibid*, p. 465.

7. For details see http://www.aseansec.org/15268htm. Accessed on April 16, 2010.

8. For details see http://english.people.com.cn/90001/90776/90883/6857416.html;and also http://english.sina.com/china/2010/0101/296958.html (accessed on April 16, 2010).

9. **For details see Xu Yi-chong, "China's Energy Security",** *Australian Journal of International Affairs*, **Volume 60, Issue 2, June 2006.**

10. ***Newsweek***, December 3, 2007, p. 46.

11. 'Myanmar Pact with Petro China for Sale of Gas', The Shwe Gas Movement, 11 January 2006 [http://www.shwe.org/news/2006/01/myanmar-pact-with-petro-china-for-sale.html].

12. Gideon Lundholm, **"China Trumps India in Myanmar Gas Stakes",** ***Asia Times***, 11 September, 2007. See also http://www.atimes.com/atimes/Southeast_Asia/ II11Ae02.html.

13. For details see http://www.apcss.org/core/BIOS/malik/India-China_Relations.pdf.

14. For details see http://www.armscontrolcenter.org/policy/securityspending/articles/fy09_dod_request_global/; see also www.sipri.org/media/media/pressreleases/8june_ yearbook _launch.

15. "Oil Group Seeks to Skirt Malacca Strait," *Taipei Times*, May 27, 2007, http://www.taipeitimes.com/News/worldbiz/archives/2007/05/29/2003362966.

16. **Xenia Dormandy, "India's Foreign Policy",** *November 5, 2007, for details* see http://belfercenter.ksg.harvard.edu/publication/17778/indias_foreign_policy.html

17. MILAN, meaning meeting in Hindi, is a biennial conglomeration of Asia-Pacific Maritime Navies that is hosted by the Indian Navy. The aim of this exercise is to foster understanding and cooperation in the areas of common interest and safeguard SLOCs (sea-lanes of communication) from poaching, piracy and terrorist activities, promote interoperability to the extent possible and engage in joint search and rescue and humanitarian operations. Opportunities to promote understanding and camaraderie amongst the navies are encouraged through ship visits, social interactions and cultural presentations by the participating countries. MILAN has grown from a small congregation of five nations to nine during 2006 (with 20 ships attending from eight countries) to 11 nations (of 13 invited) and 16 ships in 2008. For details see www.bharat-rakshak.com/NAVY/Articles/Article11.pdf

18. *The Chicago Tribune,* December 20, 2004.

19. Joseph Nye Jr., *Soft Power: The Means to Success in World Politics*, Public Affairs Books, USA, 2005.

20. For details see China's "Soft Power" in Southeast Asia (Report) by Thomas Lum, Wayne Morrison, Bruce Vaughn, Congressional Research Service (CRS) Reports and Issue Briefs, January 2008.

21. A recent discussion on China's advocacy of Chinese language. Sheng Ding and Robert A. Saunders, "Talking Up China: An Analysis of China's Rising Cultural Power and the Global Promotion of the Chinese Language," *East Asia: An International Journal*, Vol. 23, No. 2, 2006, pp. 3-33.

22. Brian McCartan, **"A helping Chinese hand", April 30, 2009,** http://www.atimes.com/atimes/Southeast_Asia/KD30Ae01.html (accessed on 26/4/2010).

23. **Alan Hunter, "Soft Power: China on the Global Stage"**, *The Chinese Journal of International Politics*, Vol. 2, No. 3, 2009. For details see cjip.oxfordjournals.org/cgi/content/full/2/3/373.

24. Tridib Chakraborti, "India's Look East Policy: Time for Stock-Taking", N. 5, p. 467.

15

Geo-Strategic Concerns and Geo-Economic Prospects in the Trans-Himalayan Region: Implications for India – China Relations

B.C. Upreti

Regional approach has gained much currency in international relations during the last few decades, particularly in the context of New International Order characterised by globalisation and liberalisation. The process of globalisation has in-fact encouraged regional economic interlinkages so that a particular region becomes adaptive to market forces. The security concerns, increased awareness to environmental conservation and management and the need for multilateral cooperation have also laid greater emphasis on regionalism in the arena of international relations.

A region is a compact geographical unit having its independent identity on the basis of history, society, culture, economy, etc. Stronger are these distinguishing factors, stronger a region would be. However, the importance of a particular region would rest upon its viability and utility for the countries of the region as well as the outside forces. The importance of a region may be in politico-strategic or economic terms. Where both the factors are prevalent that region would be more complex in the arena of international politics because of the fact that in that case it would become the focal point of the politics of the world powers.

This paper seeks to highlight the geo-strategic significance and the economic potential of the trans-Himalayan region (THR). Two important constituent countries of this region are India and China and, therefore, it also intends to reflect on the political, strategic and economic issues that, in the trans-Himalayan borderland impinge on India-China relations.

The trans-Himalayan region has been historically important for religious, cultural, trade, migratory, relations between the countries of Central Asia and South Asia. In the contemporary period, the significance of the region is due to a number of factors, such as

(i) The region is strategically important.

(ii) It is rich in terms of natural and mineral resources.

(iii) It forms a tri-juncture of three important regions of Asia: Central Asia, South Asia and East Asia.

(iv) Various parts of the region form the nerve centre of Islamic extremism and terrorism.

(v) The world powers are excessively interested in this region, particularly, since the emergence of the independent states of the Central Asia after the disintegration of Soviet Union.

(vi) Three major countries adjoining the trans-Himalayan border land – India, Pakistan and China – have conflicting relations.

(vii) The region offers vast opportunities for mutual cooperation.

Identifying the Trans-Himalayan Region

The Himalayan ranges form a great divide and a natural demarcation between Central Asia and South Asia. The area is known as the land of snow.[1] The Himalayan borderland lying in between these two regions of Asia is termed as the trans-Himalayan borderland. The countries of the trans-Himalayan region which share borders are India, Nepal, Bhutan, China, Pakistan, Afghanistan, Kazakhstan, Tajikistan, Kyrgyzstan and Myanmar. The Himalayas, in effect, form the highest mountain range in the world. The Himalayan system as a whole stretches around 2400 kms. in length and varying in width from 240 to 330 kms. It is made up of three parallel mountain ranges: the greater Himalayas, the lesser Himalayas and the outer Himalayas. The northern most range of the Himalayas is known as the trans-Himalayan range and located mostly in the Qinghai-Xinjiang plateau, north of the great west to east trending valley of the Yarlung Zangbo river. The trans-Himalayan range is although dived from the great Himalayan range for most of its length; it merges with the great Himalayan range in the western section – the Karakoram Range where India, Pakistan and China form a tri-juncture.

Historical Significance of the Region

The trans-Himalayan region has been historically important for many reasons. It provided the Central Asian Gate Way to India. Most of the earlier invasions from Central Asia originated through this region. It also witnessed the flow of cultures, religion, languages from Central Asia to India and *vice-versa* for ages. The Fargana valley acted as a centre of religious-cultural mixing as well as the southward invasions.

The rise of the British colonial rule in India also changed the politico-strategic scenario of the trans-Himalayan borderland. In the Anglo-Russian agreement of 1873, both agreed upon mutual sphere of influence in the region. China was equally interested in the region. These three powers tried to destabilise each in the region. After the Bolshevik revolution in Russia, the British were afraid of the communist infiltration in the region. Therefore, they tried to create a chain of buffer states all along the Himalayan region. There were several small autonomous entities in the north-west Himalayan belt. The British were much concerned to the security of the region. In the 1935 agreement between government of India and Jammu & Kashmir Durbar, it was decided that the Gilgit Wazart, north of the Indus, and its dependencies, would be leased to the British for a 60-years period. It was also decided that all the civil and military administration of the region would be transferred to the government of India. Just before India's independence, the lease was, however, terminated and the region was given back to Maharaja of Jammu and Kashmir. It is a different story that soon after the accession of Jammu & Kashmir to India, Gilgit was declared as the independent republic of Gilgit that later opted to join Pakistan.

The point is that the British realised the strategic importance of Gilgit, Hunja and Baltistan area and tried to ensure the security of the region. The trans-Himalayan region was an important trade route for centuries. The famous silk route passed through this region. Two important trade routes in this region were: east Ladakh route – Khotan, Yarkand & Kashgar ; west Gilgit route – Hunja, Khunjerab and Mintoke passes. There were also numerous caravan routes. Srinagar, Leh, Skardu, Kishtawar, Kullu, Lahaul, Spiti, Nurpur and Ladakh on the Indian side, Samarkand, Yarkand, Khotan in Central Asia, Lhasa in Tibet and Xinjiang in China constituted important trade centres. Trade with Tibet from Ladakh and Kashmir was regulated by the treaty of Tingmosgang concluded in 1684.[2] India had, in effect, very old trade relations with Tibet.[3]

The Major items of trade across the trans-Himalayan region were gold, silver, hump, drug, shawls, wool, carpets, tea, leather wares, raw silk, etc. The Indian items, which were popular in Central Asia and beyond, were indigo, spices, dyed leather, opium, etc.

Geo-Strategic and Geo-Economic Importance of THR

The trans-Himalayan region has been historically important but in contemporary phase its strategic and economic importance has been multiplied due to a number of reasons. The whole of the trans-Himalayan regions forms politically a highly fragile and unstable region. Jammu & Kashmir region in India, northern parts of Pakistan, POK, Afghanistan, Xingiang region of China, Tibetan region, parts of Central Asian states form a highly unstable and conflict-ridden zone. There are challenges of political instability, conflicts and disorder. The societies in the region are traditional and lack openness. The region is faced with ethno-religious uprising. There is lack of economic development despite huge unexploited resources, religious extremism and terrorism; arms and drug trafficking are becoming serious problems in the whole of the region. Pakistan's patronage to Islamic terrorism and fundamentalism, cross border terrorism in Jammu & Kashmir, terrorism and destabilising tendencies in Afghanistan, Islamic extremism in Xinjiang and ethno-religious uprising in Central Asia are major causes of concern.[4] It is due to these multiplied problems of stability and sustenance that most of the countries of the region look for external support.[5] This approach of the countries of the region have given an edge to the superpowers to play a role in the region. The United States, Russia, China and other powers are immensely interested in the region in the name of containing terrorism and ensuring political stability. As a result, the trans-Himalayan region has become the focal point of the renewed 'great game'.[6] The economic resources of the region is a very prominent factor behind the external interference in the region. The region offers vast scopes for trade, economic, cooperation, investments, exploitation of natural and mineral resources. The development of north-south transport corridor would facilitate trade in the region. The region also has vast prospects for tourism.

Changing Scenario in Central Asia

The emergence of the independent states of Central Asia in the wake of the disintegration of the Soviet Union has changed the geo-strategic and geo-economic complex of the trans-Himalayan region. Three states of Central Asia: Kazakhstan, Kyrgyzstan and Tajikistan form part of the trans-Himalayan region, but the region also forms a gate-way to the rest of the states of Central Asia. The Central Asian states are passing through a complex process of nation building. Most of them are witnessing the revival of the militant Islam. The region is becoming a haven for international terrorism.[7] The Islamic extremism is gaining new forms in Central Asia. The states adjoining the trans-Himalayan region are faced with ethnic uprisings and conflicts. In Kyrgyzstan sharp division between southern Kyrgyz and northern Kyrgyz is seriously threatening the integrity of the country. Jhus and Hordes are engaged in power politics in Kazakhstan. Tajikistan is yet to overcome from the onslaughts of civil war that claimed 50,000 lives. Islamic extremism is becoming a difficult problem in Uzbekistan and other countries. Narco-terrorism and arms trafficking are a serious problem in Afghanistan and Kyrgyzstan.

Central Asia offers vast prospects for trade, cooperation and investment. The huge oil and gas reserves and other rich mineral and natural resources have attracted the major powers towards this region.[8] The United states tried to make its presence felt in the region in the name of war on terrorism, while China and Russia are in search of creating a balance of power. India is also in search of its stakes in the Central Asian region.

Thus, the power politics is taking new shape in Central Asia.[9] America, Russia and China have given millions of dollars of aid to the region. The power politics in Central Asia has direct implications for the trans- Himalayan region. The issues for which Central Asia has become significant to-day are:

(i) Struggle against terrorism and Islamic extremism

(ii) Control over energy resources

(iii) Trade and transport corridor

China's Stakes in the Trans Himalayan Region

China's major concern in the trans-Himalayan region is its Xinjiang province which forms part of the region. The Xinjiang Uighur Autonomous Region (XUHAR) shares common border with Russia, Mongolia, Tajikistan, Kyrgyzstan, Kazakhstan, Pakistan and India. It is the largest province of China and forms 1/6 part of the territory of the country. It produces cotton. IT is also endowed with the largest oil gas reserves in China. Xinjiang is a Muslim majority region and Uighur, Han, Kazakh are in majority. Their integration has been problematic for China. Xinjiang region has been an important **trade hub** and it provides a gateway to China in Central Asia. China's entry to Central Asia is through this region. Therefore, peace and stability are important for this region. The region is currently becoming a centre of Islamic extremist activities due to its proximity to Afghanistan and Pakistan. A number of Muslim extremist groups are active in the region. There is also problem of illegal migration in the region.

China's major interest in Central Asia is its energy resources. China also wishes to contain the hegemonic influence of the United States in Central Asia.[10] Therefore, China is trying to cooperate with Russia. Both China and Russia have their stakes in the region and they would not like the US to make its dent in the affairs of the region in the name of war on terrorism. Therefore, China's strategy in Central Asia is peace, security and cooperation. China concluded a boundary demarcation protocol with Kazakhstan on 10 May 2002; and a cooperation pact was concluded with Kyrgyzstan on 24 June 2002.

In 2001, Kazakhstan, Kyrgyzstan, Tajikistan and Uzbekistan were made members of Sanghai Cooperation Organisation (SCO) which was renamed as Commonwealth Countries of SCO. The SCO offers multilateral cooperation with Central Asia including terrorism, arms and drug trafficking. China is interested in Central Asia in the areas of infra-structure development, gas pipelines, exploration of energy resources, and development of transport corridor, railway link between Central Asia and China by linking Fargana valley to Xinjiang. China has made huge investments in some of these sectors. China's long term strategy seems to be closely integrating Central Asia's energy resources with China right up to western China. China is in an advantageous position as it has access to Indian Ocean through Karakoram highway. China enjoys friendly relations with Pakistan which adds to its advantageous position in the trans-Himalayan region.

India's Interest in Trans-Himalayan Region

India also has its interest in the Central Asian region both politico-strategically and economically. India is equally concerned to the rising Islamic terrorism in the region. India is in a strategic disadvantage due to Chinese occupation of Aksai Chin and POK. Due to Karakoram highway, India does not have any direct access to the areas to the north. India has border dispute with China and Pakistan. There have been inimical postures and deep rooted mistrust between these countries. India's security risks are quite high in the region.

India can be an important partner for trade in the trans-Himalayan region with China and Pakistan. The old trade route can be revived. India is in search of a durable cooperation with China and Russia so that its stakes in the trans- Himalayan region are protected both strategically and economically. India got a observer status in SCO in its fifth summit meeting on 5 July 2005 in Astana. India's collaboration with SCO would not only be beneficial for her in terms of trade and investment but would also help easing tensions with China.

India-China-Russia collaboration in the region can be useful in dealing with the challenges of terrorism, Islamic extremism, drugs and arms trafficking. India and China have already made some headway towards controlling narco-terrorism in the region. Further, India-Russia and China collaboration can also be helpful in containing US and NATO presence in the Central Asian region.

On the whole, it can be said that there are vast opportunities for India-China cooperation in the trans-Himalayan region which may help in developing mutual understanding between the two giant powers of Asia. Apart from trade and commerce, security, peace, stability, terrorism, illicit trade, ethnic unrest are the other issues where India and China have mutual stakes. Islamic terrorism alone is a serious issue which needs to be addressed urgently and it is also a fact that the anti terrorism drive needs mutual cooperation.

Some of the areas where India and China can enter into a broad based collaboration in the trans-Himalayan region are:

1. Trade, commerce and investments,
2. Peace, security and stability,
3. Terrorism and Islamic extremism,
4. Infra-structure development, particularly transport corridor,
5. Neutralising the US and NATO influence,
6. Exploitation of energy resources and gas pipeline.

References

1. Ram Rahul. *The Himalayas as a Frontier*, Vikas Publishing House, New Delhi, 1978, p. 1.

2. K.Warikoo, "India's Gateway to Central Asia: Trans-Himalayan Trade and Cultural Movements through Kashmir and Ladakh (1846-1947)", in K.Warrikoo (ed.) *Himalayan Frontiers of India: Historical, Geopolitical and Strategic Perspectives*, Routledge, New York, 2009, p. 5.

3. See for details, Phanindra Nath Chakrabarty, *Trans-Himalayan Trade: A Retrospect, 1774-1974*, Classics India Publication, Delhi, 1990, pp.47-91.

4. Ahmad Rashid, *Jihad: The Rise of Militant Islam in Central Asia*, Hyderabad, 2002.

5. Nirmala Joshi (ed.), *Central Asia: The Great Game Replayed*, New Century Publications, Delhi, 2003, p. 7.
6. *Ibid.*
7. P. Stobdan, "Strategic Trends in Central Asia", in S.D. Muni (ed.), *Asian Strategic Review*, New Delhi 2008, p. 269.
8. R.G. Gidadhubli, "Oil Politics in Central Asia", *Economic and Political Weekly*, January 30, 1999.
9. See, David Shambaugh (ed.), *Power Shift and Asia's New Dynamics*, California University Press, Berkeley, 2005.
10. Sujit Dutta, "China's Emerging Ties with Central Asia", in Nirmala Joshi, **N.5**. p.144.

16

India China – Conflict and Co-operation in the Indian Ocean Region

R. S. Vasan

On 1 October 2009, China celebrated the 60th anniversary of the revolution. Coincidentally, some 600 years ago the Chinese displayed a great interest in maritime trade and commerce and wielded maritime influence in the far corners of the globe. The exploits of a Chinese Admiral Zheng illustrate the range and spread of activities supported by the Navy. India likewise did possess ships that sailed to countries to its west and east to establish trade relations. The spread of Buddhism happened both through the land routes and through the sea routes. Both the countries slowly lost out the preeminence of their maritime prowess with the colonisation.

It is evident that the Chinese exhibited enormous interest in the maritime neighbourhood not just in the South China Sea but also in the distant corners of both the Pacific and the Indian Ocean. After more than six centuries, it is evident that there is a resurgence of the PLA –Navy, which has given the Chinese Navy the option to revisit their past and reassert their maritime prowess in the areas of interest. Some years ago, the Chinese did just that by replicating the entire voyage in a smaller sized Junk to revisit the past and to cherish the memories of the successful voyages undertaken by the Admiral from a bygone era.

That both India and China did understand the importance of the seas and made determined attempts to conquer the seas and exercise control in far off areas has never been doubted. However, India's maritime prowess did diminish with the preoccupation of the Mughal emperors with land borders. In the case of China too the preoccupation with the littorals in the South China Sea had limited expansion till the eighties. Powered by the sustained GDP growth and robust economy, all that is changing for both the Asian giants.

Coming to the present day situation, the sustained modernisation of the PLA Navy with heavy funding has caused a lot of consternation in not just its neighbourhood but also in the far corners of the world. China's maritime prowess is growing from strength to strength with sustained economic positives. The Chinese have a well orchestrated policy to increase the maritime clout particularly in the Indian Ocean. The maritime interests of the Chinese today mainly stem from:

(a) A requirement of Strategic nuclear deterrence. The Chinese are indeed worried about the Taiwan factor and the possible intervention of the West led by US. It has, therefore, heavily invested in the military modernisation and is also building up a credible nuclear force. The nuclear submarines (Xia, Jin, Han and Zhang class) number over ten and more would be built with the capability to strike targets in the US. While no official figures are available, the military spending has been put at any thing from 70 to 200 billion dollars. With the political leadership not willing to take any chances with the adversaries both in the immediate neighbourhood and the extended neighbourhood, China has taken every precaution on land, over water, in the air and in the cyber space.

(b) Energy Dependence. The acute dependence of China on energy products from around the world is yet another factor that has compelled the Chinese to start stepping out of the confines of the Malacca Straits. Over 80 percent of the energy flow into China is through the Malacca Straits. China's economy is dependent on the ability of the Chinese Government to maintain sustained energy supplies from far corners of the world through the medium of the seas. That large quantities of oil and gas need to be imported bring in the factor of energy chain vulnerability that obviously engages the attention of the political and military planners of energy dependent countries. It is a challenge indeed to be able to operate in far off areas and wield influence by using the maritime forces as instruments of national policy. China is addressing these challenges in a well calibrated strategy along with a foreign policy that aims to bring the Indian Ocean Region nations under its influence one way or the other. The most popular handle used is the investment in the target country and a dedicated effort to build linkages that could serve as leverages in hour of need.

The two diagrams, from IMF reproduced below, illustrate the kind of energy consumption and dependence on sea routes for the carriage of oil/ gas/raw materials in India's neighbourhood. The Chinese would need to be concerned about the vulnerabity of the Sea Lines of Communication.

Also instead of putting all its eggs in one basket, it is also exploring the possibilities of finding alternate viable routes for the trans-shipment of oil and gas. Thus, it is seriously contemplating cutting across the Kra Isthamus to bring down the dependence on Malacca Straits.

However, even the Kra Isthmus would be under the surveillance of India and this thought would be discomforting as it bares a factor of vulnerability in the Indian Ocean due to the strategic positional advantage enjoyed by India.

(c) India's emergence as a Regional Power center. The Indian Navy's growth in the region has been quite impressive and there is no one within the immediate neighbourhood, who could match the might of the Navy. At the time when the Indian Navy was growing at a rapid phase, China went to the extent of publicly declaring that Indian Ocean is not India's ocean clearly indicating that it would challenge the maritime supremacy of India in its backyard. China which is dependent on the critical Sea Lines of Communication (SLOCs) would want to address issues of vulnerability of SLOCs that criss cross under the watchful eyes of Indian surveillance architecture. With the predominant presence and power of the Indian Navy, the Chief of the Naval Staff has identified the Indian Ocean as a "weak area" for the Chinese.

(d) Policy of Encirclement. China has been assiduously building spheres of influence in India's neighbourhood to further its national objectives. Pakistan has remained a strong ally for over five decades and there is convergence of ideas and thoughts about containing India. In a calculated move, China has invested heavily or is planning to buiid deep water ports not only in Pakistan but also in Sri Lanka and Myanmar. It is also looking at Bangladesh as a friend who would perhaps open up its ports for use by the Chinese in hour of need. This has been described as dependency ports by the outgoing Navy Chief Admiral Suresh Mehta: "They are not happy and are concerned with our presence in the Indian Ocean. And, therefore, they have to do this, i.e., build dependency. That is their strategy and they are doing it to come over here and be present in the Indian Ocean in larger numbers." While acknowledging the Chinese efforts to build on future options, this author also does not entirely subscribe to the idea of the so called 'string of pearls strategy'. The vast limitations of the extended support line and the fact that any presence in large numbers is not an easy option for the present till the blue water capability is fully developed.

(e) Fears of Strategic alliance of those perceived as inimical to the growth of China. China has always viewed, with suspicion, the US led initiatives in the Indian Ocean/Bay of Bengal for coordinated naval exercises. The combined exercise conducted in 2007 among US, Japan, Australia, UK, Singapore and India was seen as grouping of those who wanted to convey a message to China about the coming together of democracies against what was perceived as an undemocratic Government that ignored human rights. The declaration of promotion of democracy was perceived by China as a scheme to belittle the progress of China by highlighting the human rights abuses.

(f) Requirement to tackle maritime terrorism and piracy. Though the number of piracy attacks in the Malacca straits has come down drastically, the increasing incidents of piracy particularly in the Somalian waters is a matter of serious concern for all maritime nations including China. While many nations did send their men of war to patrol the waters off Somalia, India sent a strong message to the pirates by assertive action by sinking a commandeered vessel that was being used for hijacking ships. China did not want to be left behind as the opportunity presented itself for China to test out its own capability to operate in distant waters and also to send a strong message to observers around the world not just about the capabilities of PLA-Navy but also its intentions. By its successful and sustained operations in the Gulf of Aden, since December 2008, China has flexed its muscle and declared that it is here to stay as an Indian Ocean power whenever the circumstances so demand.

(g) Peaceful development. The Chinese have publicly adopted a strategy of peaceful development for growth. However, under the garb of peaceful development, China is spending a lot of money towards military modernisation with a view to be able to possess the military might that would provide the essential powerful tool of foreign policy. The main adversary is the US with its known displeasure with China on many counts including the human rights record. However, both China and the US have dependent economies and there are limits to posturing that would remain within a certain sphere of actions that would not go out of hand. Depending on the situation, definitive amount of sabre rattling would be witnessed with self imposed restraint on both sides to see that the situation does not go out of hand. The peaceful development as a strategy appears to be paying rich dividends to China as it knows that it has put its adversaries at ease with these proclamations which only provide some additional time to all to refine their strategies.

Indian Ocean, therefore, forms part of this peaceful development in which China would continue to invest in the neighbourhood of India economically, politically and also in other spheres of mutual interest. The response of India and other nations would depend on how they view the military modernisation and the economic growth as threats or as opportunities for mutual cooperation.

(h) Ship Building and Mercantile trade. China is at least 15 years ahead in terms of its ship-building capacity and in terms of its merchant marine growth. The ports with capacity to handle throughput of more than 100 million tons has gone up to 20 ports. These big ports and other smaller ports meet the import and export needs of the country not merely for energy but also for receiving raw materials and exporting finished products which have captive markets in the west and also in many other parts of the globe. Unlike India, China's shipping is completely state-owned and is fully supported in its expansion plans. Chinese are competing with the best ship-yards for ship production. It may be recalled that in a global tender, China was kept out of a port only on security considerations.

When a similar examination in the case of India is undertaken, it would reveal somewhat similar pattern in the perception of the Indian planners. Indian Navy started growing only after the successful attacks on Karachi during the liberation of Bangladesh. The additional funding support and some sound planning enabled the Indian Navy to grow to be a potent force to be recognised as such. India has also started reaching out to far corners of the world in a show of strength on its visit for power projection and cooperation with the navies of the world including China.

The mercantile marine growth has not been very impressive, despite the large dependence of the seas for export and import of various products. Slowly, the face of ship building and refit industry are also changing and there is lot of promise for the future as more and more operators have shown interest in the maritime related industry in the country. India's maritime industry's growth was stagnant for a long time. The long gestation period for infrastructure and lack of funds prevented the growth in this sector at the desired phase. However, there are more and more private operators who are now interested in Ports, Ships, off shore installations and infrastructure.

A study of the India's stated/perceived foreign policy goals in the Indian Ocean region would be in order to understand the power play in the region in which both India and China have serious strategic interests.

India's Maritime Engagement in the Indian Ocean Region

Many analysts seem to think that 'China has an edge in the IOR region. However, a dispassionate analysis clearly illustrates a slightly different point of view. A closer examination of the maritime relations in the IOR would reveal the facts which may actually place India in a slightly better place.

Sri Lanka. Both due to historical and cultural relations that have existed for centuries, the relations between the two neighbours have been good. There were of course phases of strained relations due to Tamil factor. However, this remained a factor only till the assassination of the former PM of India Rajiv Gandhi. Successive Governments including coalition governments at the Center have not given any quarter to supporters of the LTTE. The defeat of the LTTE at the hands of the Sri Lankan military forces has a major share of contribution from India due to the Rajiv Gandhi's assassination. India provided material and moral support to the fight against the LTTE, despite some resistance by some regional parties who continued to support the LTTE with full knowledge of its track record of violence, extortion, child recruitment, illegal trade and drug peddling.

While the development of Hambantota in southern Sri Lanka has been claimed as a win for the Chinese in the power play in the IOR, the facts are that India did not capitalise on the opportunity to develop this port that was offered to it in the first place. India cooperated actively during the tactical phase of its sea battle with the LTTE and the intelligence inputs provided by Indian surveillance proved crucial in neutralising the logistic ships of the LTTE which were carrying military hardware that was difficult to get across to the LTTE controlled areas. The Chinese also provided essential military hardware. During the entire phase of war, the Indian Coast Guard and the Indian Navy were in constant dialogue with their Sri Lankan counterparts to sort out issues as and when they developed. The Chinese had no such interaction when it came to maritime military cooperation. Even after the development of Hambantota, it is unlikely that it would be offered for military use by the Chinese while the intention of the Chinese would indeed be to use this facility as a dependency port in times of crisis.

Sri Lanka has gained from its friendly relations with India, Pakistan and China in its war against the LTTE. However, as asserted every now and then by the leaders on both sides, India does enjoy special relations and it is unlikely that Sri Lanka would want to break this mutually beneficial association. Sri Lanka, however, can not be faulted for using the China/Pakistan card as leverages for getting a little more from its bigger neighbour. There is another dimension to the relations between the two countries and that relates to Fishing in the Palk Bay. The fertile fishing grounds around the Kachchativu Island which was ceded by India about 35 years ago has remained an Island of contention for fishermen from Tamil Nadu and Sri Lanka. However, this is localised and is unlikely to involve China in the immediate neighbourhood in any perceivable manner.

Bangladesh. If Gwadar in the Arabian Sea is the port of origin in the scheme of things for the Chinese, ports in Bangladesh are on the radar scan of China for developing 'dependency' ports. There is talk of accessing some of the ports of Bangladesh through the network of roads and rivers from China. Depending on the Government in power, the relations with India go through a cycle of ups and downs. The Chinese would have plans for engaging Bangladesh in investments and also by supplying essential military hardware including ships. Bangladesh also has maritime border disputes with both India and Myanmar. With the criticality of energy products, and the expectations of such finds in the EEZ, there would be territorial disputes over sea areas. Bangladesh would be looking for support and also would be in the process of equipping itself with a decent sized navy that could intervene should it be necessary. It is not that the Bangladesh Navy would be in a position to take on the might of the Indian Navy, but she would like to have a minimum deterrence vis-à-vis its maritime neighbours. It is here that the Chinese initiatives are of importance in the Bay of Bengal.

With the sharing of maritime and land borders, India has a joint role to play with Bangladesh in providing Search and Rescue in the sea areas in the Bay of Bengal. The fact that the Indian Coast Guard ships visited Bangladesh only after being in existence for over a quarter century does not augur well for the maritime relations.

Myanmar. India distanced itself from the Military Junta for a long time, as it felt that the democratic processes were suppressed and human rights were constantly abused. The Chinese had no great respect for human rights and found it easy to engage with the military rulers of Myanmar. The supply of arms and ammunition and the excellent relations that China enjoyed with Myanmar was not comforting for India. Overruling itself on its stand on Myanmar, India was compelled to engage with the military Junta to prevent total control of the Myanmar Government by the Chinese who were looking for foothold in the Bay of Bengal. Chinese had already leased the Coco Islands for setting up their listening posts much to the discomfiture of Indian strategists. It appears that not much can be built on the Coco Island, yet, it is significant that this Island became the first foot-prints of China in the BoB.

Pakistan. China and Pakistan have enjoyed excellent strategic and military cooperation for many decades due to India being identified as a common enemy. The opportunity for getting a foot-hold close to the Straits of Hormuz came the Chinese way when Pakistan was looking at developing another Port along the Makaran coast. The devastating attacks by the Indian Navy in 1971 had clearly brought out that having just one port was counter productive as the blockade of such a port could be easy for a determined Navy supported by its Air force. China readily jumped at the opportunity and invested heavily in the port development. Unlike Sri Lanka, Pakistan has no qualms about providing all facilities to China who has stood by Pakistan in its hour of need through the sixty two years of Pakistan's existence.

However, the deployment of the Chinese units from Gwadar would not escape monitoring by the US led task force close to the Straits of Hormuz. With the increased strategic realignment with India, it is quite likely that the US would provide the necessary intelligence on the actions of the Chinese.

West Asia. Many analysts have felt that the western neighbours were ignored in the quest for gaining diplomatic and political ground in the east with the look east policy. This can be analysed to the predominant presence of US led forces who have been in and around the Straits of Hormuz for monitoring the activities in Iran and Iraq and also for intervening as and when required. India has been content with visits and some exercises with the regional navies to engage the regional navies.

Singapore: The relations between the two countries have been very good and there has been regular interaction between the maritime forces of the two countries. Singapore has consistently attempted to have good relations with both India and China and has by and large succeeded in balancing the relations. The trade relations are growing and many Singapore based marine companies are using Indian sea farers and their skills for even managing their maritime enterprise. Singapore has also been actively participating with Malaysia, Indonesia and Thailand to combat piracy in the Malacca Straits.

Other Southeast Asian Countries: There is good interaction at both the working and the top level in terms of extending the spheres of cooperation mainly in the areas of search and rescue and disaster management. The positive and timely assistance provided by the Indian maritime forces post Tsunami to the affected countries, has bolstered the image of India as a capable country which has the wherewithal to manage large scale disasters simultaneously in different theatres.

South China Sea/Spratly Islands: Different areas of over 4, 00,000 Square kilometers of area has been a bone of contention between the Littoral states and China. China seems to have differences with all the states in the region on the ownership. However, in 2002 all the claimants agreed to defer resolving of the disputes to a later date. Despite such understanding, China has been pursuing an aggressive policy towards its neighbours and keeps the maritime forces in the neighbourhood on tenterhooks despite some formal declarations to maintain peace.

In the past, China and Vietnam have exchanged gun-fire over the Spratly Island chain, which even resulted in the death of over 70 Vietnamese sailors. China has managed to enforce strict fishing regulations without any concern for its neighbours by even fining those found fishing in troubled waters. China also manages to coerce foreign companies carrying out exploratory work in the disputed waters. The various disputes in this sensitive area are given below:

Coastal Area - disputed by Thailand, Vietnam, the Philippines and China.

Gulf of Tonkin - disputed by China, Vietnam.

Paracel Islands - disputed by the People's Republic of China, Republic of China (Taiwan) and Vietnam.

Spratly Islands - disputed by People's Republic of China, Republic of China (Taiwan), Malaysia, the Philippines, Vietnam, and Brunei.

Vietnam - While there have been historical differences and wars between China and Vietnam, presently there is a climate for economic cooperation. Vietnam has a decent maritime force and also is a claimant to many of the disputed areas in the Spratly Islands.

Indonesia. The past legacy of Sri Vijaya Empire has visible influences even today. This is another country that could be developed as an independent power center along with Vietnam to provide the counter balance in the region to China's growth.

Thailand - Has also had its differences with China on ownership issues in Spratly Islands. However, the peaceful development concept adopted by China has reduced the tension in the areas of conflict. Due to historical reasons, Thailand has good relations with India. It is the only country in the region besides India that operates an aircraft carrier and has shown a keen interest in developing its maritime potential.

Maldives. For military and strategic analysts particularly in India who have been apprehensive of the recent Chinese overtures in the Indian Ocean, the news of the impending defence/security pact between India and Maldives likely to be concluded in end August by the Defence Minster Mr. Anthony would provide a certain degree of assurance that China can not have a cake walk in our maritime neighbourhood.

The Chinese have been wooing Maldives too by providing aid and investing in that country. There was talk about the likely use of Marao one of the largest atolls by the Chinese to promote their commercial and military interest. However, both due to historical and cultural relations with Maldives and the active role played by India in thwarting a coup attempt by launching 'Operation Cactus' in Maldives in November 1988, the ties between the two countries remain very strong. During the Presidency of Gayoom, India gave lot of importance to the improvement of relations with Maldives. The relations with the new president Mohammed Nasheed, popularly called Anni, have also been extremely productive and the intention of the new Government to get into a security ambit with India is indicative of the continued importance that both countries have attached to the strategic dimensions in the Arabian Sea. The perceptions of both the Governments also appear to converge when it comes to tackling terrorist attacks sponsored by the radicals.

India also readily reached out to its neighbours including Maldives immediately after the Tsunami on 26th December 2004. The humanitarian aid and relief was provided under 'Operation Castor'. With low lying atolls, the threat of inundation due to Tsunami is quite high and there is a need to provide quick relief to the victims in the event of such an eventuality. The fears of getting submerged with the rising heights of the seas due to global warming, have prompted the Government of Maldives to seriously scout for real estate for its citizens in other parts of the world. India obviously enjoys the positional advantage and has the wherewithal and material advantage to provide help and succour in the event of a natural calamity or man-made disaster in the Islands.

In more specific terms, India would be transferring two helicopters to Maldives for surveillance and would also install an integrated radar network with linkages to naval command centers on the West coast of India. As per reports, the first of the Helicopter would be handed over by the Defence Minister during his visit from 20-22nd August. The second from the Navy would be transferred at a later date. It is evident that these helicopters would also be used for disaster mitigation related tasks.

From the point of view of Indian security, in a post 26/11 scenario, this is an important development as India augments its Maritime Domain Awareness (MDA) potential in the Arabian Sea by the expanded surveillance/response capability. The strategic location of Maldives that straddles the Sea Lines of Communication (SLOCs) would enable the combined surveillance mechanism to detect, identify, track and prosecute targets on establishing the threat potential. India gifted INS Tillanchang, a Fast Patrol Vessel (named after one of the Islands in the A&N group of Islands), in April 2006 to the Maldives National Security Service (NSS). The vessel is now named Huravee after a Hero and a freedom fighter and would be an effective component of the response mechanism in Maldives waters.

The air elements of the Indian Navy and the Indian Coast Guard have been undertaking reconnaissance sorties in the EEZ and would now be in a position to augment the surveillance efforts of the Maldivian security forces. There has been active and positive cooperation between the security forces of the two countries and many security personnel from Maldives are being trained in India. It has also been reported that the team of experts from Maldives would be visiting Andaman and Nicobar group of Islands to be exposed to means, methods and the manner in which security of over 524 Islands is being coordinated by the tri services Commander. While it is always not necessary to look at all these developments in the Indian Ocean through the Chinese prism, this development in the Arabian Sea has enormous significance for India's maritime posturing vis-à-vis China, whether intended or not.

It may appear that China has encircled India. In reality, forward posturing, despite the friendly bases, would be a challenging task given the long distances from Chinese waters and the long vulnerable supply chains. In the long run, the PLA-Navy would be looking at Gwadar, Hambantota and similar ports in Myanmar and Bangladesh as forward posts that could help in extending logistic support. The Chinese recently did operate for extended periods off the Somalian coast on anti piracy patrols demonstrating the capabilities of a blue water navy. Since leaving Hainan for the fist time on 26th December 2008, tasked for anti piracy task in the Gulf of Aden, the Chinese fleet has maintained an active patrol in the Gulf of Aden by rotating its units every 2-3 months. It is also interesting to note that one of the Chinese guided missile destroyers Shenzhen (DDG 167) called at the port of Kochi on its return passage last week (10th August 2009) and exchanged notes with the Indian naval counter parts. There are no doubts that the Chinese would have fine tuned their procedures for such extended operations and their confidence in such operations would have gone up tremendously.

Extra Regional Powers: Despite some efforts in the past to declare Indian Ocean as a zone of peace, in reality there is nothing to suggest that any one was serious about this declaration of the few. During the cold war, both the western led NATO and the Soviet Union led WARSAW forces manoeuvred in the Indian Ocean guarding their assets and stalking each other to prevent a nuclear war. With the near unipolar world of today, it is the US writ that largely runs in the IOR. The Combined Task Force 150 has been active in the Straits of Hormuz and the Task Force 151 has come to tackle the piracy menace off Somalia. After the break-up of the Soviet Union, Russia is slowly trying to be a force to reckon with and some of the old prejudices appear to be returning to restart the cold war.

There are no doubts that Indian Ocean would continue to be a centre of gravity in the present century and no one would like to miss a party here as Asia leverages its economy and power of the people in the Asian Century.

Areas for Cooperation: The world is witnessing increased attacks on maritime trade notably both in Malacca Straits and also in Somalian waters. While the menace appears in control in the Malacca Straits, there are many attacks endangering lives and property in the waters off the African coast in the Gulf of Aden. Both India and China have been sending their own warships for protecting the mercantile commerce and safe passage of ships from the Gulf of Aden. There is not much synergy and this is one area which offers avenues for cooperation between the two countries. The other areas that open up for cooperation is in terms of ship-building and energy-tapping in different corners of the world.

Areas of Conflict: The major areas of conflict in the maritime arena stem from the desire of China to be a dominant power in the IOR. India looms large in the Chinese calculus of maritime equations in this part of the world. China is fully aware of the maritime potential and the strategic advantages conferred on India by its geographic location overlooking the Sea Lines of Communication and thus being in a position to challenge the flow of goods through the medium of the seas. It is this fear that explains the Chinese economic engagement in our neighbourhood. China in its stated objective of peaceful development has invested heavily in countries around India. The expectations that such investments and economic activity would provide the necessary leverages for future, are not out of place in a globalised economy. The developing countries including India are constantly looking out to attract investments for improving the economic potential of the country. China does not loose any opportunity to invest in countries around the world to improve its standing and clout. China would plan to ensure that the situation in the South China Sea never goes out of control. India's engagement of the neighbouring countries in this region would indeed be a source of worry for China which would look such relations with suspicion. From the point of view of India, it would be doing to China in South China Sea what China itself is planning in the Indian maritime neighbourhood.

The salient discussions could be summarised as indicated below:

(a) From the Indian view point, the counters should also include better relations with the Littoral states in the South China Sea and active engagement with the navies and the Coast Guards. The Indian Navy and the Indian Coast Guard have been visiting countries in this area and are engaging the maritime forces in joint exercises. Good relations with these countries would serve a two-fold objective of keeping our options open in the South China Sea and also to bring about a sense of balance in the smaller navies in the region who do not exactly endorse all the moves of China in the region. The 21st century would witness acute competition between the two Asian neighbours.

(b) Conflict for supremacy in IOR and cooperation (anti piracy/counter terrorism) where convenient would continue.

(c) The geo strategic advantage enjoyed by India would need to be supported by maritime military might, astute policies and assertive engagement with stake holders, to keep China at bay.

(d) Enhanced cooperation with China's maritime neighbours in peacetime operations needs vigorous attention.

India has also done well in initiating a forum called Milan which has been active for over a decade now and has brought together the navies from the region and allowed them to interact on professional, social and cultural platforms provided at Port Blair in the Andaman and Nicobar group. Also, the offer of India for conducting training in combating terrorism has been well received and the Indian Coast Guard has been regularly conducting the necessary training to the participants from many countries identified in the ASEAN Regional Forum (ARF). From the point of maritime strategy, whatever moves are initiated by China in the Indian Ocean need to be countered not only in our back-yard but also should be complemented in our proactive but not offensive actions in China's backyard.

Conclusion

In conclusion, it appears that both China and India would continue to compete to extend the military and economic sphere of influence amongst the littorals in the Indian Ocean Region. The fact that China and India would be in the top three slots by 2020 in economic terms, does not necessarily mean that there would be total estrangement between the two countries. The vexed border issue would remain a thorn in the relations between the two countries. However, there is space for both the countries to prosper together without seriously undermining their economic growth.

It is safe to assume that both the countries would avoid confrontation as long as possible to consolidate their respective positions. The keen sense of competition would prevail as was witnessed in the efforts of both the countries to scout and acquire energy fields in many parts of the world. China would increase its efforts to prevail in the maritime neighbourhood of India. It has succeeded in Pakistan in a big way. It would continue to build spheres of influence in Bangladesh, Myanmar and even Sri Lanka. Maldives would be difficult proposition for China due to the historical relations with India and the recent security pact that was signed by the two governments.

17

India-China Relations: Economic Harmony or Defense Hostility

G. Vijay Kumar Reddy

India and China are neighbours- each with a billion population together accounting for 38 per cent of the world's population, with the fastest GDP growth rates for large economies, with China already the world's second largest economy and India set to become the third largest in the future. The interaction between the two big neighbours is bound to reflect the global order in the future.

The two neighbours, until 300 years ago were considered by the then prevailing criteria as the most developed in the world, accounting for 50 per cent of world's GDP. However, India and China underwent a two century long decline by the mid 20th century, thanks to the foreign aggression and imperialism. Despite being neighbours with flourishing economies, the two nations never went to war until 1962. The two countries traded goods, exchanged visitors and borrowed ideas, and generally respected each other at the ruler and the ruled level. There are number of recorded incidents in the history where visitors from China visited India and Indian visitors who visited China – until foreign invasion and imperialism cut off normal interactions and the relations became frozen. They were revived only in 1950 but fizzled out by 1959. War followed in 1962, for the first time in the millennia. It took lot of efforts, thereafter to restore normal relations between both the nations. Although relations have been normalised, it is not that easy for India to deal with the Chinese. On the one hand, the trade between both the nations has been on the rise and India has become China's tenth largest trade partner and China has replaced the US as the second largest trading partner of India. On the other hand, tensions continue even today on the undemarcated border of 4000 km between India and China as Chinese intrusions into Indian Territory have grown significantly over the years. The rivalry between these nations in the Indian Ocean region is always a cause for concern. As the two largest consumers of energy in the world, the competition for energy is growing between these two Asian giants.

They have lately received a lot of international attention being viewed as emerging giant economies as they both play the key roles at the international level. For example, China has been a permanent member of the UN Security Council, while India who has led the Non-Aligned Movement for years, is still vying for a similar position. Furthermore, India has been one of the founding members of the WTO and has played a prominent role as one of the developing nations whereas China has had to fight for decades to obtain its admission into this international organisation.[1]

While both China and India have an extended history of international trade, tracing back to centuries, both their economies were until recently highly protected and controlled to a large extent despite that their political systems being very different. China is still a very unique case in the sense that while it has allowed its economy to be opened to Capitalists, it is still governed by the Communist Party with a strong leadership not giving away state power.[2]

The Border Issue

4000 km of common border which India and China share – one of the longest inter-state borders in the world, which covers some of the most difficult terrain in the world, remains undefined or undemarcated either on maps or on the ground. This has inevitably led to a long standing dispute regarding the precise territorial division between the two countries.

The boundary issue became prominent with China annexing Tibet in 1950. India's role in providing sanctuary to the Dalai Lama and his Tibetan government in exile in Dharmashala, aggravated the problem between the two nations. In 1956 China published the first official map of Chinese territory rejecting the McMahon Line drawn by the British Colonial Authorities in 1914 to demarcate the borders between India and China. The map showed large territories held by India as being within China's borders.[3] The Indian government reacted angrily, accusing China of arbitrarily extending China's borders. In 1959, in his reply to Nehru's letter, the Chinese Premiere Zhou Enlai rejected Nehru's contention that the Chinese–Indian border was based on treaty and custom. Rather, he pointed out that China had never accepted the McMahon line drawn up during the 1914 Shimla Convention, which delineated the eastern section of the border between British India and Tibet. Zhou Enlai made it clear that Tibet is an integral part of China.[4]

After 1959, border skirmishes intensified on the border which escalated into full scale war when People's Liberation Army launched an assault on Indian positions on 20th October 1962. Indians suffered heavy losses at the hands of the Chinese. On 21st November, China declared unilateral ceasefire and a formal peace agreement was signed between India and China and the ceasefire line up to which the Chinese withdrew was converted into Line of Control. But the exact location of the Line of Actual Control (LAC) remains under dispute even today. After the war, the diplomatic relations were almost suspended and all manner of formal contacts between the two nations reached a plateau.

The visit of Rajiv Gandhi to China in 1988 was the first by an Indian Prime Minister since 1962. This visit was made possible only when India dropped its decades long insistence that there could be no real improvement in relations between the two countries until Beijing returned all the territories forcibly taken in the 1962 war. India meaningfully adopted a broad position and no longer pressurised for the settlement of border issue.[5] After two decades of talks, India and China exchanged maps on the least controversial middle segment of their frontier in 2000 and three years later special envoys were appointed to map out a resolution of the dispute. Chinese premier Wen Jiabo and Indian Prime Minister Manmohan Singh signed an agreement on the "guiding principles" to resolve the dispute in 2005. China formally abandoned its claim to the Himalayan state of Sikkim. But, there have been no concrete efforts on demarcating the border. Even after the signing of the "guiding principles" agreement, not much development has taken place as both the sides are rigid in their approach. China unexpectedly upped the ante by demanding more territorial concessions, and India replied that some boundary matters are 'non-negotiable". The core area of contention remains India's long standing claim that China is illegally occupying some 38,000 square kilometers of Indian territory in North Western Jammu and Kashmir known as Aksai Chin (which has been held by China since 1962 war). This border area known as Actual Line of Control borders the Indian state of Himachal Pradesh, where the Tibetan leader, fourteenth Dalai Lama has established his government in exile in the town of Dharmasala[6].

India also claimed the 5,180 square kilometers of Jammu and Kashmir ceded to China by Pakistan under 1963 Sino-Pakistan Boundary Agreement. The ceded area, known as the Trans–Karakoram Tract, subsequently became part of the land bridge linking Pakistan to China's Xinjiang along the Karakoram Highway. For its part Beijing claims sovereignty over 90,000 square kilometers of Sumdorong Chu Valley in India's northern state of Arunachal Pradesh (In fact in some of the Chinese maps Arunachal Pradesh itself is shown as part of China) including non descript area known as Tawang, which is important to Tibetan Buddhism because it is believed that the sixth Dalai Lama was born there. To make matters even worse, New Delhi has suggested that the area around the Sacred Mount Kailash-Manasarovar in Tibet be returned to India, because it has been a sacred Hindu pilgrimage site for centuries[7].

In May 2007, an Indian Administrative Service official from the state of Arunachal Pradesh was denied a Visa by the Chinese government to attend a mid-career training programme that China was hosting. Chinese claim was that he is residing in Chinese territory and did not require a Visa. The Indian government in a tit-for-tat move, immediately stopped the 107 – person official delegation from going to Beijing and also extended an invitation to Taiwan's opposition Kuomintang Party Presidential candidate Ma Ying-jeou to visit India in June 2007. China voiced its displeasure to Ma's visit and called on India to abide by the "one China policy". Further, in August 2007, Beijing demanded that the Indian government remove its military bunkers situated in a junction between Sikkim, Bhutan and Tibet, claiming that these were located on Chinese territory, thereby indicating and backtracking on its earlier declared policy of treating Sikkim as part of India.

Eventually, in January 2008, during Manmohan Singh's visit, China recognised "Sikkim state as part of the "Republic of India" in its official map. The two countries also reached agreement on the "modalities" to implement the confidence building measures along the LAC. But, even after three decades of negotiations, only modest progress has been made. India and China remain as divided as ever on the core territorial issues. The border issue remains a bone of contention between the two countries.

Tibet Problem

On October 7 1950, the Chinese PLA invaded Tibet and occupied it and from then on, it became an important issue on the border between India and China. China's Tibet policy has significant security implications for India. It has led to the border dispute and the 1962 Chinese war. On 21st October 1950, the Indian government raised objection to the Chinese invasion of Tibet but the Chinese criticised India for interfering in matters relating to domestic affairs. After 1950, relations were normalised and the first trade agreement between the two nations was signed on 29th April 1954. Under the agreement India gave up all extra territorial rights and privileges that it had inherited from the British Indian Government and recognised Tibet as part of China. The first official Chinese statement on the Sino-Indian border dispute came on January 23, 1959. Replying to Nehru's letter of December 14, 1958, in which he had drawn attention to the incorrect Sino-Indian border alignment shown in Chinese maps, Zhou Enlai said that the Sino-Indian border was never demarcated and that China had never recognised the McMahon line.[8]

The Chinese occupation of Tibet ended buffer zone between the two countries and Nepal and Bhutan serve as limited buffer today, removal of Tibet as buffer brought India and China face to face. This has led to frequent skirmishes between the two nations which continue even today. With the shifting of buffer from Tibet to Nepal, the latter has become very important in China's Foreign Policy. Tibet has a 1500 kilometer border with Nepal, and China has been steadily consolidating its relations with the Nepalese government. China reached an agreement with King Gyanendra in August 2002 to cease any 'anti-China activities' in Nepal and has asked Nepal to close down the Tibetan Refugee Welfare office in Kathmandu. In May 2005, the two countries opened their first bus service between Lhasa and Kathmandu (1000 km). China also supplied arms to Nepal when India froze military assistance to the Royal Nepalese Army in the wake of royal coup in 2005.[9]

Close analyses of Chinese policies reveal that China's primary objective of holding Tibet is to gain strategic capability. The construction of the Qinghai-Tibet railway project is central to such policy. Through this project China aims at achieving strategic capability against India. The Qinghai – Tibet railway line will enable China to quickly increase its military deployment near the India-Tibet border region – when needed. The rail link reduces travel time from the Chinese province of Gormo to Lhasa from 72 hours to 16 hours. The Chinese military arsenal on the larger Tibetan plateau is reported to have eight missile bases, with at least eight inter-continental ballistic missiles, 70 medium range and 20 intermediate range missiles and 25 airfields and airstrips. Enhanced military capability will not only be a direct security concern for India but also enable the Chinese to approach the border dispute with India from a position of greater strength.[10]

The Indian Ocean Region

Given the geographical structure of the Indian Ocean, with landmasses on all the three sides, there are only three major entry points which are of strategic importance. The south-east entry point is the Straits of Malacca, the south-west entry point is around the Cape of Good Hope and the third one is north-west entry point which is the Suez Canal. There are a few other routes, through the straits if Sunda, Lombok and Makaasar and around Australia (Cape York in the north-east and Base strait in the south-east); but these waters are more difficult to navigate or for a longer journey. The major east-west sea lanes from the Indian Ocean pass through the Straits of Malacca in the east and the Gulf of Eden and Suez Canal in the west. The above two points as well as the Strait of Hormutz (connecting the Persian Gulf and the Gulf of Oman) comprise the three major strategic points in the Indian Ocean.[11] Malacca Straits, being one of the important routes for the transport of oil, more than 15 million barrels per day passes through it. The countries of Japan, China and South Korea rely on the safe transit of ships through these sea lanes. Over 50,000 vessels transit the Straits of Malacca per year compared to that of 20,000 through Suez Canal. Therefore, it is very important for these countries to keep the sea lanes free of problems and any disruption can cause major problems for International economy.

Indian Ocean Region is also very important in terms of natural resources. Its littoral states contain more than two thirds of the world's oil reserves, 35 per cent of the world's gas reserves, 60 per cent of uranium, 40 per cent of gold and 80 per cent of all diamond deposits. Japan imports nearly 90 per cent of its oil from Indian Ocean Region, Italy 85 per cent, Britain 60 per cent, Germany 60 per cent and France 50 per cent. Other than oil, the region is enlaced with many important industrial raw materials. These include lithium, beryllium, circonium, cobalt, vanadium and phosphates. According to one analyst "40 out of 54 types of imported raw materials used by American industry are supplied by the Indian Ocean Region". The continental shelves contain enormous amounts of mineral deposits such as nickel, cobalt and manganese much of which remain untapped. Recently geological surveys have revealed the presence of gas and oil reserves on the coasts of Myanmar and Bangladesh.[12]

For India and China, the two Asian nations, the Indian Ocean is of great importance. For China, the second largest oil importing country, the Indian Ocean and the transit of oil from West Asia through the Straits of Malacca are increasingly a top priority. Currently, over 80 per cent of the oil China imports transits the Straits of Malacca and 25 per cent of the Chinese exports to the

Gulf and Europe pass through the same Straits. It is estimated that by 2015, 70-80 per cent of India's foreign trade transits the Indian Ocean.[13]

String of Pearls

To safeguard its Sea Lines of Communication (SLOC's) for transportation of oil and other materials, China has embarked upon a "string of pearls' strategy, building ports and listening posts around Indian Ocean rim. Beijing's projects span from the Malacca Straits to the Cape of Good Hope and many places in between, including countries that were once in India's sphere of influence. Realising the strategic importance of Sri Lanka in the Indian Ocean, a massive port is being developed by China at Hambantota, at the southern tip of Sri Lanka. The Gwadar port in Pakistan is also built by China. Some reports also suggest that China has become increasingly interested in the Bangladeshi port of Chittagong and in constructing airfields in Bangladesh. Some reports also continue to surface in the international press that China has come to a secret arrangement with the Maldives for the construction of a submarine base there. Eventually, the strategy of China is to possess key naval choke points around the sub-continent that could disrupt Indian lines of communication and shipping.[14] Some Indian analysts are growing increasingly anxious about China's growing influence in Sri Lanka. As one notes, referring back to remarks made by Napoleon, "if China acquired control over the northeastern Sri Lankan port of Trincomalee, Beijing would be in a position to convert Bay of Bengal into a veritable Chinese Lake"[15]

Energy and Oil

China and India are the two major consumers of oil in the world. While China imports 40 per cent of its oil, India imports 70 per cent of its oil. Neither country has the domestic oil fields capable of supplying their domestic needs, making them equally dependent on oil from abroad. Therefore, the race for equity oil is on, and given the highly aggressive nature of the Chinese bidders, India has learned the hard way, that it needs to act quickly to seal its oil contracts.[16]

India is in competition with China for more and more oil and natural gas around the world. Following China's example, India is also pursuing oil in remote areas. With 37 per cent of worlds population, India and China are both in a desperate race to catch up with the U.S., Europe and Japan Industrially. To meet its growing demand, India, like China, is tapping into countries that have been abandoned by the West, giving China more competition in those areas.[17]

On several occasions India has lost significant oil bids to China which includes Angola, Kazakhstan, Ecuador and Myanmar. On the other hand

Chinese oil firms are reputed to have made several deals in which they overpaid because of competition from India. Therefore, the Indian petroleum Minister Mani Shankar Aiyer during his visit to China in January 2006, has called for cooperation in the energy sector. He said that "we look China not as a strategic competitor but as a strategic partner". He also said: "The Chinese have learned that if we constantly compete, they have to pay more than a billion dollars over ideal price. As, it is the assets they acquire are often of uncertain value in risky countries." Aiyar also warned that competition for energy resources, if not checked, could enflame relations between Asia's two rising powers. Aiyar's call for cooperation between India and China in the energy field was also supported by the Director of the China Energy Strategy Centre, a government think-tank Mr. Xia Yisehn. He also said that "unbridled competition between India and China for oil and natural gas will be harmful to all concerned, and so the necessity of co-operating to share risks and reduce costs in a multilateral way is gaining currency here"[18].

State-owned Chinese and Indian energy companies have launched several joint exploration ventures, including in Russia, Iran and Sudan, with China generally taking the larger stake. In December 2006, a further step towards Sino-Indian energy cooperation was taken when CNPC and ONGC, respectively their countries largest state-owned oil companies of China and India respectively, mounted a successful $573 million joint bid to acquire Petro-Canada's 37 per cent stake in the Al-Furat oil grid and gas fields in Syria[19].

Economic Interests

Despite unresolved territorial disputes, mutual suspicions over each others' military buildup and strategic intent, potential economic competition and the changing of power and realignments, China and India have enjoyed ten years of mostly uninterrupted economic and political relationship. During his India visit President Hu Jintao put forward an ambitious 'Five Point Proposal' to promote closer Chinese-Indian economic cooperation. These included the following: (1) trade diversification to increase bilateral trade between the two countries (2) expand cooperation in key areas such as information technologies, energy, infrastructure, science and agriculture (3) improve the trade and investment environment by removing obstacles to trade and investments (4) strengthen cooperation in the multilateral arenas (in particular) that China and India should work together to strengthen coordination in the World Trade Organisation (WTO) and other multilateral economic organisations to protect the interests of developing nations (5) actively pursue trade liberalisation with the goal of establishing a preferential trade agreement and eventually a "free-trade area" between the two nations. In the area of bilateral trade, both the countries have already initiated a number of measures to remove impediments to bilateral trade and investments, including the expansion of bilateral trade through preferential tariffs (more preferential than the most favoured nation tariffs) on a range of products, including paper, steel, chemicals and food. The list includes 217 Indian exports and 188 Chinese exports facing lower than average tariffs in each others markets.[20]

China and India bilateral economic ties have greatly expanded. Bilateral trade has grown by an average of 32 per cent a year since 1996. According to Mr. Liang Shu He, Deputy – Director – General, Foreign Trade Department in the Commerce Ministry of China, India and China were on course to raise their bilateral trade to $ 60 billion by 2010, which was the target set by the Prime Ministers of both the countries in 2005. From a modest US$332 million in 1992, the two way trade volume increased to US$2.91 billion in 2000, to US$20 billion in 2006, to US$ 38.7 billion by the end of 2007 and to US$ 45 billion by the end of first quarter of 2010.[21] In fact, China has replaced the US as India's top trading partner. The volume of investments between the two countries has grown since 2000. Since 2005, trade in services, particularly in construction, engineering, education, entertainment, financial services, IT services, transport, tourism and health has seen healthy growth. The fact that both governments have committed themselves to removing administrative barriers and simplifying the regulatory trade and investment regimes will further boost trade in these areas.[22]

Conclusion

Hu's visit to India in November 2006 was a major milestone in Chinese-Indian relations. To fully realise the potential between Asia's two great powers, they must at a minimum avoid conflicts that could arise from apprehension, misperception, misunderstanding, or miscalculation. Leaders in Beijing and New Delhi are content with the current status of bilateral relations because they are stable and provide possibilities for future progress.

Beijing and New Delhi need to address their threat perceptions through greater communication, confidence building, and institutionalised conflict-management mechanisms. China's and India's growing economies and modernising militaries do not need not to be seen as aimed at each other. Greater engagement in dialogue on strategic intents could go a long way in heading off suspicion and hostility. The two countries should seek to promote common interests through the emerging China–India–United States triangle rather than using their respective bilateral ties. They can also use this communication to foster mutual interests, such as a fair and equitable international political and economic order, nonintervention, environment, disarmament, and antiterrorism in the international community.

China and India should work to capitalise on the potential of bilateral trade and technology cooperation, especially because both countries are now members of the World Trade Organization. Both should be sensitive to the issues of greatest importance to each. China should make every effort to dispel India's misgivings about the alleged Chinese assistance to Pakistan's weapons programs. China's ongoing dialogue with the Dalai Lama's representatives should be welcomed as both a good sign and worthy effort that would defuse tension over Tibet. The two countries must also set a clearly defined timetable for resolving the border dispute. The existing LAC, with minor adjustments, could be the basis for negotiating the inter-national boundary.

The two emerging Asian powers will undoubtedly have differences over a range of issues, but conflicts do not have to be inevitable if they continue regular high-level visits and official consultation, trade ties, and cooperation on international and regional issues and foster their strategic and cooperative partnership for peace and stability. Proper management by both the states can ensure stability for bilateral relations, South Asian security, and the evolving global balance of power.

References

1. Navind Beeharry, "A Comparison of the Impact of the Globalisation on the Political Economies of India and China," *Contemporary World MGX 5710.*

2. *Ibid.*

3. Shalendra D. Sharma, *China and India in the Age of Globalisation*, New York, 2009, pp. 169-171.

4. *Ibid.*

5. For more details see: www.boundaries.com/india.htm

6. For more details see : Neville Maxwell, "The Sino-Indian Border: A Scenario for Settling this Vexatious Issue," *World Affairs: The Journal of International Issues,* Volume 4, Number 3, July –September 2000, pp. 52-65.

7. *Ibid.*

8. Abanti Bhattacharya, "Chinese Nationalism and the Fate of Tibet: Implications for India and Future Scenarios," *Strategic Analysis*, Volume 31, Number 2, March, 2007, pp. 237-266.

9. *Ibid.*

10. *Ibid.*

11. Amardeep Athwal, *China – India Relations: Contemporary dynamics*, New York, 2009, pp. 30-33.

12. *Ibid.* Also see www.time.com/time/world/article/0,8599,1890251,00.html

13. For details see http://www.time.com/time/world/article/0,8599,1924884,00, html

14. http://www.hindustantimes.com/China-creates-a-pearl-in-Sri-Lanka/H1-article3

15. Athwal, **N.11**. Also see www.southasiaanalysis.org/%5Cpapers17%5Cpaper1681.html

16. The concept of equity oil, or securing acreages abroad, is not a new one. Several decades ago, the U.S. and European countries began using this idea. Exxon, Mobil and Chevron are past examples of companies that came to dominate the oil business using the concept of equity oil, and each time they pursued concessions in new oil fields abroad, they were actively aided by the respective governments. For more details see S.N.Yadav, *India, China and Africa: New Partnership in Energy Security,* New Delhi, 2008, pp. 32-35.

17. *Ibid.*

18. *Ibid*, p. 59.

19. *Ibid.*

20. Jing – dong Yuan, "The Dragon and the Elephant: China-India Relations in the 21st Century," *The Washington Quarterly,* Summer 2007, pp.131-144.

21. http://www.economywatch.com/world/economy/indo-china-trade-relations.html. Also see *The Hindu*, September 8, 2008.

22. http://business.mapsofindia.com/trade-relations/india-china.html

18

Geographical Ambivalence vis-à-vis Geopolitical Conflict in the Sino-Indian Relations

Y. Yagama Reddy

Geopolitics, as a foreign policy approach and an international relations theory, is all about "an awareness of relative position among countries and a corresponding response of statesmen to advantages and vulnerabilities that territorial and maritime space may bring to foreign affairs and national security" (Kelly, 2002). Evidently, the geopolitical discourses, as S.B. Cohen, a renowned scholar in geostrategic studies, justifiably described, have simply embarked on the analysis of geography of international studies, (Cohen, 2009). Thus, the geographical setting has all the more formed the basis for various geopolitical concepts propounded since the dawn of 20th century. Among various such theories, Heartland, Rimland and Oceanic realm have offered paradigms governing the Sino-Indian relations (Thompson, 2002).To be explicit, the Halford Mackinder's Heartland (Pivot Area) had its strength and sustenance based on the Inner (marginal) Crescent that encompassed the coastal lands of Eurasia drained by major rivers offering the inland navigation for over considerable length and facilitating the movement of goods and people, besides being endowed with the vast resource potentialities. Nicholas Spykman laid emphasis on the chances of exercising control over the Eurasian Heartland by the powers in the Rimland, while Alfred Thayer Mahan envisioned Oceanic elements as a means of power projection and control of the Sea Lanes of

Communication. Later half of the 20th century had been fraught with what John Garver aptly labels "protracted geopolitical conflict" in Sino-Indian relations. The mounting economic and geopolitical stature of China and India, lying at the base of their status as predominant powers in the region capable of wielding diplomatic clout in the context of multi-polarity (Joe, n.d.), amply reminds us of the fact "globalisation has not replaced regionalism, nor has geo-economics replaced geopolitics" (Scott, 2008). If the simultaneous emergence of India and China as Asian and global powers has made them to be sensitive to each other's interests and aspirations, these two continental-size economies and political entities are too big to contain each other or be contained by any other country (Saran, 2006).

A "balance of power game" between India and China is basically entwined with geo-political space surrounding India (Kumar, 2006). The Sino-Indian geopolitical setting is looked upon as a fundamental factor for understanding the twenty-first century which is turning out to be "the century of China and India" (Zou, 2005). The phrases frequently used in recent times, such as, 'rise of China' and 'rise of India' do testify to their prominence as potential centres of political power and economic strength and as Asian giants giving credence to the concepts of Asian Century and New Asia (Monarch and Ding, 2005). In effect, the concepts of 'China's Century' and 'India's Century' have been amalgamated giving rise to the talk of an 'Asian Century' with a thrust on the amity and cooperation between India and China (Balakrishnan, 2004; Scott, 2004; Lal, 2005). The Western media was more than ready to use the phrase 'China's/Chinese Century', Indian commentators and politicians started to talk of 'India's Century'. Even much before these phrases were gaining currency, the governmental and non-governmental cultural exchanges and friendly visits gained momentum in the 1980s from a mere 10 in 1980 to about 50 in late 1980s (Hongwei, n.d.). Of much significance was a formal visit to China in December 1988 paid by Rajiv Gandhi, the first by an Indian Prime Minister in 34 years. Deng Xiaoping told Rajiv Gandhi that "unless both India and China become well developed, there is no such thing as an Asian Century". India and China started to be talked about together; with *Chindia* coined as a term by some sources as, for instance, *Journal of World-Systems Research* (2008).

In the light of these potential prospects, it is imperative to look into the historical and geographical landscape shaping the Sino-Indian relations. While quoting the U.K-based *Guardian* newspaper as having referred to India and China as "non-identical conjoined twins, joined at the Himalayas", Niharika Chibber Joe of the Maureen and Mike Mansfield Foundation also floated the idea of "Chindia" (Joe, n.d.). Historically, the Sino-Indian border was not under dispute as Himalayas provided a natural barrier (Adityatiwathia, 2009).

Himalayas do provide us a fascinating geological history. The coalescence of Gondwana land / Indian sub-continental plate (from the south) and Angara land/ Eurasian plate (from the north) led to the mountain-building activity out of the sediments of the Thethys Sea. Further and more, movement of these land masses during the Mesozoic period (225-65 million years ago) resulted in formation of geosynclines in the form of folded mountain series trending roughly east-west direction. These Tertiary folds, thanks to syntaxial bending at the extreme eastern and western ends, got swerved and extended as parallel mountain chains into peninsular Southeast Asia on the east and branched off the Pamir Knot in southwesterly direction into Afghanistan and Pakistan on the west. Thus, the geological structure of the Himalayas has walled India off the West and Central Asian regions as well as China in the north and Southeast Asia in the northeast.

The young folded mountain ranges have throughout the history formed a formidable barrier for the movement of goods and people. If the Silk Route was a circuitous one, the Stilwell Route from Northeast India through Burma to China was of no significance to India and Burma even during the British colonial administration. That was the reason why there were no overland contacts between India and China, which had their relations maintained through maritime contacts. Similarly, the southward extensions of the Himalayas in the form of Arakan Yoma and Pegu Yoma restrained contacts between the geographically proximate regions of Northeast India and Burma; instead Bay of Bengal sustained the cultural and commercial contacts between India and Southeast Asia from the beginning of Christian era. It was in this process that Southeast Asia had become a zone of confluence of the Indian and Chinese cultural influences, which had since then become a tremendous bearing on Southeast Asian relations.

The Himalayan Tertiary series have formed the source of several perennial rivers draining many a country. The crest of these mountains including peaks which attained higher elevations has perpetually become snow-capped, seldom in the form of glaciers. The snow-thawing and the consequent glacial erosion down the steep mountain slopes have made the river courses perennial in nature. Indus and Ganges, for instance, are the international rivers flowing through China, Pakistan and India, while Brahmaputra (Tsangpo) flows through China, India and Bangladesh (wherein Ganges has its confluence with Brahmaputra). There are other Tibeto-Himalayan-origin rivers like Irrawaddy and Salween draining the territories of China and Myanmar; and Mekong has its drainage area in China, Myanmar, Laos, Thailand, Cambodia and Vietnam. Thus, the Himalayan Rivers have formed the life-line for the economic activity of the peninsular regions of the South and Southeast Asia, besides China. The sustained fluvial action has deepened the tectonically unstable synclines into deeper valleys and gorges with occasional rapids and waterfalls; and hence these perennial river courses are of no significance to inland navigation, nor could the waters be harnessed for irrigation purposes, for any intensive agriculture is a remote possibility in the mountainous topography with steep-gradient. Understandably, Himalayan geography has offered limited chances for human settlement process, but for the highly scattered settlements with very sparse population and agricultural economic activity restricted to the cultivation of fruit crops and vegetables. Environmental determinism thwarts any attempts at subscribing to the theory of Possibilism or even to chances of Probablism.

India and China are physically separated by the Himalayan Mountain chains which together with the associated mountain ranges have also got these two land masses separated from the European continent proper. Thus, it was the historical geography that insulated these two territories from the overland European influence from times immemorial. Despite their profound ethno-linguistic diversity in these two geographically expansive territories, India and China could develop their respective cultural bases for about 2.5 billion people accounting for one-third of global population. Thus, two great civilisations could survive the political dynamics of various intensities all through the history; and these cultural lands/areas could emerge as nation-states, transcending the variations based on topography, climate, language, economic structure and ways of life. Both India and China are endowed with the agriculturally potential and productive coastal lands capable of sustaining economic activity and hence the large concentration of population. India and China have their strengths based on vast area, large population, indigenous cultural base, resource potentialities and agro-climatic diversity facilitating the self-reliance in crop production, even as the variations warranting the sustained efforts for national integration and security.

The world's two great civilisations were known for resilience and prosperity for over 3000 years, even as the political contacts between them were far and wide. They were also oblivious of each other's existence for over a millennium until they began experiencing European influence from 19th century. The geography-imposed-obstacles as well as the non-expansionist nature of the Indian civilization had virtually ruled out the chances of military clash between the two Asian giants for over thousands of years. Absence of a border agreement between China and India historically led to no formal fixing of the boundary; and their border activities had been carried out on the basis of a traditional customary border. Evidently, there was no way to correctly measure the total length of the traditional customary border (Rajan, 2005).

British India, haunted by Russophobia, laid claims to the Aksai Chin area that would serve as a wedge between Central Asia and Tibet. The border was proposed and supported by British officials along the Karakoram Mountains which could form a natural boundary and set the British borders up to the Indus River watershed, while leaving the Tarim River watershed to the Chinese; and the Chinese control of this tract would present a further obstacle to Russian advance in Central Asia. In 1899, the British presented this line to the Chinese, who raised no objection to it. But, once the Russian threat receded, neither China nor the British paid attention to the occupation of Aksai Chin, virtually uninhabited high-altitude wasteland (*Origins of the Sino-Indian Border Dispute*, n.d.). India's partition in 1947 and Chinese occupation of Tibet in 1950 made them the vicinal nations as if to confront over the territorial limits. But for the bonhomie in early 1950s, the relations between the two Asian giants since the 1962 Sino-Indian border clashes were "marked by conflict, containment, mutual suspicion, distrust and rivalry". Overlapping "territory and location" has made them strive to stamp their authority on the same region, i.e., the same spatial arena (Mohan, 2009).

The message of the 1962 war was clear: "militarily the Chinese victory was complete, the Indian defeat absolute". Chinese control of the Aksai Chin plateau was confirmed. China's sweep into the northeast was not stopped by Indian military efforts. Instead, Chinese forces, after pushing India out of the disputed territory, chose to withdraw to a *de facto* line around the McMahon Line. The defeat was "a mindset-shattering event, a watershed in national psychology" (Nayar and Nayar, 2003). "The 4,056-kilometer (2,520 miles) frontier between India and China, one of the longest inter-state borders in the world, remains the only one of China's land borders not defined, let alone demarcated, on maps or delineated on the ground" (Malik, 2007). In fact, the Line of Actual Control (LAC) or the *de facto frontier* between India and China is a good example of "dull frontier" that does not provide any kind of strategic advantage to either and it has rather undermined the usefulness of an armed conflict between them, ever since the 1962 border war (Premashekhara, 2009).

Both India and China, as can be gleaned from the Table, have acquired locational significance on account of their being the land neighbours. China and India, separated by the formidable geographical barrier of the Himalayan mountain chains, share a border along the Himalayas with Nepal and Bhutan acting as buffer states lying along the Himalaya range. However, China is far ahead of India in terms of unique land borders, unique land neighbours and length of land boundary. The Sino-Indian border (3,380 km) is significantly lengthier than India's borders with 5 out of 9 countries, and is also exceedingly higher than China's borders with 12 out of 19 countries. Similarly, the Sino-Indian border is also lengthier than the land borders they shared with each of the five countries— Pakistan, Afghanistan, Nepal, Bhutan and Myanmar— to which the Himalayas have formed the frontier. Thus, the very vicinal location of these two countries in relation to their neighbours is at the base of their strategic significance and security concerns.

Absence of human habitation and known economic sources had made this bleak cold desert to remain "no man's land" right until 1950s. Like the British, India too came to a conclusion that the area of Aksai Chin was of no strategic importance. Nehru, who sought to play down the economic significance of the Aksai Chin area, described it as "barren tundra" where "not even a blade of grass grows", and even went so far as to cast doubt on the validity of the Indian claim to Aksai Chin (Bhakal, 2010). In fact, Aksai Chin was easily accessible to the Chinese, but was more difficult for the Indians to reach on the other side of the Karakorams. This line is approximately the same as the current Line of Actual Control.

The length of Sino-Indian border has been variously mentioned as, for instance, 2520 miles (4,032 km), according to Malik J. Mohan (2009) and 4,250 km according to an official document of India, *bharat rakshak* (1962). Though these figures are very much at variance with border length of 3380 km, they are, however, closer to the one referring to the Line of Actual Control (LAC), the effective border between India and China (4,057 km long) that traverses three areas of northern Indian states: western, middle and eastern (Rajan, 2005; Rehman, 2009). *The Global Times* (affiliated to People's Daily group) described the extent of disputed territory as follows: Total area in dispute— 125,000 sq. km which encompasses Eastern Sector— 90,000 sq. km; Middle Sector— 2, 000 sq. km; and Western Sector— 33,000 sq. km. Yet another source categorised the disputed area at 125,000 sq. km. into two distinct parts: (1) The Western Sector— Aksai Chin, located in the Ladakh area of north eastern Kashmir (lying beyond the Karakoram range and resting on the Kunlun mountain range), covering an area of about 37,250 sq. km— currently occupied by China, (2) The Eastern Sector— the Indian state of Arunachal Pradesh, which China calls

Table 1: Basic Features of Land Borders of India and China

	India	*China*
1. Area (million sq. km) :	2.97	9.33
2. Population (billion) :	1.17	1.34
3. No. of unique land borders :	9	19
4. No. of unique land neighbours :	7	16
5. Total length of land borders (km) :	14,103	22,147
Afghanistan :	106	76
Bangladesh :	4,053	—
Bhutan : 605	470	
Burma : 1,463	2,185	
People's Republic of China/India :	3,380	3,380
Nepal : 1,690	1,236	
Pakistan : 2,912	523	
Hong Kong (PR China) :	—	30
Kazakhstan :	—	1,533
North Korea :	—	1,416
Kyrgyzstan :	—	858
Laos : ——	423	
Mongolia :	—	4,677
Russia :——	3,645	
Tajikistan :	—	414
Vietnam :——	1,281	
6. Coastline (km) :	7,000	14,500
7. Coast/Area Ratio (km/km²) :	2.35	1.55

Source: http://en.wikipedia.org/wiki/List_of_countries_by_length_of_coastline
http://en.wikipedia.org/wiki/List_of_countries_and_territories_by_land_borders

South Tibet, covering an area of 83,743 sq. km — currently occupied by India. David Scott at the International Relations, Brunei University, termed the territorial dispute as the clearest point of divergence between the two countries, though the extent of the disputed area is found at variance with the other sources: India claims around 40,000 square kilometers of Chinese controlled territory (Aksai Chin) on the western flanks of the Himalayas; China claims around 92,000 square kilometers of Indian controlled territory (Arunachal Pradesh) on the eastern flanks (Scott, 2008a, pp. 244-270).

The Chinese built in 1950s a 1,200 km (750 miles) road connecting Xinjiang and western Tibet, of which 179 km (112 miles) ran through the Aksai Chin region claimed by India. India was not aware of the very existence of the road until 1957. It was in 1958 when China published its maps that the Chinese-built highway caused a spurt among the Indians as an issue of national prestige. The Chinese Premier, Zhou En-Lai, proposed that China relinquish its claim to most of India's northeast in exchange for India's abandonment of its claim to Aksai Chin. The Indian government, constrained by domestic public opinion, rejected the idea of a settlement as being humiliating and unequal (*Geography of Himalayas:….*). There were certain violations committed by the British. The Shimla Agreement with Tibet had violated the Anglo-Russian Convention of 1907 that restrained both parties not to negotiate with Tibet in the absence of the intermediary of the Chinese Government. The British who had doubts over the legal status of the accord did neither put the McMahon Line on their maps until 1937, nor did they publish the Shimla Convention until 1938. Tibet which refused to concede the trading town of Tawang during negotiations in 1938 controlled Tawang. Under the pretext of Japanese threat to India's east and possible threat of Chinese expansionism, British troops secured Tawang for extra defense.

Yet, the McMahon line forms the disputed border along the Arunachal Pradesh region. As the maps published at the time of India's independence did not clearly indicate whether the Aksai Chin region was in India or in Tibet, the new maps published by India in 1954 included the region well within the boundaries of India. China rejected the legality of the 1914 Agreement claiming that Tibet had no right to sign treaties as it was not a sovereign state, while India considered it to be the legal border. India maintained that the Himalayas which formed the ancient boundaries of the Indian subcontinent were traditionally Indian and associated with India; and it has been consistently proposed the high watershed of the Himalayas as the border between India and its northern neighbours. The original line drawn up by Henry McMahon on the Shimla Treaty map starts at 27°44'30", starting a tri-junction between Bhutan, China, and India, and from there, extends eastwards. Thus, India claimed the territory south of the high ridges and obviously, north of the high ridges should be Chinese territory. The Indian version of the McMahon Line moves the Bhutan-China-India tri-junction north to 27°48'N, though the actual treaty map itself is topographically vague (as the treaty was not accompanied with demarcation), and the treaty includes no verbal description of geographic features nor description of the highest ridges. The McMahon Line is a demarcation line drawn on map referred to in the Shimla Accord, a treaty signed in 1914 between the United Kingdom and Tibet, which defined the eastern section of the border between India and Tibet. Obviously, the intent of the treaty was to follow the highest ridges of the Himalayan Mountains.

While describing the inexorable logic of geography in the Sino-Indian relations geopolitical frameworks, Indian Foreign Affairs Ministers, for instance,

Jaswant Singh (1999) and Foreign Secretaries like Shyam Saran (2006) admitted the intersecting interests between these two rising powers. Undeniably, the border problem is not only relating to a dispute over territory, but also to the national dignity and people's sentiment. The difference of the two sides is large and neither side could make unilateral concessions (Shihai, n.d.). By far the biggest obstacle is the public perception of the Chinese 'betrayal' of 1962. But, Anil Athale, who claimed to have had access to the Top Secret Henderson Brooks inquiry report, termed this perception wrong, given the bureaucratic infallibility and political inertia that obscured the facts behind the history of the conflict (Athale, n.d.).

The popular slogan, "*Hindi-Chini Bhai Bhai*" (Indians and Chinese are brothers), testifying to a growing solidarity between the two nations in early 1950s, turned so much a rhetoric as to be termed as "*Hindi-Chini-Bye Bye*". The "protracted geopolitical conflict" in Sino-Indian relations for the last 50 years is reminiscent of a Cold War of its own. Of some solace in the recent times is the growth in economic links, especially the sharply rising bilateral trade that eclipsed the Sino-Indian historic acrimony so much as the '*Hindi-Chini Buy-Buy*' phenomenon is gaining currency. There are media speculations that the historic 478-mile Stilwell Road would be opened to connect India's northeast with Yunan province, besides resuming the first direct trade link between India and China through Nathu La pass in Sikkim at a height of 15,000 feet— the world's highest custom post (Joe, n.d.).

The impressive positive trends in their bilateral relations since late 1980s include: regular high level political interactions; increasing bilateral trade (from a minuscule of US $ 0.35 billion in 1993 to $30 billion in 2007) that was expected to reach the mark of $60 billion in 2009 and may likely to get doubled by 2015 (*The Times of India*, 2008) ; boundary demarcation-talks since 2003; and joint military exercises, including two 'anti-terror' exercises in 2007 and 2008 (Sakhuja, 2009). The two sides at the August (2009) border talks in New Delhi favoured 'apolitical solution' to the boundary problems and for 'safeguarding the peace and calmness in the areas along the border' (*Xinhua News Agency*, 2009). Yet, in 2008 there were reportedly "270 border violations and nearly 2,300 instances of 'aggressive border patrolling' by Chinese soldiers" (*New York Times*, 2009). Obviously, the ill-drawn boundary has been at the base of cross-border violations wittingly or unwittingly to the extent of undermining the spirit of neighbourliness. The two Asian powers, lamented Vijay Sakhuja (at the Indian Council of World Affairs in New Delhi), continue to "suffer from a trust deficit and are increasingly concerned about each other's strategic intent, particularly over their respective military developments across the Himalayas", including the "augmentation of defense forces and military infrastructure along the border", although leaders on both sides try to downplay the border sparring. The boundary dispute gains greater salience given the fact that China has resolved its boundary disputes with most of its neighbours, while its dispute with India remains unresolved (Sakhuja, 2009).

'China Threat' perceptions have been buttressed by its concerted efforts aimed at 'strategic encirclement of India'. China's direct control of Xinjiang is complemented by direct hold on Tibet since 1950. China's land threat from the north has been extended downwards through its 'all-weather friendship' with Pakistan, a link symbolised by the Karakorum Highway, currently being upgraded, which "concretises an enduring Sino-Pakistani alliance. This enabled China to threaten India's northern flank from Tibet and western flank through West Pakistan, which has long been the lynchpin of China's presence in South Asia. China's maritime multilateralism with Indian Ocean littorals from mid-1980s, by way of regular incursions into the Indian Ocean region which is regarded as India's "strategic backyard" and naval deployments in the region, has the potential to translate into strategic partnership. Through its bases in the Indian Ocean— electronic surveillance installations in Myanmar, maritime infrastructure developments in Bangladesh (Chittagong) and Sri Lanka (Hambantota) as well as at the deep-sea port in Pakistan (at Gwadar) both for commercial and naval activities— China could emerge as a stakeholder in the Indian Ocean security architecture (Rechard, 2006; Malik, 2009, Sakhuja, 2009). China's grand strategy intended to encircle India by befriending the Indian Ocean littorals, what is of late characterised by the 'string of pearls', does speak of China's "long memory", though the celebrations of 60th anniversary of the Sino-Indian diplomatic relations have for the time-being eclipsed China's distrust and hostile reaction to the developments concerning the border issue (Raman, 2010). Though both consciously downplay their differences, "the two may never be friends, but will not go to war and will not queer the pitch beyond a point" (Mahendra Ved, 2010).

China's burgeoning links with Myanmar are well established on land. Yet, as Vatikiotis points out, geography makes it hard for China and India to confront one another. The Himalayas pose a formidable barrier to military adventurism in either direction. About the same time, the Himalayas do not pose any fundamental barrier to military operations from Chinese-held Tibet against India, especially in an age of missiles and with China holding the heights (Vatikiotis, 2006). India has also been seeking to improve its infrastructure along her disputed northern border with China, facilitating future deployment of military power. Besides support to the post-Taliban Afghanistan, India has its military shadow expanded by setting up air bases in Tajikistan close to the north of Afghanistan and conducting bilateral military exercises in Mongolia. India-Vietnam defense agreement in 1994, further strengthened by a joint protocol on defense cooperation in March 2000, facilitates sharing of strategic threat perceptions and intelligence and participating in bilateral naval exercises. China's military alliances and forward deployment of its naval assets would definitely prompt India to respond by way of seeking access to ports in Vietnam (Cam Ranh Bay), Taiwan (Kao-hsiung) and Japan (Okinawa) (Malik, 2009).

The geo-economic compulsions of the New Economic Order have added a maritime dimension to the Sino-Indian geopolitical rivalry. Forging closer defense and security ties with resource-surplus nations and developing appropriate naval capabilities in pursuit of controlling sea lanes through which the bulk of commerce flows do testify to their vulnerability to deterioration in their bilateral relations. The maritime rivalry, likely to be intensified in the Indian and Pacific Oceans ostensibly to safeguard their respective sea lanes of commerce and communication, will likely to intensify their mutual distrust and tensions (Mohan, 2009). The clandestine operations of the state do bears testimony to their unmerited competition in pursuit of stock-piling arms and armaments as well as to belligerent activities which would certainly demand exorbitant budget allocation to defence-related activities. It is an undeniable fact that geography-imposed logistics would drain out huge financial resources, besides heavy toll of casualties. Paradoxically, both the nations have given little credence to the logic of geography and legacy of history pertaining to the formidable Himalayan mountain system that thwarts human efforts at exercising an effective control over the borders. The Himalayan Ranges, though formed the territorial-divide, could not offer the scientific boundaries. In fact, the McMahon line itself has been described as literally a line on paper:

The actual treaty map itself is topographically vague (as the treaty was not accompanied with demarcation), and the treaty includes no verbal description of geographic features nor description of the highest ridges. There is no protocol or scientific method which uses cartographic techniques to identify the geographical location of the line (*Wikipedia*).

The existing Borders hardly conform to the basic tenets of boundary-formation, viz., the 4 Ds: Definition, Delineation, Demarcation and Defense.

This can not be construed as a willful disregard to the scientific approach, given the terrain difficulties which deterred the efforts to accomplish the process. The water-divide (the crest/ridge of the mountainous terrain) should have been the benchmark for drawing a boundary line; but the practical problem is the permanency of such topographical feature, inasmuch as the tectonic instability of the Tertiary Series manifesting in land-sliding or water-piracy capable of dislocating the once-identified landmark in a given geographical area. The defined boundary could at the most be delineated (marked) on the paper (map). Undisputedly, the delineated-boundary line could hardly be transfixed on the steep and rugged terrain thwarting the attempts at developing land-surface communication and transport facilities, leave alone the matter of defense-of-the-boundary-line running over several thousands of kilometers.

> The border dispute is the most potentially conflict prone issue between the two countries", says Sun Shihai (n.d.) who further elaborated:
>
> There were several incidents of clashes or even crises in the border areas after 1962. These clashes happened not because of any attempt to provoke a war or change the Line of Actual Control, but because the two sides have differences in perceptions of the precise locations on the ground and on the map of several points on the LAC. Such incidents cannot be ruled out in future as long as the LAC is not clearly delineated physically on the ground.

Geography imparts locational significance of a region; while the physical setting of a country serves as a precursor to its military preparedness. Both these Asian giants have their security apparatus calibrated to the precepts of geographical causation; yet, the physiography of the Himalayas invariably stands in favour of China, as vindicated by the Sino-Indian war of 1962. The Tibetan plateau covering large part of China along the Sino-Indian border offers the advantages of higher operational and logistical capability for strategic planning during a military contingency. The expansive Tibetan plateau has also enabled China to build an extensive network of roads, railheads, forward airfields, pipelines and logistic hubs, besides deploying intercontinental missiles at Delingha, north of Tibet, capable of striking targets in northern India (*Asia Times*, 2009). On the other hand, India is constrained by geographical setting that remains always detrimental to the Indian troops deployed on high mountains. Indian armed forces have to negotiate a tougher terrain comprising snow capped peaks, deep valleys, thick jungles and difficult mountain passes.

Vijay Sakhuja, a strategic analyst, thus remarked that some of the Indian army posts can be accessed only during favorable weather conditions by animal transport and human porters and serviced by helicopters for troop induction, logistics support and casualty evacuation.

Though India and China have been involved in regular border talks regarding disputed territories along the LAC since long, the Sino-Indian border dispute, as commented by Jeff Smith of the American Foreign Policy Council, "is the canary in the coal-mine". Building mutual confidence through disengagement and relocation of troops as well as reduction of tensions in the border areas would avoid uncalled for military confrontations. The Himalayas, though remain a formidable barrier to military adventurism in either direction, do not pose any fundamental barrier to military operations in an age of missiles. Geography itself mandates India to embark on friendly relations with China. India cannot afford to have a hostile and resentful China on its borders, nor could it gain any substance by entering into an anti-China alliance. The Sino-Indian border dispute remains as a test for China without entertaining adventurous hopes to challenge India's sovereignty. Time has come for India and China to overcome differences and improve bilateral economic and trade relations as well as cultural exchanges that would only help increase trust and resolve all issues, including the long contentious border crisis. This view point gets credence from the address of Shivshankar Menon, the National Security Advisor, at the Indian Council of World Affairs, when he noted that the two (China and India) had found "a way to manage their differences over the 'most complicated and difficult' boundary dispute and had decided not to allow it to stand in the way of expanding ties in other areas" (Mahendra Ved, 2010). The principle of rapprochement would bolster their prowess in the Asian balance of power vis-à-vis new global order.

References

Adityatiwathia, "Balancer Needed in Asia", *The World Affairs Blog Network,* 6 July 2009.

Asia Times, 9 July 2009.

Athale, Anil, *India and China in the 21st Century*, at <http://inpad.org/archive.html>

Balakrishnan, Paran, 'India Joins the Asian Century', 3 January 2004, at <http://www.rediff.com/money/2004/jan/03guest.htm>

Bhakal, Maitreya, *A Brief History of the Sino-Indian Border Dispute and the role of Tibet,* 26th March 2010, at <http://blog.foolsmountain.com/2010/03/26/a-brief-history-of-the-sino-indian-border-dispute-and-the-role-of-tibet/#comment-67076>

Bharat Rakshak, at <www.bharat.rakshak.com/LAND-FORCES/..../1962 chapter01.pdf>

Cohen, Saul B. *Geopolitics: the Geography of International Studies,* 2nd edition, Rowman & Littlefield, Lanham:MD (USA), 2009.

Geography of Himalayas: Sino-Indian Relations, available at <http://wapedia. mobi/en/Sino-Indian_ relations>

Hongwei, Wang, *The Relationship between China and India Facing the 21st Century,* available at <http://iaps.cass.cn/xueshuwz/showcontent.asp?id=262>

Joe, Niharika Chibber, *Fifty Years of Sino-Indian Relations: The Idea of "Chindia"*, at <http://www.mansfieldfdn.org/pubs/commentary/niharika011006.htm>

Journal of World-Systems Research, Vol. XIII, No. 2, 2008, pp.119-41.

Kelly, P. "Geopolitics of Paraguay: Pivotal Position within a Model of Geopolitics", *Historical Text Archives*, 2002, p. 1.

Kumar, A., "A New Balance of Power Game in the Indian Ocean. India Gears up to Tackle Chinese Influence in Maldives and Sri Lanka", *Strategic Comments* (IDSA), 24 November 2006.

Lal, Rashmee, "Asian Century: West is Watching", *The Times of India*, 12 April 2005.

Mahendra Ved, India, "China need to cook up a win-win deal", *Newstraitstimes*, 19 April 2010.

Malik, Mohan, "India-China Competition Revealed in Ongoing Border Disputes," *Power and Interest News Report,* No. 695, 9 October 2007, available at <http://www.pinr.com, accessed June 15, 2008>

Mohan, Malik J. "India-China Relations", *Berkshire Encyclopedia of China*, Berkshire Publishing Co., 2009, available at <http://www. apcss.org/core/BIOS/malik/india-china_ relations.pdf>

Monarch, Barleen and Ding, Zhitao, "Asian Tigers, Hear Them Roar", *Beijing Review*, 7, 10-13 April 2005.

Nayar, Baldev and Nayar, Paul, *India in the World Order*, Cambridge University Press, Cambridge: 2003, pp. 150-51.

New York Times, 4 September 2009.

Origins of the Sino-Indian Border Dispute, available at < http://forum.globaltimes.cn/ forum/blog.php?b=658>

Premashekhara, L. "Three Frontiers Theory: An Explanation to India-Pakistan Animosity", *International Journal of South Asian Studies*, Vol.1, No.1, January-June 2009, pp.11-33.

Rajan, D.S. "Aksai Chin, Arunachal ours, says China", *South Asia Analysis Group*, Paper No. 1387, 20 May 2005.

Raman, B. *India: Caught between China and the Deep Sea*, Chennai Centre for China Studies Paper No.470, 3 April 2010, available at < http://www. c3sindia.org/ India/ 1275>

Rechard, B. "The Karakorum Highway: Opportunities and Threats", *Peace and Conflict*, 9/9, 2006, p.13.

Rehman, Iskander, "Sino-Indian Border Skirmishes towards a Limited Confrontation", *IPCS Issue Brief*, No 117, September 2009.

Sakhuja, Vijay, "Military Buildup Across the Himalayas: A Shaky Balance", *China Brief*, Vol.9, Issue 18, 10 September 2009.

Sakhuja, Vijay, "Maritime Multilateralism: China's Strategy for the Indian Ocean", *China Brief*, Vol.9, Issue 22, 4 November 2009.

Saran, S. *Present Dimensions of the Indian Foreign Policy*, available at <http:// www.indianembassy.org/newsite/press_release/2006/Jan/2.asp>

Scott, David, "The Great Power 'Great Game' between India and China: The Logic of Geography", *Geopolitics*, Vol.13: No.1, 2008, pp.1-26.

Scott, David, "Sino-Indian Security Predicaments for the Twenty-First Century", *Asian Security*, Vol. 4, Issue 3, September 2008, pp. 244-70.

Scott, MacDonald, "The Asian Century is only Delayed", *Asia Times*, 24 November 2004.

Shihai, Sun, *China-Indian Relations in the 21st Century*, Institute of Asia-Pacific Studies, CASS, at <http://www.sasnet.cn/zuixincg/showcontent.asp?iD=32>

Singh, J. "*Interview with External Affairs Minister Jaswant Singh*", 14 March 1999, available at < www.indianembassy.org/new/NewDelhiPressFile/Jaswant_ Singh_ Interview. html>

Thompson, J. "Virtual Regime: A New Actor in the Geo-political Arena", *Political Science and Politics*, Vol. 35, No. 3/3, 2002, p. 507.

The Times of India, 2008, as quoted in Mohan, Malik J., "India-China Relations", *Berkshire Encyclopedia of China*, Berkshire Publishing Co., 2009.

Vatikiotis, M. "India and China: A Delicate Dance", *International Herald Tribune*, 23 January 2006.

Xinhua News Agency, 6 August 2009.

Zou, Hanru, "The Century of China and India?" *China Daily*, 28 October 2005.

Index

D

N

O